英語でつくる和食

Recipes of Japanese Cooking

藤田裕子・ナヴィインターナショナル【編著】
Supervised by Yuko Fujita & NAVI INTERNATIONAL

完全版

ナツメ社

 # はじめに

　今、和食料理が世界中でブームになっています。和食料理は四季折々の食材をうまく利用し、季節を感じられることや、野菜類や魚介類をふんだんに使用しているため、とてもヘルシーで体によいことが人気の要因だと考えられます。

　和食は難しいと思っている方はいませんか……。本書では和食の食材、使用する道具などの基本はもちろんのこと、煮る、焼く、揚げる、あえるなどの調理法の基本、コツ、テクニックなどを詳しく紹介していますので、和食料理を初めて作る人も、ちょっと苦手という人にも親切な構成になっています。本書では、家庭で古くからよく食べられているひじきの煮もの、きんぴらごぼう、おからの炒り煮、肉じゃがなどの料理を伝統食として紹介しています。さらに、煮もの、焼きもの、揚げもの、蒸しもの、あえもの、刺し身・寿し、鍋もの、ご飯もの・麺類などに料理を分類し、レシピを紹介しています。また、ヨーロッパやアメリカで人気の豆腐料理、お弁当のレシピを紹介しています。

　レシピページは、詳しい作り方の解説はもちろんのこと、多くの工程写真や料理作成の目安時間、カロリーなどを紹介していますので、初めて料理に挑戦する人や、健康に気をつけている人にも便利な内容になっています。

　本書は和食料理を作りながら、英語が学べるよう対訳になっています。どうか本書をうまく活用していただき、おいしい和食を作ることはもちろんのこと、英語の教材としてもご利用ください。さらに、国際交流のコミュニケーションツールとして、プレゼントとしても最適です。

　　　　※本書は先に出版されている「はじめての和食」「カラー版 英語でつくる和食」「カラー版 英語でつくる和食　食の歳時記」を再編集、原稿を追加して作成しています。

 # Preface

Japanese cuisine is experiencing a boom all around the world. Japanese dishes provide a sense of the seasons by using seasonal ingredients and have a healthy appeal—using abundant vegetables and all sorts of seafood.

But, some believe the preparation of good Japanese food is too difficult to master. This book will guide you through commonly used ingredients and equipment to tips and techniques on cooking methods, including how to simmer, broil, deep-fry and marinate. Those of you who haven't tried preparing a Japanese meal will discover new skills and those who've tried and been disappointed will be surprised at the ease. This book introduces traditional Japanese menus prepared frequently at home such as simmered *hijiki*, burdock kimpira, simmered *okara* and braised meat and vegetables. Dishes are categorized into simmering, grilling, deep-frying, steaming, marinating, sashimi and sushi, hot pot, rice dishes and noodles. And each recipe is explained in each category. Also, tofu dishes and recipes for lunchboxes—very popular in Europe and the United States—are illustrated.

On every recipe page, you'll find detailed explanations of the process as well as pictures to help you along. You'll also see the estimated time and calories for each meal, useful for those cooking Japanese food for the first time and others who are watching their diet.

Since this book offers parallel translation, readers can study English while preparing their Japanese dishes. We hope this book will help you prepare delicious Japanese meals and practice your English. It also makes a great gift—share a bit of Japanese culture with your international friends.

※ This book was compiled from previously published cookbooks, "The Japanese Food for the Beginners," "Recipes of Japanese Cooking" and "Annual events of Japan and recipes of dishes" with the benefit of a newly added manuscript.

日本の四季と食彩

日本には春、夏、秋、冬の四季があります。カレンダーでは、3〜5月が春、6〜8月が夏、9〜11月が秋、12〜2月は冬になります。

春はまだまだ肌寒い日が続きますが、菜の花や桜などがいっせいに開花します。春には山菜などが食卓を彩ります。

5〜6月になると梅雨といわれる雨の日が続きま

There are four seasons in Japan; spring, summer, fall and winter. On the calendar, spring lasts from March to May, summer is from June to August, fall is from September to November, and winter is from December to February.

During the spring, chilly days continue, but the flowers of the field mustard and cherry blossoms start blooming all at once. And edible wild plants add colors to our tables.

May and June brings the rainy season, called "*tsuyu*." After the

春 は桜の開花が日本列島を北上します。花見は歴史的な慣習で、日本を象徴する花のひとつです。誰もが開花を心待ちにしています。

In spring, cherry blossoms start blooming from the south to the north throughout the Japanese islands. Viewing the cherry blossoms is a historical custom, and the flower is one of symbolic flowers of Japan. Everyone anticipates their bloom.

夏 になると多くの人が涼を求めて、渓谷や海水浴に行きます。暑い夏を伝統的な生活の知恵で楽しみながらのりこえます。

Many people go out to valleys and to the ocean to cool down. They manage the hot summers by following traditional ways of living.

す。この梅雨があけると夏の到来です。夏は伝統ある祭りや花火大会などが各地で催されます。

　秋は"読書の秋""食欲の秋""行楽の秋""スポーツの秋"などといわれるように、一年で1番すごしやすく、きのこや魚介類などの豊富な食材が出まわります。

　冬になると多くの地方で雪が降ります。12月になると"お坊さんが走りまわるほど忙しい師走"といい、12月の下旬には一年の汚れを取る大掃除をしたり、正月料理の準備をします。

　1月1日（元旦）は新年といい、神社にお参りに行き、一年の無事などのお願い事をします。2月になると梅が咲きはじめ、春が近いことを教えてくれます。

rainy season, the summer arrives. In summer, there are many traditional festivals and fireworks events in various locations.

The fall is known to be the season for reading, eating, going out and sports. It's the most comfortable season of the year, and ingredients like mushrooms and seafood become more abundant and available at stores.

In the winter, snow falls in many regions. December is known to be the busiest month—they say "even monks go running around in town." At the end of December, it's customary to do major housecleaning and preparation for the New Year's meal.

January 1st is New Year's Day, and people go to a shrine to pray for a peaceful year. Japanese plums start blooming in February, letting people know that the spring is coming soon.

秋になると紅葉が北国からはじまります。カエデなどで山が黄色や赤に染まります。休日になると多くの人が紅葉狩りを楽しみます。

In fall, leaves begin to turn red from the north. Maple leaves turn mountains yellow and red. Many tourists use holidays to enjoy the autumn leaves.

冬になると多くの地方に雪が降ります。白い雪におおわれた日本の里は、まるで水墨画を観ているかのような美しさです。

It snows in many regions in winter. Scenery of Japanese villages covered with white snow is just like a beautiful ink-wash painting.

春の歳時記と食彩
The Annual Events and Meals of Spring

日本の春は桜の開花とともにはじまります。桜前線は日本列島を北上して、春を告げます。桜が開花すると、友だち同士や職場の仲間が食べものやお酒を持って花見をします。また、女の子や男の子の成長の無事を願う"雛祭り""端午の節句"などの伝統的な行事がおこなわれます。祝いとしてちらし寿しや赤飯、柏餅などをいただきます。

Japanese spring starts with the blooming of the cherry blossoms. The cherry blossom front announces the start of spring, beginning from the south and going up to the north. When the cherry blossoms bloom, friends and colleagues from work gather with food and drinks to view the flowers. And there are traditional festivals celebrating girls' and boys' healthy growth, such as *"hina-matsuri"* and *"tango-no-sekku."* It's customary to celebrate with garnished sushi, festive red rice and rice cakes wrapped in an oak leaf.

花見には団子、桜もちなども食べられる
Rice dumplings and cherry flavored rice cakes are popular treats for cherry blossom viewing

日本の春は、桜をはじめとする多くの花がいっせいに咲きほこる。写真は桜と菜の花
In Japanese spring, many kinds of flowers including cherry blossoms start blooming all at once. The picture shows the flowers of the cherry blossom and the field mustard

Hina-Matsuri(Girl's Festival)

雛祭り

女の子の成長と健康を願う伝統文化
Traditional culture in hope of growth and health of the girl

　3月3日の"雛祭り"は、桃の花が開花する季節に催されるため"桃の節句"ともいわれます。さらに古くから桃が病気などの邪気を祓うといわれています。数日前から美しい雛人形を飾り、女の子の成長と健康を祝います。

　当日は、華やかな"ちらし寿し"、目出たい"赤飯""はまぐりの吸いもの"などをいただきます。また、甘酒、菱餅、雛あられなどを飾った後、みんなでいただきます。

"Hina-matsuri" is held on March 3rd. It's also called as "the festival of peach flower" because it's around the time for the peach flowers to start blooming. And also, the peach is believed to sweep away diseases and bad fortunes from old days. From several days prior to the festival, beautiful dolls are displayed to promote the healthy growth of girls.
On the day, they celebrate it with colorfully garnished "scattered sushi," festive "red rice" and "clam soup." And they also enjoy sweet mild sake called "amazake," rhombic-shape rice cakes called "hishimochi" and colorful rice crackers called "hina-arare" after displaying them.

写真は雛人形の七段飾り。ほかにも五段飾りなどがある
The picture shows hina dolls displayed in seven tiers. There are five-tier and others

はまぐりのお吸いもの
Clear clam soup

ひな祭りには、ちらし寿しと、はまぐりのお吸いものをいただく
Garnished sushi and clear clam soup are common dishes prepared for the girl's festival

春の歳時記カレンダー（3・4・5月）
Calendar of the events in spring (March, April, and May)

◆雛祭り（桃の節句）・3月3日
Hina-Matsuri (Girls' Festival) — March 3

◆花見（梅）・2〜3月
Hanami(Ume blossom viewing) — February to March

日本の初春を伝える梅の花
Flowers of ume plum trees are signs of early spring in Japan

◆花見（桜）・3〜5月
Hanami(Cherry Blos-som viewing) — from March to May

◆花見（桃）・4〜5月
Hanami(Peach blossom viewing) — April to May

◆端午の節句・5月5日
Tango no-Sekku (Boy's Festival) — May 5

Tangono-sekku (Boy's Festival)

端午の節句

男の子の健康と立身出世を願う伝統行事

Traditional culture in hope of health and success in life of the boy

端午の節句に兜（かぶと）を飾る家もある。これは武士の力強さを子どもに願う意味が強い
There are families who display a warrior helmet on Boy's Festival with hope that their boys will have a warrior's strength.

5月5日は"こどもの日"で祝日になります。また、"端午の節句"といわれ、男の子の健康や立身出世を願う日です。数日前から立身出世を象徴する"鯉のぼり"を庭に立てます。また、強さをイメージする"武者人形""金太郎人形""鎧""兜"などを飾ります。

当日は、薬草とされる菖蒲の葉を入れたお風呂に入り、子孫繁栄の意味が込められた"柏餅"を食べるのが、古くからの伝統です。

May 5th is Children's Day and a national holiday. It's also called "tangono-sekku" and a celebration day promoting the health and success of boys. From several days before, families with boys display colorful carp banners called "koi-nobori" that symbolize success in their gardens. They also display dolls that symbolize strength such as the doll warrior, a Kintaro doll, armor and a samurai worrier helmet.

On the day, it is an old tradition to put irises, known as a medical plant, in the bath and eat "kashiwa-mochi," a rice cake wrapped in an oak leaf, with hope for the prosperity of descendants.

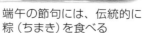

端午の節句には、伝統的に粽（ちまき）を食べる
Chimaki, a rice dumpling wrapped in bamboo leaves, is another traditional treat prepared for Boy's Festival

◆旬の食材
Seasonal Ingredients

菜の花 ● Rape blossom
春キャベツ ● Spring cabbage
わらび ● Bracken
ぜんまい ● Royal fern
たらの芽 ● Fatsia sprout
うど ● Udo
ふき ● Japanese butterbur
わさび ● Wasabi
三つ葉 ● Trefoil
にら ● Chinese chives
たけのこ ● Bamboo shoot
めばる ● Rockfish
かれい ● Flatfish
さより ● Halfbeak
さわら ● Spanish mackerel
まだい ● Red sea bream
はまぐり ● Hard-shell clam

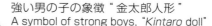

強い男の子の象徴 "金太郎人形"
A symbol of strong boys, "Kintaro doll"

夏の歳時記と食彩

The Annual Events and Meals of Summer

日本には梅雨といわれる長雨のシーズンがあります。この梅雨は稲作などには恵みの雨です。そんな梅雨がすぎると暑い夏の到来です。夏には、"冷やしそうめん"や"ざるそば"などの涼しげな料理や栄養満点な"うなぎ"などがよく食べられます。また、お祓や神幸祭として、日本各地で夏祭りや花火大会が催されます。

In Japan, there is a long rainy season called "*tsuyu*." This rainy season is a gift for rice cultivation. After the rainy season, hot summer arrives. It's common to cool down with cold dishes like "chilled *somen* noodles" or "*zaru-soba*" buckwheat noodles. Nourishing eel dishes are also popular for summer. Many summer festivals and fireworks events are held in various regions in Japan in the name of purification ceremonies and shrine rituals.

暑い夏によく食べられる "冷やっこ"
"Chilled tofu," a popular dish for hot summer

多くの人が涼を求めて、清流や海に行きます。写真は夏の清流
Many people go out on a search for cool environment like fresh streams and the ocean. The picture is a summer stream.

Natsu-Matsuri (Summer Festival)

夏祭り

お祓いや神幸祭などとして催される夏祭り
Summer festivals as purification ceremonies and shrine rituals

日本各地で夏祭りが催されますが、中でも有名なのが、京都の"祇園祭山鉾巡行"です。暑い夏の京都を代表する食べものは"はも"になります。

ほかには、揃いのはっぴで神輿をかつぐ、東京の"深川八幡祭り"、東北三大祭りの一つ宮城の"仙台七夕まつり"、青森の"ねぶた祭り"をはじめ、徳島の"阿波踊り"などの祭りが、日本の夏を彩ります。

Many summer festivals take place in various regions in Japan, but the most famous of all is "Gionsai-yamaboko-jungyo" of Kyoto. "Hamo," Common Japanese conger is a representative of the summer ingredients available in Kyoto.

There are other famous summer festivals, namely the "Fukagawa-hachiman" festival of Tokyo where participants wear the same "happi" festival costume and carry mikoshi portable shrines, "Sendai-tanabata" festival of Miyagi that is counted as one of the three large festivals in Tohoku region, "Nebuta-matsuri" of Aomori and "Awa-odori" of Tokushima.

京都の夏を彩る"祇園祭山鉾巡行"。世界各国から観光客が訪れる
"Gionsai-yamaboko-jungyo" is a famous summer festival of Kyoto. Many tourists visit from around the world to join the celebration

見物用有料観覧席有 Premium viewing seats are available : ☎ 075 (752) 7070

京都の暑い夏によく食べられる"はも料理"
"Hamo," Common Japanese conger is a famous Kyoto's summer dish

夏の歳時記カレンダー (6・7・8月)
Calendar of the events in summer (June, July, and August)

◆夏祭り・5 〜 8 月
Summer Festivals —From May to August

◆七夕・7 月 7 日
Tanabata (Star Festival)—on July 7

◆お盆・7 月 13 〜 15 日、8 月 13 〜 15 日
Bon Festival in the solar calendar—July13-15, August 13-15

◆海の日・7 月の第 3 月曜日
Marine Day—Third Monday in July

東北三大祭りの一つ"仙台七夕まつり"
"Sendai-tanabata" festival, one of the three large festivals in Tohoku region

写真提供：仙台七夕まつり協賛会

写真は東京都江東区の富岡八幡宮の神幸祭 " 深川八幡祭り "
The picture shows "Fukagawa-hachiman" festival, a shrine festival of Tsuruoka-hachiman shrine in Koto ward in Tokyo

Hanabi (Fireworks displays)・Obon

花火・お盆

夏の夜空を彩る花火。先祖供養の伝統行事が催されるお盆
Fireworks color the summer nights. During the *obon* period, traditional events are held to commemorate the ancestors

お盆の時期は、ご先祖さまにおはぎを供える
During the *obon* period, people offer sweet red bean rice cakes to their ancestors

日本の夜空を彩る花火。各地方で花火大会が催される
Fireworks color the Japanese night sky. There are many fireworks events in various regions

日本の夏を代表する風物詩の代表ともいえる花火大会は、日本各地で催されます。かつては、慰霊（いれい）と悪病退散のためにおこなわれていました。会場の近くでは、焼きとうもろこし、いか焼き、かき氷などの屋台が並びます。

お盆はご先祖の精霊（しょうりょう）を迎え、供養する期間のことです。この時期は肉類を使用しない精進料理を食べるのがならわしです。

Fireworks events represent Japanese summer traditions and take place in various places all over Japan. In the old days, they were practiced as memorial and purification ceremonies. Nowadays, stands selling roasted sweet corns, broiled squid and shaved ice line up near event sites.

Obon is a period of time to welcome ancestors' spirits and hold a memorial service. It is customary to prepare vegetarian dishes without using any meat.

◆旬の食材
Seasonal Ingredients

えだまめ ● *Edamame* (green soybeen)
そらまめ ● Broad bean
おくら ● Okra
みょうが ● *Mioga*
きゅうり ● Cucumber
にがうり ● Nigauri(bitter melon)
トマト ● Tomato
とうもろこし ● Corn
たまねぎ ● Onion
なす ● Eggplant
あじ ● Horse mackerel
いさき ● Chicken grunt
はも ● Pike eel
あなご ● Conger eel
うなぎ ● Eel
かつお ● Skipjack tuna
あゆ ● Sweetfish

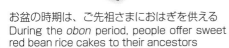

うな重
"*Unaju*," broiled eel served over rice

初夏の里山ではホタルが乱舞する
A myriad of fireflies dance around woodlands near villages in early summer

The Annual Events and Meals of Autumn
秋の歳時記と食彩

初秋になると稲穂がたわわに実り、日本の主食であるおいしい新米が市場に出まわります。また、"食欲の秋"といわれるほど、さんまなどの数多くの魚介類や野菜・キノコ類などが、食卓を賑わします。晩秋になると北国から紅葉が始まり、多くの人が紅葉狩りなどの行楽を楽しみます。また、すごしやすい秋は"読書の秋""スポーツの秋"などといわれています。

In the early fall, ears of rice grow in abundance and newly harvested delicious rice, the Japanese staple food, comes onto the market. As the fall is also said to be the season for eating, a variety of seafood such as Pacific saury, vegetables and mushrooms are served on the table. From the late fall, the leaves change to their autumn colors from the northland, and many people go out to enjoy them. The comfortable fall is also known as the season for reading and sports.

秋を代表する食材のさまざまなキノコが、食卓を楽しませてくれる
Mushrooms are autumn ingredients. Various kinds of mushrooms are served on the table

晩秋になると北国や高地から山々が赤や黄色に染まる
From the late fall, mountains become red and yellow, starting from the northland and upland areas

Shichi-Go-San (Celebration of 3, 5, and 7-Year-Old Children)

七五三

子どもの無事の成長と健康を願う伝統行事
Traditional ceremony in hope of the healthy growth of children

　七五三は、11月15日に子どもが無事に成長したお祝いや、無事に成長することを願う行事です。七は7歳の女の子、五は5歳の男の子、三は3歳の男の子と女の子のことになります。

　七五三には、神社や氏神にお参りに行き、縁起物の"千歳飴"をいただきます。地方によって異なりますが、七五三の祝いには親類を招き、真鯛の塩焼き、車えび、伊勢えび、ちらし寿しなどの料理で祝います。

Shichi-go-san is a traditional festival to celebrate children's growth and pray for their future health on November 15th. "*Shichi*" is for 7-year-old girls, "*go*" is for 5-year-old boys and "*san*" is for 3-year-old boys and girls.
On the day, families go to a shrine to pray and receive traditional candies called "*chitose-ame*." It's varied depending on each region but commonly families invite their relatives and celebrate with festive dishes such as salt-grilled red snapper, prawns, lobster and garnished sushi.

家族で子どもの成長を願い、神社へ行く
Children go to a shrine to pray for their growth with their families

千歳飴は長くのびる（末永く生きる）として、七五三に欠かせないものである
"*Chitose-ame*" is an indispensable item on shichi-go-san. Its long shape is a symbolic representation of longevity

真鯛の塩焼きは、特に3歳の祝いに"真魚（まな）の祝い"として使われた
Salt-grilled red snapper was used as a festive fish especially for 3-year-old children

鯛同様、目出たい時の祝いに用いられる伊勢えび
Lobster is also a festive ingredient like red snapper

地方によって異なるが、七五三には、えびの入った"ちらし寿し"などが食べられる
It's varied in regions, but garnished sushi with prawns is a common festive dish for *shichi-go-san*

秋の歳時記カレンダー（9・10・11月）
Calendar of the events in spring (September, October, November)

◆月見・9月中旬〜10月上旬の満月
Tsukimi (Full Moon Viewing) —on the full moon night from the middle of September to the beginning of October

◆お彼岸・9月20〜26日
Ohigan (Equinoctial Week)—from September 20 to 26

◆体育の日・10月第2月曜日
Taiku-no-hi (Health and Sports Day) —Second Monday of Octobar

◆紅葉狩り・9月中旬〜11月
Momiji-gari (Viewing the Autunm Colors)—from October to November

◆七五三・11月15日
Shichi-go-san (Seven-Five-Three)—November 15

Koraku (Holiday-making)

行楽

日本全国の観光地が賑わうシーズン

The season for tourist spots of Japan to get crowded

秋は温泉も人気
Onsen hot springs are also popular

日本の四季の中で最もすごしやすいといわれる秋は、行楽（旅行など）に最適なシーズンで、日本全国の観光地が多くの人で賑わいます。

京都は日本を代表する観光地
Kyoto is a very popular tourist spot in Japan

特に紅葉が楽しめ、歴史的建造物がある京都、奈良などが人気です。また、行楽弁当（おにぎり、いなり寿し、筑前煮）をたずさえて行く、紅葉狩りも盛んです。

Since fall is the most comfortable season of a year, it's also the best time for travel and holidays. Tourist spots in Japan get very crowded with many tourists.

Especially, it's the season for autumn leaves, and cities with historical architectures like Kyoto and Nara are popular spots. It's also common to go enjoy the autumn leaves with *"koraku-bento"* lunchboxes filled with rice balls, *inari-zushi* and simmered vegetables in *Chikuzen*-style.

近場の行楽に欠かせない "行楽弁当"
"Koraku-bento" lunchbox is good to bring to nearby sightseeing places

◆旬の食材
Seasonal Ingredients

れんこん ●	Lotus root
まつたけ ●	Matsutake mushroom
里いも ●	Taro
さつまいも ●	*Satsuma-imo* (Sweet potato)
かぼちゃ ●	Pumpkin
しゅんぎく ●	Garland chrysanthemun
ゆず ●	Japanese lime
くり ●	Japanese chestnut
ぎんなん ●	Gingko nut
そば ●	Buckwheat noodles
さば ●	Mackerel
さんま ●	Pacific saury
かつお ●	Skipjack tune
さけ ●	Salmon
かき ●	Giant pacific oyster

ぎんなん
Gingko nut

晩秋からよく食べられる "カキ"
Oysters become available from the late fall

冬の歳時記と食彩

The Annual Events and Meals of Winter

日本の冬の最大の行事は、なんといっても大晦日(おおみそか)と元旦、正月ではないでしょうか…。大晦日には、門松や注連縄(しめなわ)、鏡餅(かがみもち)などの元旦用の飾りをほどこし、正月用の料理を作ります。大晦日に年越しそばを食べます。元旦には「あけましておめでとうございます」と挨拶をします。一年の無事や願い事をするために神社に参拝します。これを初詣(はつもうで)といいます。

正月によく食べられる"ぞう煮"
"Zoni" dish is a typical New Year's meal

The biggest events during the Japanese winter are New Year's Eve, New Year's Day and the New Year Holidays. On New Year's Eve, New Year's decorations are displayed at each home, such as *"kadomatsu"* pine trees, *"shimenawa"* Shinto straw festoon and *"kagami-mochi"* round rice-cakes, and New Year's dishes are prepared. Buckwheat noodles called *"toshikoshi-soba"* are traditionally enjoyed on New Year's Eve. On New Year's Day, people greet each other saying, *"Akemashite Omedetou-gozaimasu"* and make a visit to a shrine to pray for a peaceful year. This first shrine visit of the year is called the *"hatsumode."*

元旦に神社に行くことを"初詣"という
The first visit to a shrine is called "hatsumode."

Gantan, Syogatsu (New Year's Day, the New Year)

元旦・正月

無病息災を願う元旦、一年の始まりを祝う正月

Praying for a peaceful year on New Year's Day, celebrating the beginning of a year during the New Year

元旦は新年の初日（1日）の朝（午前中）のことです。基本的に元旦に神社や寺に行くことを初詣といいます。正月は1月1〜15日までになりますが、3日までを三が日といって、休日になります。

正月には、伝統的な料理（正月料理）や伝統的な遊び（凧揚げ、コマまわし、羽根つき、福笑いなど）をします。

To be exact, "*gantan*," New Year's Day, means the morning of the first day of a new year. Basically, "*hatsumode*" means going to a shrine or a temple on "*gantan*." Traditionally, the New Year starts from January 1th to 15th, but actual New Year's Holidays are the first three days called "*sanga-nichi*."

During the New Year, people enjoy traditional New Year's meals and play with traditional toys and games such as kite-flying, spinning tops, "*hanetsuki*" badminton and make-a-face games.

正月に子どもたちにポチ袋にお金を入れた"お年玉"をあげるのが習慣
It's a New Year's custom to give children "*otoshidama*," a monetary gift enclosed in "*pochi-bukuro*," a small decorated envelop

正月には縁起ものの料理をいただく
Various New Year's festive dished are served during the New Year

三が日に女性（お母さん）が休めるように、重箱におせち料理が入れられている
Traditional New Year's food called "*osechi-ryori*" is packed in tiered food boxes. It's prepared plentifully so that women (especially mothers) can rest during the first three days

冬の歳時記カレンダー（12・1・2月）
Calendar of the events in winter (December, January, and February)

◆師走（冬至）・12月
shiwasu (*Toji*) — December

◆大晦日・12月31日
Oomisoka (New Year's Eve) — December 31

◆元旦（新年）・1月1日
New Year's Day — January 1

◆初詣・1月1〜7日
Hatsu-Moude (the First Visit to a Shrine or a Temple of the Year) — January 1

◆書き初め・1月2日
Kaki-zome (the First Calligraphy of the year) — January 2

◆七草がゆ・1月7日
Nanakusa-gayu (Porridge Mixed with the Seven Spring Herbs) — January 7

◆鏡開き・1月11日
Kagami-biraki (Cutting of New Year Rice Cake) — January 11

◆成人の日・1月の第2月曜日
Coming-of-Age Day — Second Monday of January

◆節分・2月3〜4日
Setsubun (Seasonal Division) — February 3 to 4

Kagami-biraki, Nanakusagayu, Setsubun (Cutting a kagami-mochi rice cake, Rice porridge with 7 herbs, the traditional end of winter)

鏡開き・七草がゆ・節分

体の健康を願う鏡開きと七草がゆ、家族の邪霊災厄を願う節分
A wish for a healthy life by "kagami-biraki" and "nanakusagayu"
An event to expel evil spirits out of houses on "setsubun"

1月7日は、正月に疲れた体をいたわるためや無病息災を願って、七草がゆをいただきます。1月11日には、鏡開きといって正月に供えた鏡餅を木づちで開き（割り）、一年の健康を願いお汁粉に入れたり、焼いていただきます。

2月3・4日は節分になります。節分は豆まきをして、家の邪霊災厄（鬼にみたてている）を除くための伝統行事です。

「鬼は外、福は内」といいながらする豆まきは、鬼を払います。まいた豆を歳の数だけ食べると、一年を健康ですごせるといわれています。柊挿しは、柊の葉のトゲといわしの焼いた臭いで邪鬼を払うものです。

また、めでたい七福神にちなみ七種類の具材を巻いた"恵方巻き"を願い事をしながら、無言で1本丸ごと食べる地方もあります。

無病息災を願い食べられる七草がゆ。七種類の野菜は、（せり、なずな、はこべ、ごぎょう、ほとけのざ、すずな、すずしろ）になる
Rice porridge with 7 herbs is prepared in hope of a healthy life. Seven herbs are namely seri, nazuna, hakobe, gogyo, hotokenoza, suzuna, and suzushiro.

On January 7th, people eat nanakusa-gayu rice porridge with seven kinds of herbs in hope for healthy lives. This porridge is known to be good for digestion after eating and drinking too much over the New Year. On January 11th, they break round rice cakes called "kagami-mochi," used as New Year's decoration with a wooden hammer, and eat them by adding in sweet red bean soup or toasting them.

February 3rd and 4th are called "setsubun." There is a traditional event to expel evil sprits out by throwing handful of beans out of houses on "setsubun."

People throw beans while shouting "Demons out! Good luck in!" to drive the demons out of their homes. It's believed that good health will prevail all year around if they eat the same number of thrown beans as their ages. There is another tradition to display a broiled sardine head poked into a branch of holly trees. The holly prickles and the smell of the sardine expel the demons.

A festive food for "setsubun" is sushi roll with seven kinds of ingredients called "eho-maki." Seven is derived from "shichi-fukujin," Seven Deities of Good Fortune. There is a tradition to eat a whole sushi roll silently in some regions.

◆旬の食材
Seasonal Ingredients

かぶ ●	Turnip
だいこん ●	Giant white radish
はくさい ●	Chinese cabbage
みずな ●	Potherb mustard
にんじん ●	Carrot
ねぎ ●	*Naga-negi*-onion
ぶり ●	Japanese amberjack (Yellowtaijl)
ひらめ ●	Bastard halibut
はたはた ●	Japanese sandfish
ふぐ ●	Puffer
あまだい ●	Tilefish
くろまぐろ ●	Bluefin tuna
けがに ●	Horsehair crab
ずわいがに ●	Snow crab
あまえび ●	Northern shrimp

地方によっては、節分に焼いたいわしを食べて邪霊災厄をする
Broiled sardines are served in the hope for healthy lives in some regions

豆まきは、基本的に炒った大豆を使用する
Only toasted beans are used for throwing

鏡開きをした餅をお汁粉や焼いていただく
Broken rice cakes are put in sweet red bean soup or get toasted

17

目 次・CONTENTS

第五章 Chapter 5
和食の基本・焼きもの ────── 107 ～ 126
Basic Japanese Grilled and Pan-Fried Dishes

第六章 Chapter 6
和食の基本・揚げもの ────── 127 ～ 148
Basic Japanese Deep-Fried Dishes

第七章 Chapter 7
和食の基本・お弁当 ──── 149 ～ 162
Basic Japanese Packed Lunch

第八章 Chapter 8
和食の基本・蒸しもの ──── 163 ～ 172
Basic Japanese Steamed Dishes ···················

Column・コラム

❶料理名／ Name of the dish

❷調理時間の目安／ Approximarte time required to complete cooking

❸料理のカロリー／ Calories of the dish

※カロリーは１人前です。

※ The indicated calories are for one serving.

❹材料と分量／ Ingredienes and their quantities used for the dish

❺料理の作り方の手順／ Specific recipe of the dish

❻料理の工程写真／ Cooking process photos

❼コツのコツ／ Tips useful for successful results

❽食材（料理）のバリエーション／ Other suitable ingredients (dishes)

分量の目安 ● Measurement Conversion

【容量・LIQUID MEASURE】

● 小さじ 1=1 tsp=5㎖ (cc)　● 大さじ 1=1 Tbsp=15㎖ (cc)

● 1 カップ =1 Japanese cup =200㎖ (cc)

※ 1 (U.S.) cup =240(236) ㎖ (cc)

【長さ・LINEAR MEASURE】

● 1cm=0.39 inches　● 1inch=2.5(2.54) cm

※詳しい分量の目安は 27 ページを参照にしてください。

※ Refer to p.27 for a detailed measurement conversion.

【重量・WEIGHTS】

● 1 ounce =30 (28.35) grams

● 1 gram =0.035 ounces

【揚げ油の温度 DEEP-FRYING OIL TEMPERATURES】

● 160℃／ 320℉－165℃／ 330℉=low

● 170℃／ 340℉－175℃／ 350℉=medium

● 175℃／ 350℉－180℃／ 360℉=high

Basic Knowledge of Japanese Cuisine
和食の基本知識

和食に使用する道具の名称から使い方、度量衡表、おいしい和食を作るための食材の切り方と下ごしらえ、よく使用する調味料などを紹介している。和食の基本として覚えておきたい。

In this chapter, names and how to use basic equipment for making Japanese food, measurements, cutting techniques, preparation and basic seasonings are introduced. They are the essential basics of Japanese cuisine and should be remembered.

食に使用する道具・ Things to have on hand to make Japanese food

和食に使用する代表的な道具を紹介。各道具の特徴をうまく利用して和食に挑戦したい

Here are the basic tools you'll need to make Japanese food. Get familiar with their features so you can make the best use of them.

万能包丁 ● Universal Knife

いろいろな料理に使えます。刃の長さが18〜20cmくらいのものが使いやすいです。

Can be used for various dishes. One with a 7 to 8-inch long blade is easy to use.

出刃包丁 ● Kitchen Carver

肉厚なので、魚をおろしたり、骨つき肉をたたき切る時に便利な包丁です。大出刃と小出刃があります。

Because of its thickness, kitchen carvers are often used for filleting fish or cutting chicken with bones. Two sizes, small and large, are available.

まな板 ● Cutting Board

食材を切る時に必要なまな板は、木製とプラスチック製があります。木製は食材の臭いが移りやすく、プラスチック製は水に濡れると食材がすべりやすいです。

Two types, wooden and plastic, are available. Wooden cutting boards are often left with the smell of ingredients after use while the plastic version becomes slippery when wet.

菜切り包丁 ● Vegetable Knife

大根の輪切り、桂むき、かぼちゃなどのかたい野菜を切るのに適しています。刃の長さが17cm くらいのものが使いやすいです。

Suitable for slicing giant white radish into rounds or paper-thin slices, as well as for cutting pumpkins and other hard vegetables. One with a 6 3/4-inch blade is easy to use.

柳包丁 ● Fish Slicer

別名刺し身包丁ともいわれます。魚の刺し身、薄造りなどに使用します。

Fish slicers are often referred to as "sashimi-bocho" in Japanese. As the name indicates, they are suitable for preparing sashimi.

玉じゃくし ● Soup Ladle

みそ汁などの汁ものをすくう時に使用します。

Used for scooping miso soup or other types of liquids.

穴あき玉じゃくし ● Ladle with Holes

汁ものの具だけを取る時に便利です。また、溶き卵を入れる時などによいです。

Convenient for scooping only ingredients from soup. These ladles can also be used when putting an egg into soup while whipping it.

ターナー・フライ返し ● Turner

煮魚や焼き魚など煮崩れしやすいものを裏返したり、盛りつけたりする時に便利です。

Convenient and useful for reversing delicate simmered or grilled fish that loses its shape easily in a pan or on a grill, or for arranging food on plates.

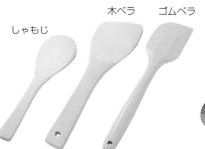

しゃもじ　　　　木ベラ　　ゴムベラ

しゃもじ・木ベラ・ゴムベラ ● Flat Wooden Spoon, Wooden/ Rubber Spatula

ご飯を盛る時や、調理中に材料を混ぜたり、裏ごしなどに使用します。

Used for putting boiled rice into bowls, mixing ingredients while cooking and straining.

計量カップ ● Measuring Cup

だし汁や小麦粉などの材料の体積を量るカップです。

Used for measuring the volume of basic stock, flour, etc.

万能こし器 ● Strainer

みそ汁を作る際、みそを溶く時に使用します。
Used for straining miso when cooking miso soup.

菜箸・揚げ箸 ● Kichen Chopsticks

和食には用途に分けて箸を使い分けます。最低2組みは揃えたいです。
Several pairs of chopsticks are usually used for different purposes. At least two pairs should always be at hand.

ザル ● Draining Basket, Sieve

ボウルと合わせて使うことが多く、食材を洗ったり、水けをきったりするのに用います。
Often used in combination with a bowl for rinsing and draining ingredients.

鉄鍋 ● Iron Pot

熱が伝わりやすいので煮ものや鍋ものによく使用します。
Because of the quick heat transfer qualities of iron, these pots are often used for simmered and one-pot dishes.

ホーロー鍋 ● Enamel Pot

酸に強く、さびにくいので煮もの、汁ものによく使用します。
Because these pots are resistant to acid, and difficult to rust, they are often used for simmered dishes and soup.

ボウル ● Bowl

食材を洗う、浸す、混ぜる、泡立てる、あえるなど、あらゆる料理の下ごしらえに欠かせません。
A utensil indispensable for cooking, which can be used for rinsing, immersing, mixing, whipping and dressing ingredients.

フライパン（鉄製）● Steel Frying Pan

熱伝導が高く、使い込むほど油がなじみます。大きなものは天ぷらにも使用出来ます。
Heat transfers quickly. The more they are used, the more easily oil can be spread thoroughly. Large-size pans can be used for deep-frying tempura ingredients.

フライパン（フッ素樹脂加工）● Fluororesin-processed Frying Pan

焦げつきにくく余計な油を使わないので人気の素材です。必要以上に加熱すると樹脂がはがれてしまいます。
Frying pans that are currently gaining popularity because they keep ingredients from scorching and require only a little oil. The resin will come off if heated excessively.

落としぶた ● Drop-Lid

煮ものを作る時に、煮崩れを防いだり、味が全体にしみ込むようにするために使います。アルミホイルでもよいです。
Used for simmered dishes to prevent ingredients from losing shape, or allow seasonings to soak into every part of the ingredients evenly. Aluminum foil can be used as a replacement.

アルミ鍋 ● Aluminum Pot

軽く熱が伝わりやすいので煮魚や炒り煮、みそ汁など和食全般に使用出来ます。
Because of their quick heat transfer qualities, these pots can be used for a wide range of Japanese dishes such as simmered fish, irini or dishes simmered until the liquid is gone, and miso soup.

ステンレス鍋 ● Stainless Steel Pot

耐久性があり煮込み料理や汁ものに最適です。
Very durable pots suitable for simmered dishes and soup.

土鍋 ● Earthenware Pot

陶器製の鍋で熱の当たりが柔らかく冷めにくい特徴があります。
These pots allow heat to transfer slowly and gently, and retain heat well.

裏ごし器 ● Fine Sieve

食材の舌ざわりをなめらかにする時に使用します。
Used for straining ingredients to smoothen their texture.

骨抜き ● Fish Bone Removing Tweezers

小骨の多い魚（あじ、さばなど）の中骨を取るのに使います。
Used for removing the fine bones of horse mackerel, mackerel, etc.

はかり ● Scale

食材の重量を量る。初めて作る料理はきちんと量りましょう。
Used for weighing ingredients. Precisely weighing each ingredient is recommended for a dish you will cook for the first time.

ふきん ● Cloth

綿、麻、レーヨンなど素材はたくさんあるが、用途によって使い分けましょう。
Materials differ widely, including cotton, jute and rayon. Always have several cloths on hand in the kitchen for different pur-poses.

おろし金 ● Grater

大根、わさび、しょうがなどをすり下ろす時に使用します。材質は銅製、陶磁器製、プラスチック製などがあります。
Used for grating giant white radish, *wasabi* horseradish, ginger, etc. They are usually made of copper, ceramic or plastic.

うろこ取り ● Fish Scale Remover

魚のうろこは包丁でも取れるが、うろこのかたい魚に使用するとよいでしょう。
Scaling can also be done with a knife, but these removers come in handy when scaling hard fish.

蒸し器 ● Steamer

茶わん蒸しなどの蒸しものに欠かせません。アルミ製のものはふたに水滴が着いて水滴が落ちるので、ふきんをはさんで使用します。
A utensil indispensable for cooking steamed dishes such as chawan-mushi savory custard. For aluminum steamers, insert a cloth between the lid and pot when steaming to prevent the moisture on the inner side of the lid from dripping onto food.

飯台 ● Wooden Sushi Bowl

ちらし寿しなどの寿し飯を作る時に使います。木製なので余分な水分を吸ってくれます。
Used for preparing vinegared rice for garnished sushi and other types of sushi. Wood absorbs excess moisture.

すり鉢・すりこぎ ● Grinding Bowl and Pestle

あえものなどのタレを作る時やすったりする時などに使用します。すりこぎは、すり鉢の直径の２倍くらいの長さが使いやすいです。
Used for grinding ingredients or when preparing dressing for dressed foods. Pestles should ideally be about twice as long as the diameter of the grinding bowl.

キッチンペーパー ● Kitchen Paper

食材の水けや油をふき取ったりするのに便利です。
Convenient for wiping off excess moisture or oil from ingredients.

フードプロセッサー ● Food Processor

細かく切ったり、みじん切りや混ぜたりも出来ます。乾物を砕いたりするのにも使えます。
These processors can handle ingredients in several ways including thin cutting, fine chopping and mixing. They can also be used for grinding dry food.

巻きす ● Bamboo Rolling Mat

巻き寿しを作る時に使う他、ゆでた青菜を絞る時などに使います。
In addition to making sushi rolls, these mats can also be used for draining boiled greens.

ラップ ● Wrap

食材を包んで保存したり、料理の保存に使用します。電子レンジに利用出来ます。
Used for storing ingredients or cooked dishes. They are microwave-safe.

アルミホイル ● Aluminum Foil

熱に強いので食材を包んでホイル焼きにしたり、落としぶたとしても使えます。
Because these foils are uninflammable, they are often used for foil-cooked dishes. They can also be used as a substitute for a drop-lid.

計量スプーン ● Measuring Spoon

少量の調味料を量るスプーン。小さじ（2.5ml、5ml）、大さじ（15ml）の三種類が一般的です。
Used for measuring the small volume of a seasoning. The most common three types are tsp (1/6 cu. in. and 1/3 cu. in.) and Tbsp (1 cu. in.).

度量衡表
Measurements

容量 ●LIQUID MEASURE

- 小さじ 1＝1 tsp＝5㎖ (cc)　● 大さじ 1＝1 Tbsp＝15㎖ (cc)
- 1 カップ＝1 Japanese cup ＝200㎖ (cc)
- ※ 1 (U.S.) cup ＝240(236) ㎖ (cc)
- ※表の数値はおよその値で換算している。
- ※ The figures in the table indicate roughly converted values.

spoons	㎖	u.s. cup	Japanese cup	ounces
3 Tbsp+1 tsp	47 ㎖ (50 ㎖)	1/5 cup	1/4 cup	1 1/2 oz
4 Tbsp	59 ㎖	1/4 cup		2 oz
5 Tbsp+1 tsp	79 ㎖	1/3 cup		
7 Tbsp-1 tsp	94 ㎖ (100 ㎖)	2/5 cup	1/2 cup	3 1/3 oz
8 Tbsp	118 ㎖ (120 ㎖)	1/2 cup		4 oz
10 Tbsp	142 ㎖ (150 ㎖)	3/5 cup		5 oz
13 Tbsp+1 tsp	200 ㎖	4/5 cup	1 cup	6 2/3 oz
16 Tbsp	236 ㎖ (240 ㎖)	1 cup		8 oz
	296 ㎖ (300 ㎖)	1 1/4 cup	1 1/2 cup	10 oz
	394 ㎖ (400 ㎖)	1 2/3 cup	2 cup	14 oz
	473 ㎖	2 cup		
	500 ㎖	2 1/8 cup	2 1/2 cup	
	560 ㎖	2 2/5 cup		19 oz
	600 ㎖	2 1/2 cup	3 cup	
	710 ㎖	3 cup		
	800 ㎖	3 1/3 cup	4 cup	
	946 ㎖	4 cup		

長さ ●LINEAR MEASURE

- 1cm＝0.39 inches　● 1inch＝2.5(2.54) cm

CENTIMETERS	INCHES
1.5mm	1/16 in
3mm	1/8 in
5mm	3/16 in
1cm	3/8 in
1.5cm	1/2 in
2cm	3/4 in
2.5cm	1 in

CENTIMETERS	INCHES
4cm	1 1/2 in
5cm	2 in
6.5cm	2 1/2 in
8cm	3 in
9cm	3 1/2 in
10cm	4 in

重量 ●WEIGHTS

- 1 ounce ＝30 (28.35) grams
- 1 gram ＝0.035 ounces

GRAMS	OUNCES	POUNDS
5 g	1/6 oz	
10 g	1/3 oz	
15 g	1/2 oz	
20 g	2/3 oz	
30 g	1 oz	
50 g	1 3/4 oz	
60 g	2 oz	
70 g	2 1/2 oz	
80 g	2 4/5 oz	
85 g	3 oz	
100 g	3 1/2 oz	
115 g	4 oz	1/4 lb
140 g	5 oz	
150 g	5 1/4 oz	
170 g	6 oz	
200 g	7 oz	
225 g	8 oz	1/2 lb
300 g	10 1/2 oz	
340 g	12 oz	3/4 lb
360 g	12 2/3 oz	
400 g	14 oz	
450 g	16 oz	1 lb
500 g	18 oz	
600 g	21 oz	
700 g	24 1/2 oz	
800 g	28 oz	1 3/4 lb

揚げ油の温度
DEEP-FRYING OIL TEMPERATURES

- 160℃／320℉－165℃／330℉＝low
- 170℃／340℉－175℃／350℉＝medium
- 175℃／350℉－180℃／360℉＝high

食材の切り方と下ごしらえ
Cutting Techniques & Preparations

野菜の基本的な切り方 ● Vegetable Cutting Techniques

輪切り ● Rounds

にんじんや大根、なすなどの材料を円形に切ります。材料の皮を薄くむき、用途によって厚さを揃え、均等に切っていきます。

A technique used for slicing *daikon* giant white radishes, carrots and other cylindrical ingredients into rounds. Peel the ingredient thinly, and slice it crosswise for rounds of uniform thickness. The thickness depends on how the ingredient is to be used in dishes.

薄切り ● Thin Slices

玉ねぎや大根を幅1mm程度の薄さに材料の端から切っていきます。スライサーを使えばより均等に仕上がります。

A technique used for slicing onions, *daikon* giant white radishes and other vegetables from one end into rounds of about 1/25-inch thickness. Slicers are handy for realizing a more uniform finish.

斜め切り ● Diagonal Cut

長ねぎ、なす、きゅうり、にんじんなどの厚さを均等に斜めに切っていきます。

A technique used for cutting *naga-negi* onions, eggplants, cucumbers and other cylindrical vegetables diagonally. Make sure that the thickness is uniform.

小口切り ● Edge Cut

細長い野菜、ごぼう、長ねぎ、きゅうりなどを輪切りの要領で切ることです。厚さを揃え、均等に切っていきます。

A technique used for slicing burdock, *naga-negi* onions, cucumbers and other long slender cylindrical vegetables into rounds. When slicing, make sure that the thickness is uniform.

せん切り ● Julienne Strips

キャベツ、レタス、青じそなどを繊維にそって、薄切りと同様に幅1mm程度に均等に切っていきます。

A technique used for cutting cabbages, lettuces, green perilla, etc. very thinly(about 1/25 -inch thick). Vegetables should be cut in the same direction as their grain.

そぎ切り ● Shaving Cut

主にしいたけや白菜に使われる切り方です。包丁を寝かせるように入れ、そぐように切っていきます。

A technique used for shiitake mushrooms and Chinese cabbages. Shave vegetables thinly using the knife in such a way that it is almost laid on its side.

半月切り ● Half-moons

にんじんや大根、きゅうりなどの円筒状の材料を縦半分に切り、輪切りの要領で半月の形に切っていきます。

A technique used for cutting carrots, *daikon* giant white radishes, cucum-bers and other cylindrical vegetables into half-moons. Cut vegetables in half lengthwise, and then slice them crosswise.

いちょう切り ● Quarter-rounds

にんじんや大根などの円筒状の材料を縦4等分に切り、厚さを均等にして、いちょうの葉のように切っていきます。

A technique used for cutting carrots, daikon giant white radishes and other cylindrical vegetables into quarter-rounds. Cut vegetables in quarters lengthwise, and then slice them crosswise. Make sure that the thickness is uniform.

くし切り ● Wedge Cut

トマト、オレンジ、レモンなど球形の材料を縦に6〜8等分に切り、くしのような形にします。

A technique used for cutting tomatoes, oranges, lemons and other spherical foods into wedges. Cut foods lengthwise in sixths or eighths

拍子切り ● Bar Rectangles

材料を長さ3〜4cmに揃えて切ります。繊維にそって厚さ5〜6mmに切っていきます。次に切ったものを横にたおし、幅5〜6mm程度に切り、拍子のような形に揃えながら切っていきます。

Cut vegetables into 11/5 to 11/2-inch lengths. Cut them in the same direction as their grain into rectangles of 1/8 to 1/4-inch thickness. Lay them on their side, and cut them into bars of 1/8 to 1/4-inch thickness.

細切り ● Thin Cut

材料を長さ4〜5cmに切ってから、繊維にそって縦に2mm程度に切っていき、そのまま横にたおして2mm程度に切っていきます。

Cut vegetables into 1 1/2 to 2-inch lengths. Cut them lengthwise in the same direction as their grain into rectangles of about 1/12-inch thickness. Lay them on their side, and cut them into thin pieces of about 1/12-inch thickness.

短冊切り ● Rectangles

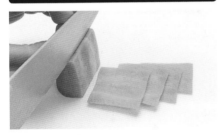

拍子切りの要領で材料を長さ4〜5cmに切り、それを繊維にそって薄切りに切っていき、それをそのまま横にたおして幅8mm程度に切っていきます。

Cut vegetables into 1 3/5 to 2-inch lengths. Cut them thinly in the same direction as their grain. Lay them on their side, and cut them into rectangles of about 1/3-inch thickness.

さいの目切り ● Cube Cut

拍子切りにした材料を端から幅1cm程度に切り、さいころ状にします。

Cut bar rectangles from one end into cubes of about 1/25-inch thickness.

乱切り ● Rolling Wedges

包丁を斜めに入れて、野菜を回し、角度を変えながら大きさをほぼ一定にして切っていきます。

Make diagonal cuts while rotating vegetables a quarter turn between cuts.

針しょうが ● Ginger Needles

皮をむいたしょうがを薄切りにし、それを4～5枚重ね繊維にそって針のように細く切っていきます。

Slice peeled ginger thinly. Then, cut a stack of 4 to 5 slices in the same direction as their grain into thin needle-like shapes.

あられ切り ● Dice Cut

さいの目切りより小さな切り方です。材料を長さ4～5cmに揃えて5mm程度の厚さに切り、拍子切りの要領で切っていきます。それを端から5mmに大きさを揃えて切っていきます。

A technique used for cutting vegetables into cubes with a size smaller than those of the cube cut technique. Cut vegetables into 1 1/2 to 2-inch lengths. Then, cut them lengthwise into rectangles of about 1/8-inch thickness as in the bar rectangles technique. Cut them from one end into 1/8-inch cubes.

ささがき ● Sasagaki Shavings

ごぼうの皮をたわしや包丁の背でこそげ落としてから端から5cmくらいのところまで十字に切り込みを入れ、鉛筆を削る要領で端からごぼうを少しずつ回しながらそぎ落としていきます。

Scrape off the burdock skin with a *tawashi* kitchen brush or using the back of a knife. Make a lengthwise cross-shape incision about 2 inches deep at one end, and cut it from that end as if you were sharpening a pencil while rotating little by little with the other hand.

みじん切り（玉ねぎ） ● Fine Chopping (Onions)

縦半分に切り、そのまま横にたおし幅5mm程度に薄切りに切っていきます。次に横から包丁を入れます。端から細かく切っていきます。

Cut onions in half lengthwise. Then, with the cut face down, slice them into pieces of about 1/8-inch thickness. Make sideway cuts. Cut them finely from one end.

切り違いきゅうり ● Cucumber Peaks

4 ～ 5cm ほどの筒切りにしたきゅうりの真ん中に切り目を入れ、切り目に届くように 45 度斜めに切り込みを入れます。裏返して同じように切り目を入れます。

Cut cucumber into 1 1/2 to 2-inch lengths. Run the knife through the center of a length, and make a diagonal cut(45°) halfway through the cucumber up to the center cut. Make an identical diagonal cut from the other side.

面取り ● Bevel-edged Cylinders

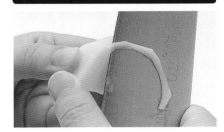

主に大根やいも類で使うことが多い切り方です。材料の角の部分を包丁の角度を一定にし、左手で大根を回転させながら包丁を送り込み、面を取っていきます。

A technique often used for giant white radishes and potatoes. Edges of ingredients are beveled for a neat appearance. Apply the knife to the edge of an ingredient at a certain angle, and rotate the ingredient with the left hand.

隠し包丁 ● Penetration-facilitating Cut

面取りしたものを煮る時に味がしみ込みやすく、火の通りを早くするため、裏面に全体の厚みの３分の１くらいまでの十字の切り込みを入れます。

Make a cross-shape incision from one end of a bevel-edged cylindrical ingredient up to about 1/3 of the length. This will facilitate the penetration of seasonings and heat when simmering them.

末広切り ● Fan Cut

4 ～ 5cm の長さに切り、一片の端を4分の１ほど残して縦に細く切り目を入れ、切り目を寝かせるように左右に広げます。

Cut vegetables into 1 1/2 to 2-inch lengths. Make lengthwise cuts at narrow, even intervals through all but 3/8 to 5/8-inch (about 1/4 of the entire length) at one end. Gently spread open the "fan."

白髪ねぎ ● Naga-negi Onion "Gray Hair" Cut

長ねぎを 4 ～ 5cm 程度の長さに切り、縦に１本の切り込みを入れてから青い部分を取り除き材料を重ねて、せん切りの要領で細く切っていきます。

Cut the white portion of naga-negi onions into 1 1/2 to 2-inch lengths. Make an incision in their center to remove the soft green core. Cut them thinly as in the julienne strips technique.

しいたけの飾り切り ● Shiitake Decorative Cut

生しいたけに３本の切り込みを入れ、切り込みに向かって包丁を左右から斜めに削るように切り込みを入れていきます。鍋料理などに使用します。

Make three incisions on top of each shiitake mushroom, and bevel these cuts by inserting the knife diagonally into them.

野菜の下ごしらえ ● Preparing Vegetables

きゅうり ● Cucumber

板ずり／まな板に塩をふり、その上できゅうりを転がします。きゅうりの緑色がより鮮やかになります。

Roll them on a board (*Itazuri*) / Sprinkle a little salt on the cutting board before you roll the cucumber on it. This will enhance the cucumber's beautiful color.

たけのこ ● Bamboo shoot

ゆでる／皮つきのたけのこはアクが強いため米のとぎ汁か米ぬかに赤唐辛子を入れたものでゆでます。大きいものは縦2つ割りにします。

Boil / Unpeeled bamboo shoots will let off a lot of scum. To avoid this, you can precook them with red peppers in the water leftover from washing rice. Or, put them in boiling water with rice bran. To make bigger shoots easier to handle, cut them lengthwise in two.

かぶ ● Turnip

泥を取る／茎を1〜2cmつけて切り落とし竹串で泥を取ります。皮の近くにアクがあるので厚めにむくとよいでしょう。

Remove the dirt / Cut off the turnip's stem leaving about 3/8 to 3/4 inch and remove the dirt with a bamboo skewer. Peel the skin deeply to reduce the turnip's bitterness.

ほうれん草 ● Spinach

水洗い／ほうれん草などは根の茎部分に、土やゴミが多いので水道水で丁寧に水洗いをします。

Wash with water / Wash your spinach thoroughly in water to remove the dirt, paying special attention to the bottom of the stems.

大根 ● Giant white radish

❶面取りをする／ふろふき大根などのように長時間煮る物は切り口の角の部分を包丁で細く削り取り、丸みをつけます。これで煮崩れがなくなります。
❷下ゆでする／大根にはアクがあるので、皮をむいて、米のとぎ汁で下ゆでしてから調理するとよいです。

❶ **Round the corners** / Round off the corners of the cut ends of your radish to maintain their firmness during a long simmer.
❷ **Precook** / Peel the radish and precook them in the water leftover from washing rice. This will help to remove the radish's bitterness.

白菜 ● Chinese cabbage

❶葉をはがす／白菜は縦に切ると持ちが悪くなるため、基本的には葉を一枚々むいて使用するとよいです。
❷下ゆでする／葉芯はかたいので包丁で薄くそいでから調理すると口当たりがよいです。

❶ **Peel the layers** / Cutting it lengthwise will cause it to spoil more quickly. It is better to peel the leaves and use them one by one.
❷ **Precook** / Slice the core part of leaves thinly and cook them to make them palatable.

かぼちゃ ● Pumpkin

❶わたと種を取る／縦に2〜4つ割りにした後、かぼちゃのわたと種をスプーンでかき取ります。
❷皮をむく／煮ものの場合はかぼちゃを使用する大きさに切り、薄くそぐように皮がまだらに残るようにむきます。全部むくと煮崩れの原因になります。

❶ **Remove the seeds** / Cut your pumpkin in two to four pieces lengthwise. Scoop out the seeds with a spoon.
❷ **Peel the skin** / For boiled pumpkin, cut the pumpkin into chunks and peel the skin thinly in patches. Removing all the skin will cause the pumpkin to lose firmness while cooking.

しいたけ ● Shiitake mushrooms

❶洗う／しいたけは基本的に香りが取れてしまうので水洗いをしないで、かたく絞ったふきんなどで軽くふいてゴミを取ります。
❷石づきを落とす／根元のかたい部分は石づきといって食べられないので包丁で切り落とします。

❶ **Clean the mushrooms** / Avoid washing mushrooms in water as this takes away their flavor. Instead, use a damp cloth to remove the dirt.
❷ **Cut away the stems** / The shiitake stems are called *ishizuki* and are considered inedible. Remove them with a knife.

じゃがいも●Potato

❶芽を取る／じゃがいもの芽には、ソラニンといわれる下痢や腹痛を起こす毒素があるので、包丁の角でえぐるように取ります。

❷水にさらす／皮をむき、使用する形、大きさに切ったじゃがいもは、アク抜きのため水にさらします。

❶ **Remove the sprouts** / Potato sprouts contain a toxin called solanine that can cause digestive problems and stomach pain. Simply cut the sprouts out with the corner of a knife.

❷ **Soak in water** / Soak the peeled and cut potatoes in water to remove their bitterness.

ごぼう ●Burdock

❶皮をむく／皮の部分に香りがあるので、包丁ではなく、たわしで軽くこすって皮をむきます。

❷酢水にさらす／ごぼうはアクが強い野菜なので使用する大きさ、形に切ったらすぐ酢水につけます。

❶ **Peel the burdock** / Use a scrubber to peel the burdock. This will preserve the flavor, most of which is found in the skin.

❷ **Soak in water mixed with vinegar** / Soak the burdock in water mixed with vinegar immediately after cutting. This will reduce their strong bitter flavor.

里いも ●Taro

❶洗う／里いもはよく洗わないと土臭さが残るため、たわしでよく洗いましょう。

❷皮をむく／ふきんなどで水けをよくふき取った里いもは両端を切り落とし、皮は上から下にむくときれいに仕上がります。

❸ぬめりを取る／塩でもみ、ぬめりを出したら水で洗い流します。

❶ **Wash the taro**/ Wash the taro thoroughly with a scrubber to get rid of the earthy flavor.

❷ **Peel the taro** / Dry the taro well with a cloth. Cut both ends of the taro and peel them from top down for a beautiful finish.

❸ **Remove the taro slime** / Rubbing salt into the cut taro will eliminate its slime. Wash with water after the salt rub.

野菜調理のポイント ●Tips on Cooking Vegetables

1 切る方向に注意
Take care in the direction of your cut

キャベツなど生で野菜は歯ざわりが大切です。繊維にそって切るとよいです。逆に煮ものように柔らかく仕上げたいときは繊維の逆に切るとよいです。

It's important to protect the firmness of fresh vegetables like cabbage. Cut these vegetables lengthwise. When you're preparing vegetables that will be cooked to a soft finish, you can cut the vegetable crosswise.

3 緑の野菜は沸騰から、根菜は水から
Put green vegetables after the boil, root vegetables before the boil

緑の葉野菜（ほうれん草、小松菜など）は沸騰してからゆでます。（大根、いも類）は逆に水からゆでると中まで火が通りやすいです。

Cook leafy vegetables like spinach and komatsuna in boiling water. It's faster to cook root vegetables and tubers before the boil while the water is cold.

5 葉菜をゆでる時の注意
Tips on boiling leafy vegetables

葉菜をゆでる時は、まず根と茎のかたい部分を先にゆで、次に葉の部分をゆでるようにするとよいです。

When boiling leafy vegetables, try to boil the stems first and the leafy parts next.

2 材料の加える順番
When to add each ingredient

火が通りにくい順に加えます。火が通りにくいのは大根、にんじんなどの根菜、次にじゃがいも、里いもなどのいも類。葉菜は最後でよいです。

Add vegetables according to the time they take to cook. Vegetables that take the longest are root vegetables like giant white radishes and carrots. Next come the tubers, like potato and taro. The last vegetables to go in are the leafy greens.

4 ゆでる時は塩をひとつまみ入れる
Add a pinch of salt when boiling

緑の野菜を鮮やかにゆでるには、塩をひとつまみ入れます。塩はビタミンCの破壊を少なくする働きもあります。

When boiling green vegetables, remember to add a pinch of salt to the water. Salt will protect the vegetable's vitamin C.

6 緑の野菜を鮮やかに煮る
Get a bright color finish on boiled green vegetables

緑の野菜は薄く作った煮汁でさっと煮て取り出し、冷まします。煮汁も冷めたら、その中に戻し味を含ませる青煮にするとよいです。

Boil green vegetables very quickly in a weak broth and take out to cool down. After the vegetables and the broth have cooled, reintroduce the vegetables to the broth for fuller flavor and a bright green finish.

基本的な魚介類の下処理とさばき方 ● Basic Preparations and Cutting of Fish and Seafood

下処理 ● Preparations

1 ぬめりを取る
ぬめりのある魚は包丁でこそげ取り、ボウルに水をため、その中でぬめりを取ります。ぬめりの強い魚は塩をふって手でこすってから水できれいに流すとよいでしょう。

❶ Remove the slime
Use a knife to scrape a slimy fish. Place the fish in a bowl of tap water and rub away any remaining slime. If the fish is still very slimy, sprinkle salt on it, rub it down and then wash it well in water.

2 腹わた、血合いを取る
胸びれの後方から包丁を入れ、腹を開き、腹わたを包丁の刃先で取り出します。血合いを手で取り、腹の中を水できれいに洗い流します。
※魚や調理法によっては腹わたなどを取らず、そのまま調理する場合があります（さんまなど）

❷ Remove the guts and blood
Cut the fish from the back of the pectoral fin to open the stomach. Remove the entrails with the tip of your knife. Use your fingers to remove the black, bloody bits and then rinse the cavity well in water.
※ Depending on the kind of fish (like saury) and the cooking method, it is not always necessary to remove the entrails.

3 うろこを取る
うろこ引きや包丁を使用して全体のうろこを取ります。うろこを取った魚は水洗いをし、はがれたうろこを完全に取り除きましょう。
※あじ科の魚はゼイゴを尾の方から包丁を入れて切り取ります

❸ Remove scales
To remove the scales, use a fish scaler or knife and scrape the fish from tail to head. Rinse the fish well in water to wash away all the scales.
※ For cavally, use a knife to cut off the hard scales known as *zeigo* from the fish's tail side.

4 飾り包丁を入れる
塩焼きや煮つけにする場合は、皿に飾りつけた時に見える側に火の通りがよいように、写真のように切り込みを入れます。
※煮つけの場合切り込みは、1本でもよいでしょう
※一般的には頭が左にくるように盛りつけます

❹ Make cuts
If you are broiling the fish with salt or boiling the fish in soy sauce, make cuts on the presentation side of the fish as shown in the picture. This will shorten your cooking time.
※ A single cut may be sufficient if you are boiling the fish in soy sauce.
※ Generally, present the dish with the fish head on the left.

二枚おろし ● Filleting in Two

1
魚の頭を左にして置き、包丁の刃先でうろことぬめりを取り、あじの場合はゼイゴの部分を尾から頭の方へ向かって取り除いていきます。

❶ Place the fish head on the left and remove the scales and slime with the tip of your knife. For cavally, use a knife to cut off the hard scales known as *zeigo* from the fish's tail side toward the head.

2
頭の部分は胸びれの根元から包丁を斜めに入れ、頭を切り落とします。

❷ Insert your knife at an angle from the base of the pectoral fin and cut off the head.

3
腹の部分に包丁を入れ、刃先を入れて内臓をかき出します。水を入れたボウルで腹の中を洗い血合いを取り、流水で洗ってからペーパータオルで水けをよくふき取ります。

❸ Use a tip of your knife to remove the guts from the stomach cavity. Rinse the cavity in a bowl filled with water and remove the black, bloody bits. Wash well in running water and pat dry with paper towels.

4
頭が右になるように向きを変え、身と、骨がついた身の二枚に切るため、中骨の少し上に包丁を当て、包丁を上下にゆっくりと動かしながら尾の方まで切っていきます。尾の手前で包丁を少し上に向け切り離します。

❹ Now, place the fish head on the right and place your knife on the backbone of the fish to separate the meat into two fillets. Slowly move your knife up and down along the bone to fillet the fish to the tail. Lift your knife just before it reaches the tail and separate the meat.

三枚おろし・刺身用さく●Filleting in Three / Sashimi Fillet

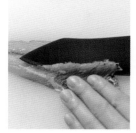

1 二枚おろしの**1〜4**までの作業をします。

❶ Follow the procedures for Filleting in Two.

2 骨のついた身の方を上にし、頭の方から中骨と身の間に入れた包丁を上下に動かしながら切ります。

❷ Place the fillet with the bones facing up. Cut out the meat while moving the knife up and down along the bone.

3 身の部分が2枚と中骨が1枚の三枚おろしの出来上がりです。

❸ You now have three fillets; two fillets with the meat and one with the backbone.

4 さらに腹骨の部分に包丁を寝かせて、すき切るように取ります。

❹ Set down your knife and remove the bones around the stomach as though you were slicing the part off.

5 中骨を骨抜きで取れば完璧です。刺身用として使用できます。

❺ Removing all the bones makes a perfect fillet that can be used for sashimi.

五枚おろし●Filleting in Five

1 ひらめは包丁を寝かせて尾の方から前後に動かし、両面のうろこをそぎ落としていきます。かれいは包丁で両面のうろこを取ります。

❶ Remove the scales of a flounder by placing your knife at an angle and scraping the scales off from the fish's tail to its head. For a sole, remove its scales on both sides.

2 胸びれの後方の方に包丁を入れ、頭を切り落とし、切り口に指か包丁の刃先を入れて腹わたを取り出し、水洗いします。

❷ Place your knife at an angle from the base of the pectoral fin and cut off the head. Use your fingers or the tip of your knife to remove the guts and rinse well with water.

3 尾のつけ根の部分に中骨のあたりまで包丁を入れ、背側、腹側とも包丁の刃先で尾にそって切り込みを入れます。

❸ Make an incision at the base of the tail toward the backbone. Using the tip of your knife, make cuts from the tail along the fin on both sides of the fish.

4 縦中央（側線）に頭から尾にかけて中骨の深さまで切り込みを入れます。

❹ At the center of the fish, make a lengthwise cut from the head toward the tail to the depth of the backbone.

5 頭の方に包丁を入れ、尾に向かって、中骨にそいながら半身を切り取っていきます。もう一方も同じように切ります。

❺ Insert your knife near the head and cut toward the tail to remove half of the meat along the backbone. Do the same on the other side.

6 裏返して腹側も**5**と同じ要領で切り、5枚おろしの出来上がりです。

❻ Flip the fish over and repeat step 5 to make five fillets.

筒切り ● Making Fish Steaks

1 表面のぬめりを洗い流し、尾の方から腹にかけてうろこを取り除いて、腹びれの後ろに包丁を入れ頭を切り落とし、尾も切り落とします。

❶ Wash the fish of its slime and remove the scales from tail to stomach. Place your knife at the back of the pelvic fin to cut off the head. Cut off the tail, too.

2 切り口から指で腹わたを抜き出し、流水できれいに汚れを取り除いたらペーパータオルなどで水けをふき取ります。

❷ Use your fingers to remove the guts from the cut you made. Rinse the cavity well and pat dry with paper towels.

3 骨ごと輪切りに切っていきます。さばなら4～5等分が適当です。さんまは2～3等分くらいがよいでしょう。

❸ Cut the fish in thick round slices with its backbone. You can divide a mackerel into five equal steaks or get two to three steaks from a Pacific saury.

背開き ● Splitting Open Along the Back

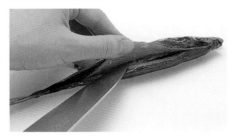

1 ぬめり、うろこ、あじであればゼイゴ（ゼンゴ）を包丁で取り除き、流水で洗い、ペーパータオルで水けをふき取ります。

❶ Clean the fish of its slime and scale it (being sure to use your knife to remove the *zeigo* from fish like a horse mackerel). Wash the fish in running water and dry it with paper towels.

2 背の方を手前にし、尾を左にして置き、頭から包丁を入れ、中骨の方まで引いていき、中骨にそって尾まで切り目を入れていきます。

❷ Position the fish with its back facing you. Placing the tail on your left, insert your knife at the head and cut along the backbone toward the tail.

3 尾まできたら切り開き、身から腹わたを取り除き、えらの根元を包丁の刃先で切り、取り出します。手で取ってもよいでしょう。

❸ Split the fish open and remove the guts. You can use the tip of your knife to cut off the gills from their base or you can remove them with your hands.

飾り包丁 ● Make Incisions

1 ぬめりやうろこ、腹わたを取り除き、下処理をしてから魚の腹の方から背にかけて、中骨のあたりまで包丁で切り込みを入れます。

❶ Clean the fish of its slime, scale and gut it and prepare the fish. Insert your knife near the stomach toward the back. Cut as deep as the backbone.

2 向きを変え、切り目が交差するように包丁で切り込みを入れます。火が通りやすく、味もしみ込みやすく、見た目も美しく仕上がります。

❷ Turn the fish around and make a crosswise cut with your knife. This cut will allow the fish to be cooked through evenly while enhancing the flavor and maintaining a beautiful look when you present the fish to the table.

かきの捌き方 ● How to Handle an Oyster

1 タオルを当てて貝殻の底が深い方を下にしてしっかりと押さえ、身を傷つけないようにステーキナイフをすき間に差し込み、ねじるようにして貝殻をこじ開けます。

❶ Steady the oyster by sitting the bigger shell on a towel. Insert your steak knife between the shells carefully. Try not to damage the oyster meat when you twist the knife to pry open the shells.

2 貝殻と身の間にナイフを差し込み、身を取り出して塩水で洗います。

❷ Place your knife between the shells and remove the meat. Rinse with salted water.

えびの剥き方 ● How to Peel Shrimp

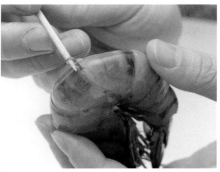

1 背に、つまようじか竹串を刺して背わたを取ります。

❶ De-vein the shrimp from the back by using a toothpick or bamboo skewer.

2 有頭えびは、頭を手でひねって胴から離します。

❷ If your shrimp still have heads, use your hands to twist off the heads from the bodies.

3 腹側から尾を残して殻をむきます。

❸ Remove the shells from the stomach side. Leave the tail untouched.

天ぷらの下処理 ● Preparations for Tempura

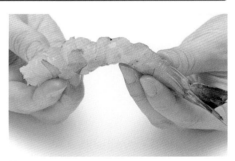

1 尾の先端を包丁で斜めに切り、尾の中の水けを包丁でしごき出します。

❶ Use your knife to make a diagonal cut on the shrimp's tail. Stroke any water from the tail with your knife.

2 えびの捌き方**3**のえびの腹側に包丁で数か所の切り込みを入れます。

❷ Follow step 3 of How to Peel Shrimp and then make several cuts along the shrimp's stomach with your knife.

3 **2**を手でのばし繊維を切ります。天ぷらで揚げた時に身が丸まらず、まっすぐに揚がります。

❸ Stretch out the shrimp to sever its fibers. This will allow the shrimp to cook straight rather than curling when deep-fried.

ほたて貝の捌き方 ● How to Handle Scallops

1 けがをしないよう、軍手もしくは濡れタオルを当てて、ほたて貝をしっかりと押さえステーキナイフなどをつけ根の方から差し込みます。

❶ Wear a cotton glove or place a wet towel underneath the scallop shell to protect your hands. Insert your steak knife into the base of the shell.

2 ステーキナイフなどで貝柱をすくうようにしながら手前に引いていき、貝殻を押し上げるようにして開きます。貝殻と身の間にステーキナイフを差し込み、身を取り出します。

❷ Apply pressure to open the upper shell while pulling your knife to sever the muscle holding the shells closed. Place your knife between the meat and the shell, cut the muscle and remove the meat.

3 ひもと貝柱を取り分ける時は、貝柱についているひもの部分を端から引っ張ってはずし、ひもは軽く洗って汚れを落とします。貝柱は表面についている薄い膜とわたを取り除きます。

❸ Pull on the string to separate the meat from the muscle. Wash the string gently to remove the dirt. Remove the membrane and dark meat from the scallop.

いか類の捌き方 ● How to Handle Squid

1 胴体に指を入れて腹わたをつぶさないように胴体と切り離し、左手で胴体をしっかり押さえ、右手で足の根元を押さえながら引っ張ります。

❶ Insert your fingers into the body and gently separate the entrails, taking care not to damage the squid. Steady the squid by holding the base of its tentacles with your left hand and pull out the guts with your right hand.

2 えんぺら（耳）を胴体に向かって皮とともに引いて取ります。

❷ Pull the squid's fin toward the body and separate it along with the skin.

3 2でえんぺらを取った部分の皮がはがれているので、左手で身を押さえながら皮を一気にはがします。皮がはがれない時は、ふきんやペーパータオルでつかんではがすとよいです。えんぺらも同様に皮をむきます。

❸ The skin will be partly peeled where the fin was separated. While holding the body with your left hand, peel off the skin with one quick pull. Peel off any remaining skin with a cloth or paper towel. Be sure to peel the skin from the fin as well.

4 胴の横から包丁を入れ、切り開き、残っていた内臓や軟骨を取り除きます。

❹ Use your knife to open the side of the body. Remove any remaining guts and cartilage.

5 足の目の上に包丁を入れ、腹わたを切り離します。新鮮な腹わたは塩辛、煮ものに使用できます。

❺ Place your knife right above the eyes and cut off any entrails. Fresh entrails can be used to make *shiokara* or salt-cured squid as well as a boiled dish with soy sauce.

6 足のつけ根に包丁を入れ、切り開き、くちばし（とんび）を指で取り、目を押し出すように取ります。くちばしの周りの身も食べられます。

❻ Cut the base of the tentacles with your knife and remove the beak with your fingers. Push out and remove the eyes. The meat around the beak is edible.

7 水の中で足の吸盤をもみ落とします。

❼ Rub the tentacles in water to remove sucking disks.

はまぐりの捌き方 ● How to Handle Clams

1 はまぐりはもみ洗いし、表面の汚れを落とし包丁を使って貝のつけ根のちょうつがいを切ります。

❶ Rub the surface of the clam. Use your knife to cut the hinge of the shells.

2 ステーキナイフを殻の薄い部分から差し込み貝を開きます。身と殻の間に包丁を入れ、貝柱を切り身を取り出します。

❷ Insert your steak knife into the thin part of the shell to open the clam. Place your knife between the meat and the shell, cut the muscle and remove the meat.

魚介類の調理ポイント ● Tips on Cooking Seafood

1 まな板を濡らす
Wet your Cutting Board

乾いたままのまな板に魚を置いて捌くと魚の臭いがまな板について、なかなか取れなくなってしまうので、必ずまな板を濡らしてから捌きはじめましょう。

Remember to get your cutting board wet before use. This will prevent your cutting board from absorbing the persistent smell of fish and seafood.

2 新聞紙を使う
Make Use of Newspapers

血合いの多い魚や魚を捌く時にまな板の上に新聞を敷いてからすると、まな板が臭くならず、頭や腹わたをそのまま新聞で包んで捨てられるので便利です。
ただし、白いまな板は新聞のインクの色がつく場合がありますので注意しましょう。

It's a good idea to spread newspapers on your cutting board especially when cleaning and gutting fish. This will help keep your board free of the fishy smell and aids in the easy disposal of guts. It's to be noted that white cutting boards may be stained by the newsprint ink.

3 うろこの引き方
How to Remove Scales

❶小・中型魚のうろこを引く場合は、魚を新聞紙の上におき、包丁の刃先やうろこ引きを使って尾から頭にかけてうろこを取ります。
❷うろこの多いものは、ボウルや流しのタンクに水をため、水の中でうろこを引くとうろこは飛びません。大型の魚も同じ方法でうろこを取る。
❸比較的身の柔らかい小魚（はぜ、しろぎすなど）は包丁、うろこ引きでは大変なので、ビールの王冠、ペットボトルのふたの裏側でうろこを引くとやりやすいです。

❶Place small or medium fish on newspaper and use your knife or a scaler to remove its scales, moving from the tail toward the head.
❷ For fish with a lot of scales, fill up a bowl with water and remove the scales in the water. This will keep the scales from getting all over your workspace. Do the same with large fish.
❸ Removing scales from small fish with tender meat, like goby and Sillago japonica, with a knife or a scaler can be difficult. Consider using the backside of a bottle cap instead.

4 手についた臭いの取り方
How to Remove the Smell of Seafood From Your Hands

魚の臭いは石鹸で洗ってもなかなか落ちないものです。そんな時は柑橘類（レモンなど）の液で洗うとよいでしょう。また、流しの臭いは酢水で洗うと殺菌効果もあり、一石二鳥です。

Even with soap, it's hard to wash away the smell of fish and seafood from your hands. Try using the juice of citrus, like lemons. Vinegar is useful for washing your sink because of its antiseptic properties.

5 まな板の処理
How to Clean a Cutting Board

魚介類と野菜などを切るまな板の面を変えることはもちろんですが、魚介類を捌くとどうしても臭いがついてしまいます。そんな時はキッチン用漂白剤につけておき、最後に熱湯をかけて殺菌すればOKです。

Remember to use different sides of your cutting board for seafood and vegetables. If the smell of seafood has lodged in your board, use bleach to clean it then wash it with hot water to disinfect it.

39

肉類の種類と特徴 ● Names of Meat Cuts and Their Characteristics

牛肉 ● Beef Cuts

 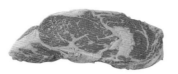  

肩ロース
牛の頭のつけ根近くにある肉で、脂肪が適度にあるが、やや筋っぽい。煮込み料理に適します。

The Chuck Eye Roll
A cut near the neck that contains a moderate amount of fat and connective tissues, often used for stewing.

リブロース
肉質がきめ細やかで柔らかく、脂肪が霜状に入っているものを最高とします。しゃぶしゃぶやすき焼きによく使用されます。

The Rib Roast
The highest grade is considered fine and tender meat with marbled fat. Thin slices are frequently used for shabu-shabu and sukiyaki.

もも肉
比較的脂肪が少ない赤身肉で、揚げものやつけ焼きなどに使用されます。

The Round
It contains lower fat and lean meat, often used for deep-frying and sauteing.

ばら肉
脂肪が肉の層に入っており、長時間煮込むとよい味になります。煮込み料理に最適です。

The Plate
It contains a fat layer between meat layers. A long stew enhances its flavor. Primarily used for stews and soups.

豚肉 ● Pork Cuts

肩ロース
豚の頭のつけ根近くにあり、適度に脂肪が入っていてコクがあって旨い肉です。とんかつなどに使用します。

The Boston Butt
It comes from near the neck and contains a moderate amount of fat with rich flavor. It's mainly used for pork cutlet.

ロース
脂肪層が外縁についています。とんかつやしょうが焼きなどによく使用します。

The Loin
It has a layer of fat along the outer edge. Primarily used for pork cutlet and ginger pork saute.

もも肉
脂肪があまりない赤身肉で、焼き豚や煮込み料理などによく使用されます。

The Legs
This part is lean meat with lower fat. Frequently used for roasting and stews.

ばら肉
三枚肉（脂肪と赤身肉が層になっているため）とも呼ばれ、脂肪が多い肉で、角煮などに使用します。

The Back Ribs
It's also called "sanmainiku," meaning three layers, since this cut is composed of layers of fat and lean meats. It's fairly fatty and primarily used for "kakuni" braised pork dish.

鶏肉 ● Poultry

手羽先
Chicken tip

手羽元
Chicken drumsticks

胸肉
脂肪が少なく、柔らかい肉質で、唐揚げなどの揚げものなどに適しています。

The Breast
These are lean and tender meats, suitable for deep-frying like "kara-age."

ささみ
脂肪がほとんどなく、淡白であっさりしており、酒蒸し、椀種などに使用されます。

The Sasami
It contains little fat and with light and plain flavor. It's good to be used for sake steaming and as an ingredient to put into soups.

もも肉
脂肪は多いのですがコクがあり、煮ものや揚げもの、焼きものなどに使用します。

The Thigh
It's fatty but rich in flavor, primarily used for simmering, deep-frying and sautéing.

手羽類
手羽類には手羽、手羽元、手羽先とがあります。煮込み料理に適しています。

The Wing
It comprises three segments; the middle, the drumstick and the tip. It's good for stewing.

肉類の下ごしらえと調理のポイント ●Meat Preparation and Tips

牛肉の下ごしらえと調理のポイント ●Beef Preparation and Tips

脂肪・筋を切る
脂肪や筋の多い牛肉は、包丁で脂肪や筋の部分を切ると熱を加えてもあまり縮みません。

Remove Fat and Cut Cartilage
Making cuts on the fat and cartilage prevents the meat from shrinking when cooked.

たこ糸でしばる
塊肉を使用する場合は、たこ糸でしばり、形が崩れないようにして調理します。

Bind with String
When using a whole cut of beef, bind it with a stout string. This will help maintain the shape.

豚肉の下ごしらえと調理のポイント ●Pork Preparation and Tips

たこ糸でしばる
塊肉を使用する場合は、たこ糸でしばり、形が崩れないようにして調理します。

Bind with String
When using a whole cut of pork, bind it with a stout string. This will help maintain the shape.

肉をたたく
厚めの豚肉は肉たたき（包丁の背、すりこぎなどでもOK）でたたいて、繊維を柔らかくします。

Pound Meat
Pound thick-cut pork with a tenderizer (or the dull side of a knife or a pestle instead) to make the meat tender.

焼いてから煮る
煮る前に肉の表面を焼くと、肉の旨味汁が流れ出ません。

Broil Before Boil
Broil pork before boiling so the meat retains its juice and flavor.

鶏肉の下ごしらえと調理のポイント ●Chicken Preparation and Tips

焼く前に皮に穴をあける
皮のついた鶏肉は加熱すると、縮んでしまうので、焼く前にフォークなどで数か所を刺して筋切りをして、縮み防止をします。また、火の通りもよくなります。

Prick on the Skin Before Cooking
When cooking chicken with the skin still on, the meat usually shrinks. Use a fork to prick the skin and cut the fibers. This will prevent the chicken from shrinking and help it to cook more easily.

臭みを取る
鶏肉のブロイラーは臭みがあります。こんな時は調理前に日本酒をふりかけてから調理すると多少臭みが取れます。

Remove Smell
Broiler chicken is sometimes smelly. Sprinkle sake on the meat before cooking to reduce the smell.

筋を切り取る
ささ身肉などについている白い筋を取らないで、そのまま加熱すると縮むので、包丁で筋の先端を肉から切り離し、筋のある肉片を下にし、指で筋をつかみ、包丁で押えながら引っぱるとよいです。

Remove a Band
When cooking sasami or the white meat of chicken, remember to remove a white band to prevent the meat from shrinking. Separate a tip of the band from the meat with your knife. Flip the meat so it is band-side down. Steady the band with your fingers and use your knife to hold down the meat. Pull out the band.

切り開く
やき鶏などに使用する手羽先を、骨にそって包丁で切り開いていきます。この作業で食べやすくなります。

Cut Open
Using your knife, cut open the chicken wings to be used for yakitori. This procedure makes them easier to eat.

41

乾物の種類と下ごしらえ ● **Dry Food Preparations**

干しわかめの戻し方 ● How to Reconstitute Dried *Wakame* Seaweed

ボウルなどに入れ、たっぷりの水につけて戻します。熱を加える場合は柔らかくなりすぎると食感が悪くなるので長時間つけないようにしましょう。

Put the *wakame* into a bowl filled with plenty of water. When cooking, avoid letting the *wakame* soak too long as this will soften the wakame too much and spoil its texture.

干しひじきの戻し方 ● How to Reconstitute Dried *Hijiki*

ボウルなどに入れ、水洗いをして汚れを取ったら、たっぷりの水につけ（約 15 ～ 20 分）柔らかく戻します。

Rinse the *hijiki* with water in a bowl. After removing the dirt, soak the *hijiki* in plenty of water for about 15 to 20 minutes to soften.

細切り昆布の戻し方 ● How to Reconstitute Shredded Kelp

ボウルなどに入れ、たっぷりの水につけて戻します。

Put the kelp in a bowl and soak in plenty of water to soften.

きくらげの戻し方 ● How to Reconstitute Dried Cloud Ear Mushroom

ボウルなどに入れ、たっぷりの水かぬるま湯につけて戻します。戻ると大きく広がります。広がったら軽くもみ洗いをして汚れを落とし、石づきを包丁で切ります。

Put the mushrooms in a bowl filled with plenty of cold or lukewarm water. The mushrooms will expand after reconstitution. When they are large, rub them gently to wash off the dirt and trim off the stems.

干しゆばの戻し方 ● How to Reconstitute Dried Bean Curd

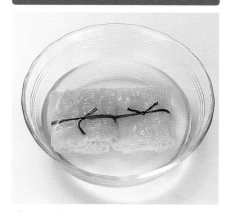

ボウルなどに入れた、たっぷりの水にさっとくぐらせます。もしくは濡れふきんの片方に干しゆばを広げて置き、もう片方のふきんで包んで戻すとよいでしょう。

Plunge the dried bean curd in a bowl filled with plenty of water. Alternatively, you can lay the bean curd flat on a wet cloth. Wrap the wet cloth around the bean curd.

寒天の戻し方 ● How to Reconstitute Agar

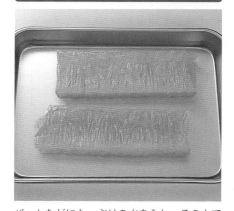

バットなどにたっぷりの水を入れ、その中で戻します。全体が柔らかくなるまできっちりと戻しましょう。

Soak the agar in a rectangular tray filled with plenty of water until it is entirely softened.

干ししいたけの戻し方 ● How to Reconstitute Dried Shiitake Mushroom

かたく絞ったふきんで干ししいたけをふいてゴミを軽く除き、水かぬるま湯に約2〜3時間つけておきます。急ぐ場合はぬるま湯に砂糖を少量入れて、漬けるとよいです。干ししいたけが浮き上がらないように、落しぶたなどで押えるとよいです。戻し汁は煮ものや麺類のだし汁に使用出来るので捨てないようにしましょう。

Use a moistened and squeezed cloth to wipe the dirt off the mushrooms and then soak them in cold or lukewarm water for 2 to 3 hours. If in a hurry, add a small amount of sugar to the lukewarm water. To avoid the mushrooms from floating, place a drop-lid over them. Save the soaking water to use in a broth for simmered dishes and noodles.

切り干し大根の戻し方 ● How to Reconstitute Dried Shredded Giant White Radish

ボウルなどに水を入れ、何度も水をかえながらもみ洗いして汚れを取ります。汚れが取れたらたっぷりの水で約20分ほど戻します。あまり長時間漬けておくと、柔らかくなりすぎるので注意しましょう。戻ったら水けを絞りザルに上げます。

To remove the dirt, rub the daikon lightly with your hands in a bowl filled with plenty of water. Change the water several times. After cleaning, soak in water for about 20 minutes. Remember not to soak for too long or the radishes become too soft. After soaking, squeeze out excess moisture and place in a strainer.

かんぴょうの戻し方 ● How to Reconstitute Dried Gourd Strips

たっぷりの水に約10分ほどつけて戻し、戻し汁を捨て、水洗いをします。もしくは、さっと水洗いをし塩をふり、手もみをします。それをたっぷりの湯で透き通ってくるまでゆでます。

Soak the gourd strips in plenty of water for about 10 minutes. Discard the soaking water and wash them with water. Or you can give the gourd stips a salt rub after washing. Then boil them in plenty of water until they become transparent.

乾麺類の戻し方 ● How to Reconstitute Dried Noodles

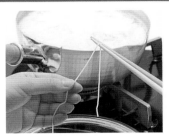

1 鍋にたっぷりの湯を沸かし、沸騰したら中火にして、使用分の麺を鍋の中に放射状になるように入れます。麺が横に入れられるほどの鍋であれば、上からパラパラと鍋に落としてもよいでしょう。

❶ Put plenty of water in a pot and bring to a boil. Reduce the heat to medium, place the noodles vertically in the pot and fan them out radially. If the pot is large enough to accommodate the length of the noodles, you can drop them in little by little.

2 麺を入れて少したったら、麺どうしがくっつかないように箸で軽くかき混ぜます。吹き上がってきたら差し水をして、再度沸騰するまで待ちます。

❷ After a short while, stir the noodles lightly with chopsticks so the noodles don't stick together. When the water bubbles over the pot, pour a little bit more water in and wait for it to boil again.

3 箸で麺を1本取り出し、水にさらしてから指で切るか、食べてみてゆで加減を見ます。冷たいままで食べる場合は麺の中央部の芯が取れ、透明になったら大丈夫です。さらに煮込む場合は芯が残るかためにゆでるとよいでしょう。

❸ Remove a noodle with your chopsticks and cool it in water to see if it's done. You can cut it with your fingers or take a bite to test it. If you're preparing cold noodles, cook until the core of the noodle is transparent. For warm dishes, they should be cooked al dente.

4 ゆで上がったら流水でよくもみ洗いをして、麺のぬめりを洗い流します。

❹ After cooking, rinse and rub the noodles in running water to wash off the slime.

豆腐の水きりの仕方●How to Drain Tofu

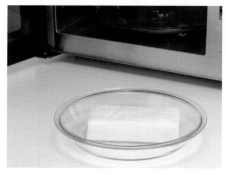

豆腐の重みで自然に水きりする

やっこや鍋もの、サラダなどには、キッチンペーパーで豆腐を包み、盆ザルにのせて自然にでてくる水けをきる程度にします。また、斜めにしたまな板の上にのせておくだけでもよいでしょう。

Drain tofu naturally under its own weight

When used for "yakko" chilled tofu served with variant sauces, one-pot dishes, or salads, wrap the tofu in kitchen paper and place on a flat sieve. Let drain as water naturally comes out. Or just let stand on a cutting board set at a slant.

豆腐を絞って水きりする

豆腐を崩して使う場合や、炒めて火を通す料理には、固く絞った清潔なふきんやガーゼなどに豆腐を包み、ふきんをねじりながら豆腐を握るようにして水けを絞ります。

Drain by squeezing

When using on breaking into pieces or for stir-flying, wrap in a wringed-out clean cloth or gauze, and squeeze the tofu while twisting the cloth.

電子レンジで温めて水きりする

しっかりと水きりしたい場合や、時間がない場合には、豆腐の表面が出ないようにしっかりとキッチンペーパーで包み、耐熱皿にのせて電子レンジで1〜2分温めて取り出して冷まします。冷ましている間に自然に水がきれます。

Drain by heating in a microwave oven

If you want to drain firmly or do not have much time, warp securely in kitchen paper without letting out any surface, place on a heat-resistant plate and heat in a microwave oven for 1 to 2 min. Take out and let stand until cool. While cooling, water naturally comes out.

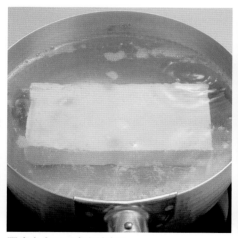

豆腐に重しをのせて水きりする

豆腐の形を崩さずにしっかりと水けをきりたい時には、豆腐をキッチンペーパーで包んでまな板の上に置き、均一に圧力がかかるように上からもう一枚まな板をのせます。また、底の平らな皿などをのせることで、さらに水けがきれます。

Drain by placing some weight on

To drain firmly without deforming, wrap in kitchen paper and place on a cutting board. Place another cutting board to put pressure equally on the surface. Or placing a plate with a flat bottom will let it drain more.

豆腐をゆでて水きりする

沸騰した湯に豆腐を入れ、弱火でゆらゆらと動くぐらいの火加減で5分ほどゆで、ざるにあけて水けをきります。形を崩して使う場合には、手で粗く崩しながら湯に入れ1〜2分ゆでます。その後、ふきんに包んでさらに水けを絞ってもよいでしょう。

Boil and drain tofu

Put tofu in boiling water and simmer over low heat for about 5 minutes. Use a strainer to drain the excess water. If you are using the tofu deformed, break it up with your fingers, place it in hot water and boil for 1-2 minutes. Drain any excess water by wrapping the tofu in a cloth.

油抜きをする ● Remove Oil

1 鍋に湯を沸かし、沸騰したら使用する材料を入れ、ひと煮たちしたら取り出します。

❶ Bring water to a boil. Place ingredients in the boiling water and take out after a boil resumes.

2 ザルに材料（油揚げ）を乗せ、上からまんべんなく熱湯をかけて油を抜きます。

❷ Lay the ingredient (deep-fried tofu) on a strainer and evenly pour boiling water over it.

下ゆでをする ● Precook

こんにゃく類には石灰臭、アクがあるため、下ゆでをしてから使用しましょう。水からゆで、沸騰したら約5分ほどで引き上げます。

By precooking *Konnyaku*, you can reduce the smell of lime and harsh taste before use. Put the konnyaku and cold water in a pot and bring to a boil. After five minutes, remove the *konnyaku* from the water.

高野豆腐を戻す ● How to Reconstitute Freeze-dried Bean Curd

高野豆腐はたっぷりの熱湯に浸し、浮き上がらないように落としぶたか皿をして、芯がなくなるまで柔らかくなったら、水の中で1個ずつ、水がにごらなくなるまで押し洗いをします。この押し洗いをきっちりしないと乾物臭いので注意しましょう。

Soak freeze-dried bean curd in plenty of boiling water and place a drop-lid or plate on top to prevent them from floating. After softening the bean curd until coreless, squeeze them one by one with your hands in the water. Repeat this process until the water does no longer get cloudy. Wash them completely or the smell of dried food remains.

ふきんでこす ● Strain Through a Cloth

おからは一度水に溶き、ふきんでこしてから絞ります。

Mix *okara* with water and strain through a cloth. Squeeze the cloth to remove any excess water.

日本の調味料
Japanese seasonings

砂糖 ● Sugar

砂糖は煮もの料理など和食に多用されます。材料に甘味をつけたり、隠し味、照り、柔らかくするなどの働きがあります。

Sugar is often used for simmered dishes. It sweetens, brings out hidden flavor and luster, and softens ingredients.

上白糖
●White Sugar

よく料理などに使用される砂糖で、精製度が高く、クセがなく、よく水に溶けるので、どんな料理とも相性がよいでしょう。

Well-refined sugar that is often used for cooking. Because of its straightforward taste and quick water-dissolvable quality, it is suitable for any dish.

三温糖
●*Sanonto* Sugar

上白糖より精製度が低く、薄い茶色でミネラルを含み、コクがある砂糖です。コクのあるこってりとした煮ものなどの料理に使うとよいでしょう。

Less refined sugar than white sugar with a light brown color. It contains ample minerals, and offers full-bodied taste. Most suitable for rich tasting simmered dishes.

黒砂糖
●Unrefined Sugar

さとうきびの絞り汁を煮つめた黒褐色の砂糖です。濃厚な風味、香りがあり甘味が強いです。豚の角煮などのこってりとした煮ものに最適です。

Dark brown sugar produced by boiling down corn juice. It features rich flavor and aroma with strong sweetness. Most suitable for rich simmered dishes such as braised pork.

ざらめ糖
●Granulated Sugar

結晶の粒が大きく糖度100%に近い高純度の砂糖です。無色の白ざらと茶褐色の中ざらがあります。大学いもなどに使うとよいでしょう。

Highly pure sugar with almost 100% sugar content with large grains. Two kinds are available: Transparent shirozara sugar and brown chuzara sugar. Most suitable for *daigaku-imo* candied sweet potatoes and other Japanese sweets.

塩 ● Salt

塩は魚介類、肉類、野菜の下ごしらえや調理によく使われるもので、味つけを大きく左右する大切な調味料と言っても過言ではありません。近年、海外の塩をはじめ、さまざまな塩が販売されているのでよく特徴をつかんで使用しましょう。

Salt is often used for preliminary arrangements of fish, meat and vegetables prior to cooking, as well as cooking itself, and it is no exaggeration to say that it determines the flavor of dishes. Various types of salt are now available including that imported from abroad, and it is important to know the characteristics of each type before use.

食卓塩
●Table Salt

塩化ナトリウムを99%以上、炭酸マグネシウムを0.4%まで含まれているもので精製塩をさらに精製したものです。まさに食卓の上にあり、料理の味を調える時に使用します。

Salt consisting of 99% plus sodium chloride and 0.4% max magnesium carbonate. This is manufactured by further refining the refined salt. It is usually placed beside prepared dishes on a table to adjust their taste.

精製塩
●Refined Salt

原塩を精製して塩化マグネシウムを取り除いてあるので、塩化ナトリウムの純度がとても高く塩辛い塩です。苦味は少なく、除湿剤が入っているので細かくさらさらしている。水に溶けやすいのであえものや過熱しない料理にも使えます。

Salt with strong acidity. It features very high sodium chloride purity, which has been realized by refining raw salt and removing magnesium chloride. It is less bitter, and fine and dry thanks to the dehumidifiers it contains. Because it is easy to dissolve in water, it can also be used for dressed dishes or other uncooked varieties.

原塩
●Raw Salt

天日製塩のことで塩化ナトリウムが95%以上含まれています。塩化マグネシウム、ヨウ素などのミネラルが多いです。基本的には柔らかい旨味があります。ただし、出産国によって辛さが異なります。

Bay salt consisting of 95% plus sodium chloride. It contains ample minerals including magnesium chloride, and iodine; its flavor is basically soft. Its acidity, however, differs depending on the country of origin.

粗製塩（あら塩）
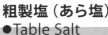
●Table Salt

海水を凝縮して作る天然塩をもう一度溶かしてゴミを取り除き再結晶させたものです。精製度が低いので、にがり（結晶させた後に出る苦い液体）が多く、塩化ナトリウム、塩化マグネシウム、ヨウ素などのミネラルを含んでいるため、柔らかい旨味と香りがあります。精製塩よりも塩けがやさしいので料理もやさしい味になります。また、魚介類の下ごしらえなどに最適です。

Salt manufactured by dissolving natural salt, condensed seawater, and re-crystallizing it after removing impurities. Because it is not so refined, it contains a relatively large amount of bittern left after crystallization. Thanks to minerals such as sodium chloride, magnesium chloride and iodine, its flavor and aroma are soft. Because it is less acid compared to refined salt, it rounds off the taste of dishes. It is also suitable for preliminary arrangements for fish dishes.

しょう油 ● Soy Sauce

日本を代表する調味料といっても過言ではないしょう油は、大豆、小麦、塩などを原料として作られます。煮もの、焼きものなど数多くの和食料理に使用します。

It is no exaggeration to say that soy sauce is the flagship seasoning of all those available in Japan. It is made from soybeans, wheat, salt and other materials, and used extensively for simmered, grilled and other dishes.

濃口しょう油
●Heavy Soy Sauce
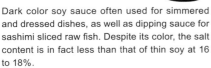

煮もの、あえもの、刺し身じょう油として使用される色の濃いしょう油です。ただし塩分は16〜18%で薄口しょう油よりも少ないです。

Dark color soy sauce often used for simmered and dressed dishes, as well as dipping sauce for sashimi sliced raw fish. Despite its color, the salt content is in fact less than that of thin soy at 16 to 18%.

薄口しょう油
●Thin Soy Sauce

濃口しょう油よりも色が薄く、料理の素材の持っている色、味わいなどを生かします。若たけ煮、吸いものなどに使用されます。塩分は18〜19%あります。

Soy sauce with a color lighter than heavy soy. This soy is useful particularly when you want to leave the color and flavor of ingredients intact. It is often used for simmered young bamboo shoots and clear soups. The salt content is 18 to 19%.

白しょう油
●White Soy Sauce

薄口しょう油よりさらに色の薄いしょう油です。上品なだし汁や茶碗蒸しなど、出来上がりを薄い色に仕上げたい時に使用します。

Soy sauce with a color lighter than thin soy. This soy is used when preparing good quality stock, chawan-mushi savory cup custard and other dishes that require a light-colored finish.

★しょう油の保存方法・How to Store Soy Sauce

しょう油は空気や日光、熱にふれると、色も風味も落ちてくる褐変現象があります。栓を開けたしょう油は冷暗所か冷蔵庫で保管するのがおいしさを長持ちさせるコツです。

Soy sauce will turn brown with the flavor deteriorated if it is exposed directly to the air, sunlight or heat. Once unstopped, it should be stored in a dark and cool place or in a fridge.

酢 ● Vinegar

酢のものや寿し（巻き寿し、にぎり寿し、ちらし寿しなど）によく使用される酢。さまざまなタイプがありますので、よく特徴を知り活用しましょう。

Vinegar is often used for vinegared dishes and sushi dishes (such as sushi roll, hand roll sushi and garnished sushi). There are various kinds of vinegar. Be familiar with the characteristics of each and make good use of them.

玄米酢 ● Brown-rice Vinegar

精白しない玄米から作る酢で、独特な香りがあります。主に飲料用として人気があります。

Vinegar made from unpolished brown rice with a unique aroma. It is popular as a drink.

穀物酢 ● Grain Vinegar

はと麦、小麦胚芽、とうもろこしなどの穀物から作られた醸造酢。クセがないので家庭でよく使用されます。

Vinegar made from adlay, wheatgerm, corn and other kinds of grain. Because of its straightforward taste, it is often used for home cooking.

米酢 ● Rice Vinegar

和食料理によく使用される米から作られた酢で、JAS（日本農林規格）で酢１ℓに対して米 400 以上使用し、酸度 4.2% 以上と決められています。

Vinegar made from rice, which is often used as a seasoning for Japanese dishes. The Japanese Agricultural Standard (JAS) requires that 40 kg (approx. 88.2 lb) rice be used per 1,000cc of vinegar, and that acidity be 4.2% or more.

果実酢（柑橘系） ● Fruit (Citrus Fruit) Vinegar

かぼす、すだち、柚子などの果汁を搾っただけの酢。焼き魚や鍋ものなどによく使用されます。また果汁（柑橘系以外）を発酵させたものもあります。

Juice freshly squeezed from *kabosu*, *sudachi*, *yuzu* Japanese lime or other sharp acidic citrus fruits, which are often used for grilled fish and one-pot dishes. There is also another type of fruit vinegar, which is made from fermented fruits other than citrus fruits.

みそ ● Miso

みそ汁、さばのみそ煮、西京焼きなど、使用用途も広いみそ、和食に欠かせない調味料の一つです。

Miso is used for various dishes such as miso soup, simmered mackerel and grilled fish in *Saikyo*-style. It's one of indispensable Japanese seasonings.

| 信州みそ（米みそ）
Shinsyu-miso
(Rice and Soybean based) | 麦みそ
Barley and Soybean based miso | 豆みそ（赤みそ）
Soybean based miso
(Red) | 仙台みそ（赤みそ）
Sendai miso
(Red) | 白みそ
White miso |

みりん ● *Mirin* sweet cooking sake

料理にコクと照り、甘みをだすみりん。筑前煮、肉豆腐、肉じゃがなどの煮もの料理によく使用されます。

It's used for adding richness in taste, glaze and sweetness. It's frequently used for simmering dishes like simmered vegetable in *Chikuzen*-style, simmered beef and tofu, and braised meat and vegetables.

料理酒 ● Cooking sake

筑前煮、さばのみそ煮、めばるの煮つけなどの煮もの料理をさらにおいしくしてくれる料理酒。うまく活用しましょう。

Cooking sake enhances the flavors of dishes like simmered vegetables in *Chikuzen*-style, simmered mackerel in miso and simmered rockfish. Make good use of this in your simmered dishes.

Basics and Techniques for Japanese Food

和食の基本・テクニック

ご飯の炊き方や基本のみそ汁の作り方などはもちろんのこと、各調理（煮もの、焼きもの、蒸しもの、酢のもの、豆腐料理など）のポイントとテクニックなどを紹介している。

This chapter introduces you to the preparation of rice and basic miso soups and provides tips and techniques for each cooking method (simmering, braising, steaming, marinating with vinegar, tofu dishes and more).

おいしいご飯の炊き方
How to Prepare Boiled Rice

【米を購入する時のポイント ● Important Point When Purchasing Rice】

米にはコシヒカリ、秋田こまち、ササニシキなどの銘柄が多いのですが、購入する時のポイントは鮮度が大切なので、袋に記載されている精製年月日に必ず目を通しましょう。

Although there are many rice brands available in Japan, such as Koshihikari, Akita-komachi and Sasanishiki, the most important point is not the brand name but freshness. Always check the polishing date indicated on the bag.

【米の保存法 ● How to Store Rice】

精米してある米をおいしく保つために、保存の仕方にも気を配りましょう。水や直射日光は米にとって大敵なので、密封容器か保存袋に入れ、冷暗所で保存します。

夏の蒸し暑い時期や梅雨の湿気の多い時期は、米が痛みやすいので少量ずつ使い切れる分だけ購入するとよいでしょう。

To maintain the taste of polished rice, special care is required for its storage. Because moisture and direct sunlight are rice's two greatest enemies, it must always be put in a tightly covered container or storing bag, and stored in a dark and cool place. During the hot summer or humid rainy season, it is recommended to purchase only the quantity that you can use up within a short period because rice is prone to go bad in these seasons.

【米の量の目安と炊き方 ● How to measure and cook rice】

■量の目安

1カップ（1合）	1人（1〜2食分）
2カップ（2合）	1人（3食分）
4カップ（4合）	2人（3食分）
8カップ（8合）	4人（3食分）

※上記の目安は多少多くなっています。また、個人差があるので注意してください。
※基本的にはその都度、炊いた方がおいしくいただけます。

■ Measuring Suggestions

3/4 cup	1〜2 servings
1 1/2 cup	3 servings
3 cup	6 servings
6 2/3 cup	12 servings

※ The up side suggestions may produce slightly more servings than indicated. Also, please note that these are only suggestions, and may vary depending on the appetite of an individual.
※ Rice tastes better if cooked each time you have a meal.

1 カップ（1〜2 食分）▶ ▶ ▶ ▶ ▶ 3/4 cup (1〜2 servings)

2 カップ（3 食分）▶ ▶ ▶ ▶ ▶ ▶ ▶ 1 1/2 cup (3 servings)

4 カップ（6 食分）▶ ▶ ▶ ▶ ▶ ▶ ▶ 3 cup (6 servings)

■炊き方

1 ボウルに水をため、その中に米を入れて素早くかき混ぜてさっと洗い、にごった水を素早く捨てます。
※素早くしないと、米が水に溶けたぬかを吸ってしまうので注意しましょう。

2 手のひらのつけ根部分を押し返すように 20 〜 30 回します。にごった水を捨てます。水がにごらなくなるまで（約 3 〜 4 回）繰り返します。

3 2 の米をザルなどに上げて、真ん中をくぼませるようにしておきます。夏は約 30 分、冬は約 40 〜 60 分が目安です。
※といですぐ炊くと、ふっくら炊き上がりません。

4 3 の水けをよくきり、炊飯器に入れ、分量の水を入れスイッチを入れます。現在の炊飯器は蒸らしも自動的にしてくれます。

※蒸らし機能がないものは炊き上がってもすぐにふたを開けず、そのまま約 10 分ほど蒸らすといいでしょう。

5 炊けたらふたを開け、水で濡らしたしゃもじを中釜とご飯の間に入れて底から全体をふんわりと混ぜます。蒸気がとぶことにより、ご飯がべったりとせず、ふんわりとしたご飯に仕上がります。

■ Directions

1 Fill a bowl with cold water and add rice. Stir it quickly, and pour off the opaque liquid immediately.
※ Quick washing is essential. Otherwise, rice will absorb bran dissolved in water.

2 Fill the bowl with fresh water from the tap. Press the rice repeatedly 20 to 30 times with the heel of the palm to make the grains rub against each other. Pour off the opaque water. Repeat this procedure about 3 or 4 times until the water becomes almost clear.

3 Drain the rice washed in 2. above on a sieve. Make a shallow cavity at the center of the rice heap, and let it rest for about half an hour in summer and about 40 to 60 min in winter.
※If you cook rice immediately after washing, the grains will not become full and plump when cooked.

4 After draining the rice thoroughly, transfer it to a rice cooker. Add water to cover the rice, and turn on the rice cooker. Rice needs to settle after the heat is turned off, but modern rice cookers handle the whole cooking process up to settling automatically.
※If your rice cooker has no settling function, allow the grains to settle with the cooker covered for about 10 min after it is switched off.

5 Open the lid of the rice cooker. Insert a wet *shamoji* or flat wooden spoon between the rice and the inside walls of the cooker, and gently overturn and mix the rice. This finishing process will allow the steam trapped inside the rice to escape, and make the rice crisp and plump.

基本的なだしの取り方
How to Prepare Basic Stock

【だし汁の材料 ● Ingredients of Basic Stock】

かつお節

Katsuo-Bushi or Dried Bonito Fillet

かつおを乾燥させて作ったのが、かつお節です。表面が赤っぽく黒ずんでいてつやがあり、よく乾燥したものがいいでしょう。使うたびに削り器で削って使用しましょう。

Katsuo-bushi is a fillet of bonito dried to a wood-like hardness. The surface is a dark reddish color and glossy. Choose one that is completely dried. It must be shaved into flakes before use with a *kezuri-ki* or bonito shaver. Shaving should preferably be done each time the basic stock is prepared, making only the necessary amount of flakes instead of shaving it all at once.

削り節

Kezuri-Bushi or Packaged Dried Bonito Flakes

かつおを薄く削ってパックしたものです。かつお節より香りが落ちますが手軽なので家庭でよく使用されます。花がつお、だし節、さば節などがあります。

Convenient packages with pre-shaved bonito flakes. Although the aroma is somewhat inferior to that of *katuso-bushi*, they are often used in modern Japanese households due to the convenience they offer. Many variations are also available including *hana-katsuo* with larger flakes, *dashi-bushi* with finer flakes and *saba-bushi* or dried mackerel flakes.

煮干し

Niboshi or Small Dried Fish

一般的には片口いわしや真いわしの稚魚を煮て干したもので、ジャコ、いりことも呼ばれます。腹が切れていたり、油焼けしたものは避けましょう。小ぶりのものがよく、大きいものはクセのある味や臭みが強くなります。

Generally, the fry of anchovies or sardines boiled and dried. They are also called *jako* or *iriko*. Avoid those with a rip in the belly or oxidized oil stains. Smaller ones are better as bigger niboshi may taste and smell too strongly.

昆 布

Konbu Kelp

昆布はよく乾燥していて、表面に白い粉がふいた肉厚のものがよいでしょう。利尻昆布、羅臼昆布、日高昆布などがあります。

Choose completely dried thick konbu with white powdery substances on its surface. *Konbu* harvested in the waters off the Rishiri, Rausu and Hidaka regions of Hokkaido are particularly famous.

干ししいたけ

Dried Shiitake Mushroom

しいたけを乾燥させたものです。生よりも香りが強くなり、煮ものなどのだし汁にするとよいです。

Because the aroma of dried shiitake mushrooms is stronger than raw ones, they are often used for simmered dish stock.

52

【だし汁の保存方法 ● How to Store Stock】

基本的には作りおきせず、使い切った方がよいですが、密封容器に入れ冷蔵庫で2〜3日は保存出来ます。

In principle, the basic stock should be used up each time it is prepared. However, it can be stored for a few days if it is put in a covered container and kept cool in a fridge.

Konbu Kelp Stock

昆布の水だし汁

■材料（4カップ分）

昆布（約20cmの長さ）…………… 1枚
水…………………………………… 4カップ

■ INGREDIENTS (Makes 4 Cups)

Konbu kelp about 8 inches in length
3 1/3 cups cold water (800㎖)

■作り方

1 昆布の汚れをふきんで落とします。

2 ボウルに水を入れ、**1**の昆布を2〜4時間（夏は約2時間、冬は約4時間）入れておきます。

3 昆布のだしが出たら、昆布を引き上げます。

■ Directions

1 Wipe *konbu* kelp with a cloth to clean.

2 Fill a bowl with cold water and add the kelp cleaned in 1. above. Let stand for about 2 hours in summer and about 4 hours in winter.

3 Remove the kelp when the stock is ready.

★昆布の水だし汁は、煮もの、鍋もの、炊き込みご飯などに使用します。
★使用した昆布は捨てないで、煮ものや佃煮、おでんに使用するとよいでしょう。

★ This stock is particularly suitable for simmered dishes, one-pot dishes and *takikomi-gohan* (rice cooked with some other ingredients).

★ The used kelp can be reused as an ingredient for a simmered dish or *tsukudani* (salt-sweet preserves).

おでん *Oden* stew

五目炊き込みご飯
Mixed Rice

煮干しのだし汁

■材料（4カップ分）

煮干し ………………………… 約 15 ～ 20 尾
水 ………………………………… 4 カップ

■ INGREDIENTS (Makes 4 Cups)

15 to 20 pieces of *niboshi* small dried fish
3 1/3 cups cold water (800㎖)

■作り方

1 煮干しは 1 尾ずつ頭と腹わたを取ります。
※頭と腹わたは、苦味になりますので必ず取りましょう。

2 ボウルに水を入れ、**1** の煮干しを入れたら約 30 分漬けておきます。

3 **2** をそのまま鍋に移し、中火で煮たたせたらすぐに弱火にし、アクを取ります。

4 **3** を 5 ～ 10 分程弱火で煮たら、ペーパータオルかふきんを目の細かいザルに広げてこします。

★煮干しのだし汁は、よくみそ汁に使用します。

★ This stock is suitable for miso soups.

■ Directions

1 Pluck off heads and pinch away entrails of the small dried fish.
※ Always remove the head and entrails since they produce a bitter taste.

2 Fill a bowl with cold water and add the small dried fish. Let stand for about 30 min.

3 Transfer the liquid prepared in 2. above to a pot, and place it over medium heat. When the liquid comes to the boil, turn down the heat to low immediately. Skim the surface to remove foam.

4 After simmering the liquid over low heat for 5 to 10 min, strain it through a paper towel or a cloth placed over a sieve of fine mesh.

煮干しの原料と作り方

Ingredients of *niboshi* and how it's made

◆原料は主にカタクチイワシの体長 5cm ほどのものになります。他にはマイワシ、ウルメイワシも使用します。水洗いした後、食塩水で煮て天日か乾燥機で乾燥させて作られます。カルシウムが豊富です。

The common ingredients of *niboshi* are 2-inch long anchovies. True sardines and round herrings may also be used. To make the fish into the *niboshi*, they are rinsed in water, boiled in salted water and dried in the sun or a drying machine. They are rich in calcium.

昆布とかつお節のだし汁

■材料（4.5 カップ分）

昆布（約 10cm の長さ） ……… 1〜2 枚
かつお節（削り節）……………… 20〜30g
水 …………………………… 4 と 1/2 カップ

■ INGREDIENTS (Makes 3 3/4 Cups)

1 or 2 pieces of 4-inch *konbu* kelp
20 to 30g *katsuo-bushi* (*kezuri-bushi*)
dried bonito flakes
3 3/4 cups cold water (900㎖)

■作り方

1 昆布の汚れをふきんで落とす。ボウルに水を入れて約 20 分漬けておきます。

2 1 の昆布と水を鍋に入れ中火にかけ、鍋底から細かい泡がたってきたら、すぐに昆布を取り出します。

3 2 の汁が沸騰してきたら、かつお節（削り節）を一気に入れ、火を少し弱め、表面に浮いてくる泡やアクを丁寧に取りながら約 2〜3 分煮ます。

4 3 の火を止め、かつお節が鍋底に沈んだら、目の細かいザルやペーパータオルなどでボウルに静かに注いでこします。

★煮もの、汁ものによく使用します。

★最後のかつお節の汁けは絞らないようにしましょう。

★昆布を鍋に入れたまま煮たたせると味が落ちるので注意しましょう。

★ This stock is suitable for simmered dishes and soups.

★ Do not squeeze liquid from the remaining dried bonito flakes.

★ Do not boil the liquid while the kelp is inside the pot.

■ Directions

1 Wipe *konbu* kelp with a cloth to clean. Fill a bowl with cold water and add the kelp. Let stand for about 20 min.

2 Transfer the kelp and water prepared in 1. above to a pot, and place it over medium heat. When small bubbles appear from the pot bottom, remove the kelp immediately.

3 When the liquid begins to boil, add all the dried bonito flakes all at once. Turn down the heat a little, and simmer the liquid for a few minutes while removing the foam thoroughly.

4 Turn off the heat. Wait until all the dried bonito flakes sink to the pot bottom. Strain the liquid through a sieve of fine mesh or paper towel slowly to obtain the clear soup in a bowl.

基本のみそ汁の作り方

Basic Recipe of Miso Soup

■作り方

1 鍋にだし汁 (P53 ～ 55 参照) か水を入れ、火にかけます。

2 火が通りにくいもの (根菜類の大根、かぶ、じゃがいもなど) から入れます。あさりなどの貝類や豆腐は最初から入れます。

3 鍋を強火にかけ、沸騰したら中火にします。

4 具に火が通ったら弱火にし、おたま、万能こし器などに適量のみそを入れ、少しずつ溶かしながら入れます。

5 再度中火にし、煮たってきた煮えばなに長ねぎ、三つ葉、万能ねぎなどを散らし、すぐに火を止めます。

★みそを溶かし入れてからは、みその香りがとぶので煮たたせないようにしましょう。

★みそを一度に鍋に入れてしまうと、味の調整がうまくいかないので少しずつ入れながら好みの味にしていきましょう。

★みそは 2 種類ほどの合わせたみそを使用すると味わいが増加します。

★ Never boil the liquid once you have dissolved miso into it because boiling will spoil the flavor.

★ Add miso gradually while adjusting the taste. You cannot make adjustments if you put the miso in all at once.

★ If two different types of miso are combined and mixed, the flavor of the soup will be further enhanced.

■ Directions

1 Fill a pot with the dashi stock (See P.53 to 55) or cold water, and place it over heat.

2 Add ingredients. Put anything solid that will take time to cook thoroughly (giant white radish, turnip, potato and other edible roots) first. When using clams such as short-necked clams or tofu as an ingredient, put them from the outset.

3 Turn up the heat to high. When the liquid comes to the boil, turn down the heat to medium.

4 Make sure that the ingredients are thoroughly cooked, and turn down the heat to low. Soften an appropriate amount of miso in a ladle or strainer, and gradually dissolve it into the liquid.

5 Turn up the heat to medium again, and sprinkle chopped *naga-negi* onion, trefoil or *bannou-negi* onion all over the soup. Turn off the heat immediately before it begins to boil.

【みそ汁の具のバリエーション ● Variations of miso soup ingredients】

大根と油揚げ（万能ねぎ）
Daikon radish and deep-fried tofu (*banno-negi* onions)

かぶと油揚げ
Turnip and deep-fried tofu

あさりと長ねぎ
Short-necked clams and *naga-negi* onions

しじみ
Fresh water clams

豆腐となめこ（万能ねぎ）
Tofu and *nameko*-mushrooms (*banno-negi* onions)

豆腐としいたけ（三つ葉）
Tofu and shiitake mushrooms (trefoils)

豆腐とわかめ（長ねぎ）
Tofu and wakame seaweed (*naga-negi* onions)

キャベツと油揚げ（長ねぎ）
Cabbage and deep-fried tofu (*naga-negi* onions)

じゃがいもとわかめ（長ねぎ）
Potatoes and wakame seaweed (*naga-negi* onions)

ほうれん草と油揚げ（長ねぎ）
Spinach and deep-fried tofu (*naga-negi* onions)

なすと豆腐、油揚げ（万能ねぎ）
Eggplant, tofu and deep-fried tofu (*banno-negi* onions)

お麩とわかめ（長ねぎ）
"*Fu*" wheat gluten and *wakame* seaweed

【みその種類と特徴・Types of miso and their characteristics】

分 類・Categories	特徴・Characteristics	代表みそ・Representative examples
米みそ Rice miso	大豆、米、食塩が原料です。色によって白、淡色、赤みそ、味によって甘、甘口、辛口にわけられます。 Ingredients are soybeans, rice and salt. It's further categorized into white, plain and red misos depending on the color. Also, there are sweet and salty misos depending on the taste.	京風白みそ、江戸甘みそ、信州みそ、仙台みそなど Kyoto white miso, Edo sweet miso, Shinshu miso, Sendai miso and others
麦みそ Barley miso	大豆、麦、食塩が原料。田舎みそともいわれます。赤みそと白みそがあります。 Ingredients are soybeans, barley and salt. It's also called as "inaka miso." There are red and white misos.	瀬戸内麦みそ、長崎みそ、薩摩みそなど Setouchi Barley miso, Nagasaki miso, Satsuma miso and others

基本の吸いものの作り方
Basic Recipe of Japanese Clear Soup

はまぐりの吸いもの
Clam Clear Soup

■材料（4人分）

はまぐり	4 個
三つ葉	6 本
ゆずの皮	1 片
だし汁	3 と 1/2 カップ
塩	小さじ 2/3
薄口しょう油	小さじ 1
料理酒	少々

■ INGREDIENTS (serves 4)

4 clams
6 stalks trefoil
1 piece *yuzu* rind
3 cups broth (710 ㎖)
2/3 tsp salt
1 tsp light soy sauce
Small quantity of cooking sake

■作り方

1 はまぐりは表面の汚れを洗い落とし、三つ葉は食べやすい2cmくらいの長さに切っておきます。

2 鍋にはまぐりとだし汁を入れ、中火にかけて煮たったら弱火にしてアクを取り、はまぐりの殻が開くまで火を通します。

3 殻が開いたら、まず塩、薄口しょう油、料理酒を入れて味つけをします。味つけは必ずひと口味見をしてみて、少し薄く感じる程度にするとよいでしょう。

4 再び煮たったら火を止めて、三つ葉を入れます。器に盛って、ゆずの皮をのせます。

■ Directions

1 Wash off the dirt from the surfaces of clams. Cut trefoils into 3/4-inch lengths.

2 Put the clams and broth into a pot and place over medium heat. When it reaches a boil, turn the heat low and remove the foam. Boil until all the clams are open.

3 After the shells are all open, season with salt, light soy sauce and cooking sake. Always try a taste after you season and keep the flavor subtle.

4 After boiling again, turn off the heat. Add the trefoils and transfer to individual bowls. Garnish with *yuzu* rind.

★はまぐりは火を通しすぎると身がかたくなってしまうので、煮たたせすぎないようにしましょう。

★濃口しょう油を使ったり、しょう油の量を多くしてしまうとせっかくの吸いものの味が半減し、色合いが悪くなってしまうので、薄口しょう油で香りづけ程度にしましょう。

★ The clams get hard if they are cooked too much. Remember not to boil too long.

★ Don't use dark soy sauce instead of light, or don't add too much soy sauce since it spoils the flavor of the soup. It also affects the color. Use only light soy sauce and try to keep the seasoning subtle.

【吸いものの具のバリエーション ● Variations of Clear Soup Ingredients】

はんぺんと生しいたけ、三つ葉
Hampen fish cakes, fresh shiitake mushrooms and trefoils

しめじとお麩、三つ葉
Shimeji mushrooms, *"fu"* wheat gluten and trefoils

かまぼこと三つ葉
Kamaboko fish cakes and trefoils

とろろ昆布と万能ねぎ
Thin-sliced kelp and *banno-negi* onions

鶏肉とかまぼこ、かいわれ大根
Chicken, *kamaboko* fish cakes and *daikon* sprouts

たけのことわかめ、木の芽
Bamboo shoots, *wakame* seaweed and *sansho* leaf bud

えびとそうめん、かいわれ大根
Prawns, somen noodles and *daikon* sprouts

手まり麩とわかめ、きぬさや
Temari-fu wheat gluten, *wakame* seaweed and snow peas

Column ・ コラム

雛祭りとはまぐりの吸いもの

"Hina-matsuri" and Clam Clear Soup

　雛祭りに、雛人形を飾るのはもちろんのこと、ちらし寿しとはまぐりの吸いもの（はまぐりの潮汁）が、祝いの膳としてよく食べられます。

　はまぐりは、二枚貝を代表する貝で、二枚ある殻が他のはまぐりの殻とは絶対に合わないため、"よい伴侶に巡り会える"といわれ、我が子がよき伴侶に巡り会え、幸せになりますようにと願いを込めて雛祭りに食べられるのです。

To celebrate *hina-matsuri*, *hina* dolls are arranged into a beautiful display, and garnished sushi and clam clear soup are commonly offered as dishes to celebrate the festivities.

Clams are bivalve molluscs. Since it's believed that the two identical shells of a clam are exceptional, these bivalves were thought to resemble a loving couple. Families with girls prepare clam clear soup with hope that their daughters will meet good partners and live in happiness.

59

和食のテクニック
Techniques for Preparing Japanese Food

【道具を使用した調味料などの計り方 ● How to measure seasonings with tools】

料理は材料の下ごしらえと調味料の量、つまり味つけによって決定するといっても過言ではありません。ここで計量スプーンとカップの正しい使用の仕方を覚えましょう。

It is no exaggeration to say that the amount of seasoning will determine your success in cooking. Learn and remember the proper way to use your measuring spoons and a cup.

計量スプーンとカップの容量
Capacities of measuring spoons and a cup

小さじ…5cc
Teaspoon…5cc

大さじ…15cc
Tablespoon …15cc

1 カップ…200cc
1 Cup…200cc

★小さじ 1/5 は手ばかりの少々とほぼ同じです。
★計量スプーンを利用して、正しく分量を量ると料理の味つけがうまくいきます。
★ 1/5 tsp salt is about the same amount as a pinch of salt.
★ Using measuring spoons to measure the right amount leads to successful seasoning.

調味料の計り方
How to measure seasonings

すり切り1杯 ● A Level Spoonful		1/2 杯 ● A Half Spoonful	1/4 杯 ● A Quarter Spoonful

塩、砂糖のような粉状のものは、すり切りヘラを計量スプーンの縁に直角にあて、余分な量をすり切ります。

Level off powder seasonings such as salt and sugar. Place a leveling paddle perpendicularly onto the edge of a measuring spoon and then level off.

みそなどは計量スプーンにきっちり詰めてから、すり切りヘラを計量スプーンの縁に直角にあて、余分な量をすり切ります。

Pack paste seasonings like miso into a spoon, place a leveling paddle perpendicularly onto the edge of a measuring spoon and then level off.

計量スプーンの2分の1杯を計る時は、1杯分を入れ、すり切りヘラでスプーンの半分の位置にヘラをさし込み、余分な（2分の1分）を払い落とします。

When measuring a half spoonful, fill the spoon with seasonings first, put a leveling paddle at center of a spoon and then remove the excess (half) amount.

計量スプーンの4分の1杯は、2分の1杯をさらに、すり切りヘラで半分払い落とします。

To measure 1/4 of a spoonful, remove another half of the half spoonful of seasonings.

【手ばかりの調味料の計り方 ● Measuring Methods with Fingers and Hands】

料理のなれた人やプロは計量スプーン・カップなどを使用することなく、塩、砂糖などは手の感覚で計ります。初心者には難しいが、ひとつのテクニックとして知っておきましょう。

Good cooks and professionals measure salt and sugar by using their hands and fingers—they don't have to use measuring spoons and cups. Such methods may be difficult for the beginners but it's worth remembering them.

塩少々 ● A Little Salt

親指と人さし指の2本で塩をつまみ取れる量です。

An amount of salt you can pinch with your thumb and forefinger.

塩ひとつまみ ● A Pinch of Salt

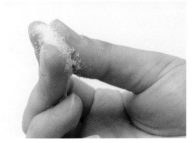

親指、人さし指と中指の3本でつまめる量です。人によって異なりますが約1gになります。

An amount of salt you can pinch with your thumb, forefinger and middle finger. The weight differs depending on the person, but it weighs about 1 g.

ひとにぎり ● A Handful of Salt

人によって異なりますが、軽くひとにぎりすると、約大さじ2ほどの量になります。

It also depends on the person, but a handful of salt is about equal to 2 tablespoons of salt.

【目ばかりで材料を計る ● Measuring Ingredients Visually】

スーパーなどの買いもの時は重量を記載しているのでよいのですが、1～2個だけ必要な場合は目ばかりができるととても重宝するでしょう。

The weight of ingredients sold at stores is usually provided, but it's convenient if you can estimate weight when you are buying one or two pieces.

じゃがいも中1個 ● 1 medium size potato

じゃがいも1個は約150gになり、小さいものは約100gになります。

One potato weighs about 150g and a small one is about 100g.

玉ねぎ中1個 ● 1 medium size onion

玉ねぎの中1個は、約200gになります。

One medium size onion weighs about 200g.

トマト中1個 ● 1 medium size tomato

手のひらの部分にのるトマトは、約100～150gになります。

A palm-size tomato weighs about 100～150g.

キャベツの葉1枚 ● 1 cabbage leaf

キャベツの葉1枚（大きめなもの）は、約80gになります。

One large cabbage leaf weighs about 80g.

煮ものの基本
Basics of Simmering

【鍋 ● Pot】

鍋は、分量（人数分）に合ったものを選択しましょう。鍋が材料の分量に比べてあまりに大きいと、鍋の中で材料が踊る状態になり、煮崩れの原因になりますし、鍋が小さすぎると材料に煮汁がきっちりと回らず芯が残ってしまう原因になりますので注意が必要です。鍋底に材料がきちんとおさまり、材料と材料の間に適当なすき間が出来るぐらいがよいとされます。

Select a pot with a size appropriate for the number of servings. If the pot is too large for the quantity of ingredients, it causes the ingredients to roll and tumble while being boiled, resulting in the loss of their shape. If the pot is too small, on the other hand, the simmering liquid cannot soak into the ingredients deep enough, and their core parts are likely to remain hard and unflavored. Ideally speaking, all ingredients should neatly sit at the bottom of the pot with some space left between each of the ingredients.

【材料を入れる順番 ● Order of Placing Ingredients】

材料が何種類かある煮ものは、かたく、熱がなかなか入りづらい材料から順番に煮ることが、おいしい煮ものを作るコツです。

When using several kinds of ingredient, put those that are solid and hard-to-cook in first.

【落としぶた ● Drop-lid】

落としぶた（鍋の大きさの紙やアルミホイル）をすることにより、材料に熱が均等に伝わり、味をしみ込む役割をしてくれます。

By covering with a drop-lid(pot-sized paper or aluminum foil),the ingredients can be heated equally and seasoned thorought.

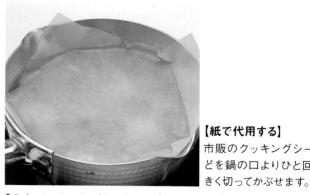

【紙で代用する】
市販のクッキングシートなどを鍋の口よりひと回り大きく切ってかぶせます。

【 Substituting Backing Paper for Drop-lid 】
Cut backing paper into a circular shape with a size slightly bigger than the pot, and put it over the liquid.

【アルミホイルで代用する】
アルミホイルを鍋よりひと回り小さく切り、真ん中に穴をあけてかぶせます。

【 Substituting Aluminum Foil for Drop-lid 】
Cut aluminum foil into a circular shape with a size slightly smaller than the pot, and make a vent at its center. Put it over the liquid.

【アク取り ● Removing Foam】

材料から出たアクはこまめに取りましょう。これをおこたると、出来上がりの色や味が落ちます。

Remove foam that comes out of the ingredients thoroughly. Otherwise, the color and taste when cooked will be spoilt.

水を入れたボウルを用意し、玉じゃくしについたアクを落としてから次のアクを取ります。

Place a water-filled bowl beside you, and clean the soup ladle used for removing the foam with the water in the bowl each time you scoop the foam out. Remove other foam after cleaning the ladle.

アクは鍋の中心に集めて取るとすくいやすくなります。

This foam removing is much easier if you gather all the foam into the center of the pot and scoop it out.

【調味料の順番 ● Order of Adding Seasonings】

昔から伝わる和食の味つけの基本になるさ（砂糖）、し（塩）、す（酢）、せ（しょう油）、そ（みそ）の五つの調味料があります。砂糖は他の調味料に比べて浸透が遅いので最初に加え、塩は材料の水分を出して引き締めてくれる働きや、味を引き締める役割をします。酢、しょう油、みそは長く煮ると香りが飛んでしまうので、数回に分けて加えたり、最後の仕上げに加えるとよいでしょう。

The basic and traditional seasonings that are often used when cooking simmered dishes consist of the 5S's. *Sato* (sugar), *Shio* (salt), *Su* (vinegar), *Shoyu* (soy sauce) and *Miso* (soybean paste) .and these should be added in this order. Sugar should be stirred into the stock first because it is hard to penetrate into solid ingredients while salt extracts their surplus moisture to tighten the food texture and make the taste more intense. Vinegar, soy sauce and miso should be added several times or when finishing off cooking.

【煮魚のコツ ● Tips for Simmering Fish】

煮魚は煮汁が沸騰してから、魚を鍋に入れます。魚の表面がかたまり、旨味が煮汁に出ることなくおいしい煮魚が出来ます。沸騰していない状態から魚を入れると、生ぐささが煮汁に出てしまうので注意しましょう。煮崩れや鍋底に魚を焦げつかせない方法として、鍋底に竹皮を敷いて、その上に魚をのせて煮つけることがあります。

Put fish into a pan only after the simmering liquid begins to boil. This will harden the fish surface to prevent the best taste of fish from exuding out into the liquid. If fish is put in a pot before the liquid boils, the smell of fish will permeate the simmering liquid and make it too fishy. To prevent fish from losing its shape or scorching and sticking to the bottom of the pot, placing a bamboo sheath over the bottom of the pot first and then placing the fish on it is recommended before simmering.

焼きものの基本
Basics of Grilling and Pan-frying

【焼き魚（姿焼き）● Grilled Fish (*Sugata-yaki* or Grilled Whole Fish)】

焼き魚に使用するものは新鮮なものを選択しましょう。調理が単純なので材料のよし悪しでおいしさが決定するといっても過言ではありません。

飾り包丁を入れたら、水けをよくふき取り、ふり塩、化粧塩をしてから焼きます。原則は強火の遠火ですが、一般家庭ではガスレンジがほとんどになります。それでも片面（盛りつけて表になる方から焼きます）を強火で焼き、裏側は最初強火で、仕上げを中火でじっくり焼くと中までしっかり火が通ります。

Choose grilled fish that is as fresh as possible. It is no exaggeration to say that the quality of fish determines the success of the finished dish when considering this simple cooking method. Score the body surface slightly with a knife to ensure the thorough penetration of heat, wipe the whole fish to remove moisture, sprinkle salt and put salt over the fins to prevent scorching. The ideal way to grill fish is to place it over "intense yet distant heat" using charcoal. In modern households, however, gas stoves are commonly used for fish grilling. These gas stoves still suffice if one side of the fish that will be face up when served is grilled over high heat, then the other side over high heat first before reducing it to medium to allow heat to penetrate to the center.

【焼き網】
焼き網を使用する場合は、網をよく焼き、サラダ油を少量網に塗ると魚が網にくっつきません。

【Cooking Grill 】
When using a cooking grill, preheat it thoroughly and apply a small amount of salad oil all over the surface to prevent fish from scorching and sticking to the grill.

【ガスレンジ】
魚をガスレンジで焼く場合は、魚焼き器に水を入れておくと、後かたづけに便利です。

【 Gas Stoves 】
When using the broiler compartment of a gas stove to grill fish, put some water in the broiler pan prior to grilling. This will facilitate subsequent cleaning.

【焼き魚（切り身）● Grilled Fish (Grilled Fillet)】

切り身の場合は皮のついている表から焼き、美しい焼き目をつけます。器に盛りつけた時に表を見せるためです。裏側は最初強火で、仕上げは中火でじっくり焼くと中まで火が通ります。

Grill the skin side first, and ensure that the beautifully scorched grid marks are left on the fish. This skin side will face up when served. Grill the other side over high heat first before turning down to medium to ensure the thorough penetration of heat to the center.

【フライパン（卵焼き）● Frying Pan (Omelet)】

卵焼き用のフライパンはよく油がなじんだものを使用し、他の調理には使用しないようにしましょう。卵が他の材料の臭いを吸収してしまうからです。

Apply a good coating of oil to omelet pans before use. Omelet pans should be used exclusively for making omelets to prevent the smell of other food from affecting eggs.

揚げものの基本
Basics of Deep-frying

【油の適温と見分け方 ● Adequate Oil emperatures and Their Determination Method】

　揚げものをカラッと揚げるためには、材料に適した油の温度を知る必要があります。油の温度はてんぷら専用の温度計で見るのが一番よいですが、あまり家庭には用意されていません。そんな時は使用する衣を油に落としてみる方法がよいでしょう。160℃くらいですと油に落とした衣は、底に沈むがすぐに浮き上がってきます。170℃くらいですと、油に落とした衣は、油の中ほどまで沈みすぐに浮き上がってきます。

To make crispy deep-fried dishes, it is important to know which temperature is most adequate for what ingredients. The best way to determine the oil temperature is to use a special thermometer, but this kind of tool is not usually available at home. The alternative way is to put a few drops of batter into the oil and see how they react. Sink to the bottom of the pan, and float up to the surface quickly-About 320°F. Sink halfway to the bottom, and float up quickly-About 340°F

野菜の適温	肉類の適温	
約 160 ～ 170℃	約 160 ～ 170℃	約 170 ～ 180℃
―	厚くて大きいもの	ひと口大の小ぶりのもの

Vegetables	Meat	
320 to 340° F	About320 to 340° F	About340 to 360° F
―	Thick and large	Small bite-size

【揚げものをカラッと揚げるコツ ● Tips for Making Deep-fried Dishes Crisp】

1 衣の水分をきっちりふき取り、材料に衣をつけたら、すぐに揚げます。

2 鍋にたっぷりはった油の中で、材料を泳がせるように揚げます。

3 油かすは油を汚し、揚げものがきれいに揚がらない原因になるので、こまめに取りましょう。

4 一度にたくさんの材料を入れると、材料が重なり揚げむらが出来たり、温度が急激に下がるので注意します。温度が下がったら、少し火を強め、再度適温にしたら火を弱めて、温度を一定に保つようにしましょう。

5 揚げた揚げものを鍋上で軽く2～3度ふり、網つきのバットに重ねないようにのせて油をきります。

1 Pat dry all ingredients. When coated, they must be fried immediately.

2 Use plenty of oil, and fry ingredients in such a way that they are tossed around in the oil.

3 Thoroughly remove the fried batter bits left after each ingredient is fried before frying another ingredient. These remnants will cause the oil to lose clarity, and thereby spoil the finished look of the dishes.

4 If you put too many ingredients into the pan all at once, they will overlap with each other preventing heat from distributing evenly, and lower the oil temperature rapidly. Should the temperature be lowered, turn up the heat until it becomes sufficiently hot again. Maintain a constant temperature in this way.

5 When retrieving, shake the fried ingredients lightly a few times above the pot, and drain them on a draining pan with a rack without stacking them.

蒸しものの基本
Basics of Steaming

【蒸し器の使い方と蒸しかげんの見方 ● How to Use Steamers and Determine Whether Steaming Is Completed】

1 蒸し器に水を入れてふたをし、火にかけ沸騰させます。

2 1が蒸気を出したら、材料を入れた上段の鍋を1の下段の上にしっかりとかぶせます。

3 2の鍋にふたをしますが、ふたの水滴が材料に落ちると、水っぽくなったり、表面に穴があいたりして仕上がりが悪くなりますので、蒸し器のふたの下に布巾をはさみましょう。

4 蒸しかげんは竹串を刺してみて、澄んだ汁が出てきたら出来上がりです。にごった汁が出てくるのは、中がまだ生煮えの状態ですので、もう少し蒸しましょう。

1 Put some water in a steamer water pot, and cover. Bring it to the boil.

2 When steam begins to be expelled from the water pot, remove the lid and place another pot on top of this with *chawan-mushi* cups laid inside.

3 Cover the pot with *chawan-mushi* cups placed inside. When covering the pot, insert a cloth between the lid and pot. This cloth will prevent moisture from dripping from the lid onto the food. Moisture causes food to become watery or creates dents on their surface.

4 Chawan-mushi is ready when an inserted bamboo skewer comes out clean. If the skewer is not clean, it means that the inside is still half-cooked, so continue to steam the custard a little longer.

【すがたたないようにするには ● How to Prevent Chawan-mushi from Becoming Spongy】

蒸気がよく出ている蒸し器を弱めの中火で蒸すと、すがたちません。強火で長時間蒸すとすがたってしまうので気をつけましょう。

To prevent the custard from becoming spongy, steam the custard over a lower medium heat while ensuring that a lot of steam is being expelled from the steamer. It becomes spongy if it is steamed over high heat for a long time.

すがたってしまった茶碗蒸しの表面。見た目も美しくないうえ、舌ざわりが悪く、味も落ちます。
Spongy chawan-mushi surface. Unsuccessful *chawan-mushi* does not look attractive, and has a coarse texture. It does not taste good either.

【器ごと蒸すには ● How to Take Hot Cups out of the Steamer】

器ごと蒸すと、取り出す時に熱くて大変ですが、そんな時は蒸し器の上段（器を入れる鍋）に布巾を敷いて、その布巾の上に器を置いて蒸せば、取り出すのに便利です。もしくは鍋つかみ用の手袋をつけて取り出してもよいでしょう。

Lay a cloth over the bottom of the pot, and place the *chawan-mushi* cups on it prior to steaming. This cloth will keep the cups from coming into direct contact with the hot bottom of the pot. Or you can also use a pair of pot gloves.

あえもの、酢のものの基本
Basics of Preparing Vinegared and Dressed Dishes

【材料の水けをよく絞る ●Squeeze out excess water from ingredients】

使用する材料の水けが残っていると、仕上がりが水っぽいものになり、味もぼやけてしまうので、必ず材料の水けをよく絞ってからあえます。また、材料をゆでてから使用する場合は、特に水けをよく絞ってから使用しましょう。酢のものもあえもの同様、使用する材料の水けをよく絞らないと水っぽくなってしまいます。材料を下処理したら、必ずペーパータオルなどでふき取ってから使用しましょう。

If ingredients contain excess water, the dressing would be diluted, spoiling the taste of the finished dishes. So, do not forget to squeeze off excess water before dressing. If ingredients are boiled, water should be squeezed out more carefully. Like dressed dishes, vinegared dishes would be diluted, unless excess water is squeezed out. After preparing ingredients, thoroughly remove water, using kitchen paper.

【あえ衣、タレを作っておく ●Prepare dressing or sauce】

材料にあえ衣、タレの材料を別々に加えるのではなく、材料の下処理が終了したら、あえ衣、たれの材料をボウルに入れ、あえ衣、タレを作ります。

After preparing ingredients, mix seasonings in a bowl to make dressing or sauce, instead of adding the seasonings separately onto the ingredients.

合わせ酢の基本・二杯酢の作り方
How to Prepare Basic Vinegar Dressing-*Nihaizu* or Two-Flavor Vinegar

■作り方

1 ボウルに大さじ2杯の米酢を入れます。

2 1のボウルに薄口しょう油大さじ2杯を加えます。

3 昆布とかつお節で取っただし汁（P55 参照）を約30ccを**2**のボウルに加えます。

4 **3**をさっとかき混ぜて出来上がりです。

■ Directions

1 Put 2 Tbsps rice vinegar in a bowl.

2 Add 2 Tbsps light soy sauce to the bowl.

3 Add about 30cc konbu kelp and dried bonito stock (See P. 55) to the bowl.

4 Stir the mix briefly.

【材料をよく冷やし、食べる直前に調味料と合わせる ●Chill ingredients well and dress them shortly before serving】

あえものや酢のものは、作ってから時間をおくと野菜から水が出て、水っぽくなったり、ぬるいとおいしさが半減しますので、材料をよく冷やし、食べる直前に調味料と合わせるとおいしくいただけます。

If dressed dishes are let stand for a long time, water would come out from vegetables, diluting the dressing. Also, warm ingredients would spoil the taste of dressed dishes. So, for delicious dressed dishes, chill the ingredients well, and dress them with the mixed seasonings shortly before serving.

豆腐料理の基本
Basics of Preparing Tofu Dishes

【豆腐の種類 ●Varieties of Tofu】

ひと口に豆腐といっても
さまざまな種類が作られて
いますが、代表的なもの
をあげると、しっかりと食
べごたえのある「木綿豆
腐」、柔らかく上品な口当
たりの「絹ごし豆腐」があ
ります。

木綿豆腐は煮ものや鍋
ものなどに向き、絹ごし
豆腐は冷ややっこやみそ汁などに向いています。また、かために作っ
た木綿豆腐に重しをして水きりをし、約半分の厚さになったら、直
火で焼き目をつけた「焼き豆腐」もあり、煮ものや鍋ものに使用され
ます。料理に合わせてこれらの豆腐を使い分けるといいでしょう。

また、水分を絞ったり、水にさらさないため絹ごし豆腐より柔らか
く、大豆の濃厚な旨味を楽しめるおぼろ豆腐、おぼろ豆腐をざるに
すくい、水分がきれたのをざる豆腐といいます。これは冷ややっこ
のように、薬味につけていただきます。さらに豆腐を薄く切り、冬に
一晩外に吊るして凍らせて作った凍り豆腐（凍み豆腐）ともいわれる
高野豆腐があります。

Although it is only a word, tofu is in fact available in various forms. Typical forms are "cotton" tofu, relatively firm and filling, and "silken" tofu, soft and delicate in its texture. The "cotton" tofu is suitable for simmering and one-pot dishes, and the other is for "yakko" chilled tofu and miso soups. In addition, there is "scorched" tofu, also suitable for simmering and one-pot dishes, made from more-firmly produced "cotton" tofu; pressed to drain until about half-thick of its original size, and scorched over a direct heat. Remember it is better to select the suitable tofu for what you're preparing.

There are other types of tofu such as "oboro" tofu, which has rich soy taste since it's made without being squeezed or exposed to water, and "zaru" tofu that is scooped and drained "oboro" tofu on a bamboo basket. They are served with condiments as "yakko" chilled tofu is. "Koya" tofu is also called "koori" tofu or "shimi" tofu and is made by slicing tofu thinly and hanging the slices outside on a cold winter night to freeze.

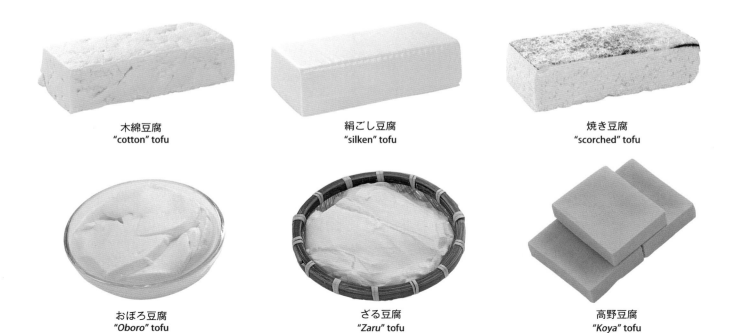

木綿豆腐
"cotton" tofu

絹ごし豆腐
"silken" tofu

焼き豆腐
"scorched" tofu

おぼろ豆腐
"Oboro" tofu

ざる豆腐
"Zaru" tofu

高野豆腐
"Koya" tofu

【豆腐の水きりの仕方 ●How to Drain Tofu】

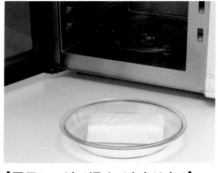

【豆腐の重みで自然にきる】
変わり種のやっこや鍋もの、サラダなどには、キッチンペーパーで豆腐を包み、盆ザルにのせて自然に出てくる水けをきります。また、斜めにしたまな板の上にのせておくだけでもよいでしょう。

【Drain tofu naturally under its own weight 】
When used for "*yakko*" chilled tofu served with variant sauces, one-pot dishes, or salads, wrap the tofu in kitchen paper and place on a flat sieve. Let drain as water naturally comes out. Or just let stand on a cutting board set at a slant.

【豆腐に重しをのせて水きりする】
豆腐の形を崩さずにしっかりと水けをきりたい時には、豆腐をキッチンペーパーで包んでまな板の上に置き、均一に圧力がかかるように上からもう一枚まな板をのせます。また、底の平らな皿などをのせることで、さらに水けがきれます。

【Drain by placing some weight on】
To drain firmly without deforming, wrap in kitchen paper and place on a cutting board. Place another cutting board to put pressure equally on the surface. Or placing a plate with a flat bottom will let it drain more.

【電子レンジで温めて水きりする】
しっかりと水きりしたい場合や、時間がない場合には、豆腐の表面が出ないようにしっかりとキッチンペーパーで包み、耐熱皿に乗せて電子レンジで1〜2分温めて取り出して冷まします。冷ましている間に自然に水がきれます。

【Drain by heating in a microwave oven 】
If you want to drain firmly or do not have much time, warp securely in kitchen paper without letting out any surface, place on a heat-resistant plate and heat in a microwave oven for 1 to 2 min. Take out and let stand until cool. While cooling, water naturally comes out.

【豆腐を絞って水きりする】
豆腐を崩して使う場合や、炒めて火を通す料理には、かたく絞った清潔なふきんやガーゼなどに豆腐を包み、ふきんをねじりながら豆腐を握るようにして水けを絞ります。

【Drain by squeezing 】
When using on breaking into pieces or for stir-flying, wrap in a wringed-out clean cloth or gauze, and squeeze the tofu while twisting the cloth.

【豆腐をゆでて水きりする】
沸騰した湯に豆腐を入れ、弱火でゆらゆらと動くぐらいの火加減で5分ほどゆで、ざるにあけて水けをきります。形を崩して使う場合には、手で粗く崩しながら湯に入れ1〜2分ゆでます。その後、ふきんに包んでさらに水けを絞ってもよいでしょう。

【Boil and drain tofu】
Put tofu in boiling water and simmer over low heat for about 5 minutes. Use a strainer to drain the excess water. If you are using the tofu deformed, break it up with your fingers, place it in hot water and boil for 1-2 minutes. Drain any excess water by wrapping the tofu in a cloth.

器と盛りつけ方
Serving Vessels and Presentation

【基本的な器 ● Basic Vessels】

西洋の食器に比べ、和食器は少々無骨に見えるかもしれないですが、土で作られたものも多く何とも温かみのある器が多く、料理ごとに多くの器を使い分けるため華やかな印象を与えます。ここでは代表的な食器を6つ紹介していますが、最低限このセットが揃っていれば一汁三菜の和食の基本の献立が出来ますので、揃えておいて損はないでしょう。

Japanese serving vessels may look rustic compared to their Western counterparts, but they are generally made of clay, and create a warm feeling. Because a variety of vessels are used with each containing different dishes, they also create a sumptuous atmosphere at the table. This section introduces 6 types of vessels, which represent the basic set of Japanese tableware. This basic set should be sufficient for a basic traditional Japanese menu consisting of "three dishes with one soup."

長角皿 ● Rectangular Plate

長方形の細長い器で、主に焼き魚や刺し身などに使います。

Used mainly for grilled fish and sashimi dishes.

平皿 ● Flat Plate

底の浅い平らな器で、丸や四角のものなどさまざまな形があります。主に焼きものや刺し身などに使います。

Various shapes including round and square are available. Used mainly for grilled dishes and sashimi.

小鉢 ● Small Bowl

深く小さめの器で、主に酢のものやあえもの、おひたしなどに使います。

Used mainly for vinegared and dressed dishes, as well as for marinated greens.

ご飯茶碗 ● Rice Bowl

ご飯を食べる時に使います。夫婦で同じ柄のものを"夫婦茶碗"といいます。

A pair of bowls with the same design is called "meoto-chawan" (bowls for a married couple).

お椀 ● Soup Bowl

吸いものや汁ものなどに使う器。ふたがついているものが一般的です。

Used for clear soup and other liquid forms of dishes. The covered type is most common.

どんぶり ● Domburi Bowl

麺類や親子丼などのどんぶりものに使用します。

Used for noodles and rice bowl dishes such as chicken'n'egg on rice.

【基本的な盛りつけ方 ●Basic Presentation Method】

「料理を目で楽しむ」という言葉があるように、見た目も料理のおいしさを決める大切な要素です。美しく盛りつけることが出来れば、いつもの食卓もいっそう華やかになります。基本のコツさえつかんでしまえば、料理がさらにおいしく感じられるでしょう。

The Japanese often say "Enjoy dishes with the eyes." As this implies, presentation is also one important element in determining the taste of Japanese cuisine. When beautifully arranged, even daily meals will look gorgeous. The following basic tips should help make your dishes even more mouthwatering.

盛りつけの基本
Basic Form of Presentation

盛りつける時は器の中心に3点に（盛りつけた料理が三角形を描くように）盛りつけるとよいでしょう。材料の種類が多い場合には、3種類や5種類など必ず奇数にします。

Arrange ingredients in such a way that they form a triangle at the center of the plate. When you have a variety of ingredients, they should be in sets of 3, 5, or any other odd number.

四角い器の場合には対角線上と中心に盛りつけます。

When using a square plate, arrange ingredients along the diagonal lines and at the center.

手前が低く、奥が高くなるように立体的に盛りつけます。

Arrange ingredients in a three dimensional manner with lower at the front and higher at the back.

刺し身の三点盛り
Three-Point Presentation of Sashimi

1 器の奥側につまをこんもりと盛ります。その上にしその葉を置きます。

2 しその葉の上に刺し身を盛り、次にその脇に刺し身を置きます。最後に正面に刺し身を盛りつけます。
※三角形を少し崩したように盛りつけるとバランスがよくなります。
※刺し身の切り身は必ず奇数になるようにしましょう。

3 仕上げにわさび、みょうが、花穂じそなど彩りのきれいな季節の香りものを添えます。

1 Put plenty of shredded giant white radish at the back of the plate. Put perilla leaves on top of it.

2 Arrange sashimi slices at three points–on top of the perilla leaves, beside the first point, and at the front of the plate.
※ Arrange the slices in a slightly irregular triangular form as this will look more balanced.
※ The sashimi slices should be in an odd number.

3 Arrange *wasabi*, *mioga*, spikes of young budding perilla and other colorful condiments that will add a seasonal touch to the dish.

1

2

3

そのほかの盛りつけ方
Other Forms of Presentation

【焼きもの】

焼きものは長角皿や平らな平皿に盛りつけます。つけ合わせを添える場合には、手前に置くようにします。

※皮つきの切り身魚の場合には皮を上に、薄い切り身の場合には皮つきのものを奥になるように盛りつけます。

※姿のままの魚の場合には、頭が左に、腹が手前になるように置きましょう。

【Grilled Dishes 】

Use a rectangular or flat plate for grilled dishes. When adding relish to the plate, place it at the front.

※ In the case of grilled fish fillets with skin, the skin side should face up. When fillets are thin, the skin side should be hidden.
※ When presenting the whole fish, place it on a plate with the head facing left and the belly side at the front.

【煮もの】

煮ものは深めの器に立体的に盛ります。また、煮ものの材料が大きい場合には、浅い平皿などに四隅をあけて平らに盛りつけるようにするとよいでしょう。

【Simmered Dishes】

Arrange ingredients in a three-dimensional manner at the center of a deep bowl. When ingredients are large, however, place them flat on a flat plate. In this case, don't fill the spaces at the four corners of the plate.

【あえものやおひたしなど】

あえものやおひたしなどは、底の深い器にこんもりと立体的に盛りつけます。

※器いっぱいに盛らず、量を少なめに盛るとよいでしょう。

【Dressed and Marinated Dishes 】

Arrange ingredients in a deep and three-dimensional manner at the center of a small deep bowl.

※ Serve only a small quantity.

【天ぷら】

天ぷらのように魚介と野菜が混ざった料理の場合にはメインになる材料を中心に盛りつけます。

※一般的にはメインとなる魚介類（えび、しろぎすなど）を中心に盛りつけることが多いです。

【Tempura】

In the case of dishes for which both fish and vegetable ingredients are used, such as tempura, arrange in such a way that the main ingredients are placed at the center.

※ Generally speaking, main seafood ingredients such as shrimp or crab are presented at the center.

第三章
Chapter 3

Japanese Traditional Dishes
日本の伝統食

母親から代々伝えられてきた、古くから日本の食卓を飾る "おふくろの味" といわれる伝統食の数々。一口食べるとほっとする日本の味をうまく作りたい。

There are a variety of Japanese traditional dishes that have been handed down from mother to daughter for generations. Prepare these dishes of Japan deliciously, providing great comfort to those who taste them.

Simmered *Hijiki* Seaweed
ひじきの煮もの

about **20**min 約20分

103kcal 103キロカロリー

栄養価が高く、古くから愛される日本の伝統食の定番
Rich in nutrients, a long-loved classic of Japanese traditional food

■材料（4人分）

ひじき（乾燥）…… 30g	しょう油 ……… 大さじ3
にんじん …1/4本（50g）	塩………… 小さじ1/4
油揚げ………… 1/2枚	
冷凍枝豆………… 50g	
サラダ油…… 大さじ1	
だし汁 …… 3/4カップ	
料理酒 …… 大さじ1	
砂糖 … 大さじ2と1/2	

※豚もも肉や鶏むね肉の薄切りを加えれば、ボリュームのあるおかずに仕上がります。また、油抜きしたさつま揚げの薄切り、グリーンピースなどを加えて、具だくさんにしてもおいしいです。

■ INGREDIENTS (serves 4)

30g dried *hijiki* seaweed	3 Tbsps soy sauce
1/4 (50g) carrot	1/4 tsp salt
1/2 cake *abura-age* deep-fried tofu	
50g frozen green soybeans	
1 Tbsp vegetable oil	
3/5 cup stock (150㎖)	
1 Tbsp cooking sake	
2 1/2 Tbsps sugar	

※ Additions of thinly-sliced pork hum or chicken breast will make the dish more filling. Thinly-sliced *satsuma-age* deep-fried fish paste that preliminary removed excess oil, green peas can be added to make the dish full of ingredients.

■作り方

1 ひじきをザルに入れ、水につけてふり洗いした後、大きめのボウルに入れてたっぷりの水で戻します。

2 にんじんは、皮をむき3cmの長さの拍子切り、油揚げはザルにのせて熱湯をかけて油抜きをし、3cmの長さの細切りにします。

3 冷凍枝豆はさっとゆでて、さやから出しておきます。

4 鍋にサラダ油を熱し、2のにんじん、1のひじき、2の油揚げの順に入れて炒め、だし汁、料理酒、砂糖、しょう油、塩を入れて中火で煮ます。

5 4の煮汁がほとんどなくなったら、3の枝豆を加えて、軽く混ぜたら火を止め、器に盛ります。

！コツのコツ

★冷凍枝豆の代わりに缶詰めの大豆の水煮を使ってもよいでしょう。

★ひじきを水で十分に戻さないと口当たりがかたくなります。

★ひじきをあまり煮すぎると、柔らかくなりすぎて食感が悪くなりますので注意しましょう。

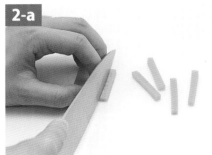

■ Directions

1 Place the *hijiki* seaweed on a sieve, immerse in cold water together with the sieve and wash while shaking the sieve. Transfer to a large bowl, and soak in plenty of cold water to soften.

2 Peel the carrot, and cut into 1 1/5-inch bar rectangles. Place the *abura-age* on a sieve, pour on boiling water to remove excess oil and cut thinly into 1 1/5-inch lengths.

3 Boil the frozen green soybeans briefly, and take the beans out of the pods.

4 Heat the vegetable oil in a pot, add the carrot, *hijiki* and *abura-age* in this order, and fry. Add the stock, cooking sake, sugar, soy sauce and salt, and simmer over a medium heat.

5 When the simmering liquid is almost completely gone, add the soybeans, and mix. Turn off the heat, and arrange everything in a bowl.

！Tip on Tips

★ Instead of frozen pod soybeans, canned boiled soybeans can also be used.

★ Soften *hijiki* seaweed sufficiently, otherwise the texture will be hard and unpleasant on the tongue.

★ Take care not to simmer hijiki too long. This will cause it to get too soft and lose its texture.

Simmered *Kiriboshi-daikon*
切り干し大根煮

about
20min
約20分

130kcal
130キロカロリー

切り干し大根のほのかな甘味と干ししいたけの旨味がおいしい
A flavorful dish combining the slight sweetness of *kiriboshi-daikon* and tasty dried shiitake

■材料（4人分）

切り干し大根（乾燥）… 40g	干ししいたけの戻し汁
干ししいたけ ……… 2枚	……………… 1/2 カップ
にんじん … 1/2 本（50g）	だし汁 ……… 1/2 カップ
ちくわ ……………… 2本	料理酒 ……… 大さじ 1
炒りごま（白）… 小さじ 1/2	砂糖 … 大さじ 2 と 1/2
サラダ油 ……… 大さじ 1	しょう味 ……… 大さじ 3
切り干し大根のつけ汁	塩 ………… 小さじ 1/4
…………… 3/4 カップ	

■ INGREDIENTS (serves 4)

40g *kiriboshi-daikon* giant white radish strips, dried	2/5 cup water used for softening shiitake mushrooms (100㎖)
2 dried shiitake mushrooms	2/5 cup stock (100㎖)
1/2 (50g) carrot	1 Tbsp cooking sake
2 cakes *chikuwa* fish paste	2 1/2 Tbsps sugar
1/2 tsp white parched sesame	3 Tbsps soy sauce
1 Tbsp vegetable oil	1/4 tsp salt
3/5 cup water used for soaking *kiriboshi-daikon* (150㎖)	

■作り方

1 切り干し大根は、水を入れたボウルの中でもみ洗いし、水けを絞ります。その後、ひたひたの水に 30 分くらいつけます。切り干し大根が戻ったら水けを絞り、食べやすい長さに切ります。つけ汁はこして 4 分の 3 カップ分取っておきます。

2 干ししいたけは水で戻し、軸を切って薄切りにします。干ししいたけの戻し汁 2 分の 1 カップ分は、こして取っておきます。

3 にんじんは皮をむいていちょう切りに、ちくわは 5cm の厚さの小口切りにします。

4 鍋にサラダ油を熱し、3 のにんじん、2 のしいたけ、3 のちくわ、1 の切り干し大根の順にさっと炒めます。1 のつけ汁、2 の戻し汁、だし汁を入れて煮たて、料理酒、砂糖を入れて 3 分くらい煮ます。

5 4 の鍋にしょう油、塩を入れ時々かき混ぜながら煮含め、炒りごま（白）をふり、器に盛っていただきます。

！コツのコツ

★切り干し大根のつけ汁と、干ししいたけの戻し汁を使用するのが、おいしさの秘訣です。

★切り干し大根と干ししいたけを早く戻したい時は、ぬるま湯に砂糖（少量）を入れて漬けると早く戻ります。

★食材を炒める時は、かたいものから炒めましょう。

 1-a 1-b
 2
 4

■ Directions

1 Wash the *kiriboshi-daikon* in cold water while rubbing, and squeeze out moisture. Put just enough cold water into a bowl to cover the radish strips, and soak the radish strips in the water for about 30 min. When finished reconstituting, squeeze out the moisture and cut into bite-size pieces. Strain the water in which the radish strips have been softened, and set aside 3/5 cup of strained water for later use.

2 Soften the dried shiitake mushrooms in cold water, chop off the stems and cut thinly. Strain the water in which the mushrooms have been softened, and set aside 2/5 cup of strained water.

3 Peel the carrot, and cut into quarter-rounds. Cut the chikuwa fish paste into 1/8-inch pieces using the edge cut technique.

4 Heat the vegetable oil in a pot, add the carrot from step 3, shiitake mushrooms from step 2, *chikuwa* from step 3, and *kiriboshi-daikon* from step 1 in this order, and fry briefly. Add the liquids set aside in 1. and 2. above, as well as the stock, and bring to the boil. Add the cooking sake and sugar, and simmer for about 3 min.

5 Add the soy sauce and salt, and continue to simmer while stirring occasionally until the ingredients have almost completely absorbed the seasonings. Sprinkle on the white parched sesame, and arrange everything in a bowl.

！Tip on Tips

★ The key to enhancing the flavor is using the soaking water from *kiriboshi-daikon* and dried shiitakes.

★ If you are in a hurry, soak the *kiriboshi-daikon* and dried shiitakes in lukewarm water with a small amount of sugar added. The radish and mushrooms will soften more quickly.

★ Add harder ingredients first when frying.

Simmered *Okara* Tofu Lees
おからの炒り煮

about **15** min / 約15分

153 kcal / 153 キロカロリー

ほのかな甘さがおいしく、体によいおからを家庭で作る
Enjoy the delicate sweetness of healthy homemade *okara*

■材料（4人分）

おから	200g
干ししいたけ	4 枚
にんじん	1/4 本 (50g)
長ねぎ	1 本
ごぼう	1/3 本 (50g)
こんにゃく	1/2 枚
サラダ油	大さじ 1
だし汁	1 カップ
干ししいたけの戻し汁	1/2 カップ
料理酒	大さじ 1
砂糖	大さじ 3
しょう油	大さじ 3

※その他の具材として、細切りにしたきくらげ、油揚げ、あさりのむき身、鶏肉などを好みに合わせて使ってもおいしいです。

■ INGREDIENTS (serves 4)

200g *okara* tofu lees
4 dried shiitake mushrooms
1/4 (50g) carrot
1 *naga-negi* onion
1/3 (50g) burdock
1/2 devil's tongue
1 Tbsp vegetable oil
4/5 cup stock (200㎖)
2/5 cup water used for softening
shiitake mushrooms (100㎖)
1 Tbsp cooking sake
3 Tbsps sugar
3 Tbsps soy sauce

※ Thinly-sliced cloud ear mushroom, aburaage or deep-fried tofu, stripped shellfish and poultry can be added.

■作り方

1 干ししいたけは水で戻し、軸を切って薄切りにします。戻し汁 2 分の 1 カップ分は、こして取っておきます。

2 にんじんは皮をむき 3cm の長さの拍子切り、長ねぎは 1cm 幅の小口切りにします。ごぼうは包丁の背で皮をこそげてから、ささがきにし水にさらしてアクを抜きます。

3 こんにゃくは 3cm の長さの拍子切りにし、熱湯をくぐらせてアクを抜きます。

4 鍋にサラダ油を熱し、2 の長ねぎを炒め、にんじん、ごぼう、3 のこんにゃく、1 のしいたけを入れて全体に油がなじむように炒めます。

5 4 の鍋におからを入れてさっと炒め合わせ、1 の干ししいたけの戻し汁、だし汁、料理酒、砂糖、しょう油を加えて汁けがなくなるように炒り煮にします。

コツのコツ

★あまり炒めすぎてパサパサにならないようにするとよいでしょう。

★干ししいたけの戻し汁は、必ず使用しましょう。

★焦がさないよう、しっとりとした炒り煮しましょう。

■ Directions

1 Soften the dried shiitake mushrooms in cold water, chop off the stems and cut thinly. Strain the water in which the mushrooms have been softened, and set aside 2/5 cup of strained water.

2 Peel the carrot, and cut into 1 1/5-inch bar rectangles. Cut the *naga-negi* onion into 3/8-inch pieces using the edge cut technique. Scrape off the skin of the burdock with the back of a knife, cut using the *sasagaki* shaving technique and soak in cold water to eliminate bitterness.

3 Cut the devil's tongue into 1 1/5-inch bar rectangles, and expose to hot water to eliminate bitterness.

4 Heat the vegetable oil in a pot, and fry the *naga-negi* onion. Add the carrot, burdock, devil's tongue and shiitake mushrooms, and fry until their surfaces absorb the oil.

5 Add the tofu lees, and fry briefly. Add also the liquid set aside in 1. above, stock, cooking sake, sugar and soy sauce, and simmer while stirring until all the liquid is gone.

Tip on Tips

★ Be careful not to fry too much, otherwise the ingredients will become dry and tasteless.

★ Remember to use the soaking water left over from the dried shiitakes.

★ Try to keep it moist while simmering. Pay attention so they do not burn.

Burdock Kimpira
きんぴらごぼう

ご飯や酒のつまみにも最適で体にもよい伝統食の代表

Nice accompaniment to rice or sake and good for the body. It is representative of traditional Japanese dishes

■材料（4人分）

ごぼう	150g
にんじん	50g
赤唐辛子	1本
炒りごま（白）	小さじ2
サラダ油	大さじ1
砂糖	大さじ1と1/2
しょう油	大さじ1
みりん	大さじ1
料理酒	大さじ1

■ INGREDIENTS (serves 4)

150g burdock
50g carrots
1 red pepper
2 tsps white parched sesame
1 Tbsp vegetable oil
1 1/2 Tbsps sugar
2 Tbsps soy sauce
1 Tbsp *mirin* sweet cooking sake
1 Tbsp cooking sake

◆ きんぴらに適した食材◆
Other ingredients suited to kimpira

◆れんこん・lotus root
◆うど・*udo*
※うどは皮の部分も
　使用できます。
※ The *udo* skin
　is also edible.

れんこん
lotus root

■作り方

1 ごぼうは皮をこそげて水で洗い、4cm の長さの細切りにして水にさらす。

2 にんじんは皮をむき1のごぼうと同じ くらいの細切りにします。

3 赤唐辛子はへたを切り、種を取って輪 切りにします。

4 鍋にサラダ油を入れ、熱して1のごぼ うを入れて丁寧に炒め、2のにんじん を加えさっと炒めます。

5 4の鍋に3の赤唐辛子、料理酒、砂糖、 しょう油、みりんを加え煮汁がなくなる まで炒め、炒りごま（白）をふります。

❗ コツのコツ

★ごぼうの皮に香りがあるので、 程度にします。

★作り方4は鍋を動かしながら炒めると 油が均一にからみ、早く炒まります。

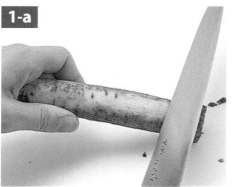

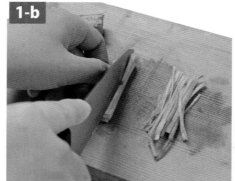

■ Directions

1 Scrape off the skin of the burdocks, rinse in cold water, cut into 1 1/2-inch-long strips and keep in cold water.

2 Peel the carrots, and cut thinly into strips of a similar size to that of the burdocks.

3 Remove the stalk and seeds of the red pepper, and cut thinly.

4 Place the oil in a pot, and fry the burdocks gently. Add the carrots, and fry briefly.

5 Add the red pepper from step 3, cooking sake, sugar, soy sauce and *mirin*, and fry until all the liquid is gone. Sprinkle on the white parched sesame before serving.

❗ Tip on Tips

★ Since the skin of the burdocks adds a good aroma to the dish, don't remove it completely. Just scraping is sufficient.

★ Shake the pot when frying burdocks and carrots (Step 4 of the recipe). This will make the oil spread out over all the ingredients evenly, speeding up the frying process.

Chicken and Vegetables. *Chikuzen*-style
筑前煮

about **35**min 約35分 | **252**kcal 252キロカロリー

味がしみ込んでおいしい、お惣菜を代表する滋味あふれる一品
A flavorful and nutritious dish that is one of the most common meals on the table

■材料（4人分）

鶏もも肉 … 1枚（200g）	しいたけの戻し汁 … 1/2 カップ
にんじん … 1/2 本（100g）	だし汁 …………… 1 カップ
ゆでたけのこ …… 100g	砂糖 ………… 大さじ 3
ごぼう …… 1/3 本（50g）	料理酒 ………… 大さじ 2
れんこん … 1/2 節（100g）	しょう油 ……… 大さじ 3
さやえんどう …… 12 枚	みりん ………… 大さじ 2
干ししいたけ ……… 4 枚	【下ごしらえ用】
こんにゃく ……… 1/2 枚	塩・酢・料理酒 … 各少々
ごま油 ………… 大さじ 1	

■ INGREDIENTS (serves 4)

1 (200g) chicken thigh	2/5 cup liquid used for softening
1/2 (100g) carrot	shiitake mushrooms (100㎖)
100g bamboo shoots, boiled	4/5 cup stock (200 ㎖)
1/3 (50g) burdock	3 Tbsps sugar
1/2 (100g) lotus root	2 Tbsps cooking sake
12 snow peas	3 Tbsps soy sauce
4 dried shiitake mushrooms	2 Tbsps *mirin* sweet cooking sake
1/2 cake devil's tongue	〈**For preliminary preparations**〉
1 Tbsp sesame oil	Small quantity of salt, vinegar and cooking sake

■作り方

1 干ししいたけを戻し、軸を切り落として半分にそぎ切りにします。戻し汁は捨てずに2分の1カップ分取っておきます。

2 こんにゃくを3cm幅くらいの棒状に切ってからひと口大にちぎり、塩をひとつまみふりかけ、手でもんで水洗いします。鍋にこんにゃくと水を入れて強火にかけ、沸騰したら5分ほど中火でゆでてザルに上げます。

3 皮をむいたにんじん、れんこん、ゆでたけのこを乱切りにします。

4 ごぼうは包丁の背で皮をこそげて乱切りにし、酢少々を入れた水に4～5分さらして、水洗いします。

5 鶏もも肉は余分な皮、脂肪を取り除き3cm角に切ります。少量の料理酒をふりかけ臭みを取り、1～2分おいたら別の皿に移しておきます。

6 さやえんどうは軸を折って筋を取り除き、塩少々を入れた熱湯でさっとゆで、冷水に取り、半分に切ります。

7 鍋にごま油を熱し、4のごぼう、3のれんこん、にんじん、2のこんにゃく、3のたけのこの順に入れて強火で炒めます。油がなじんだら、1のしいたけと5の鶏もも肉を入れて炒めます。

8 鶏もも肉に火が通ったら、1のしいたけの戻し汁とだし汁を入れて中火にします。煮たったらアクを取って砂糖、料理酒の順に入れて10分くらい煮ます。しょう油を入れて落としぶたをし、味を含ませます。

9 8の煮汁が半分以下になったら強火に戻し、みりんを加え、照りをだします。最後に6のさやえんどうを軽く混ぜ合わせます。

⚠ コツのコツ

★こんにゃくは、手でちぎると表面積が増えて味が入りやすくなります。

★鶏もも肉は酒につけたままだと旨味がにげてしまうので注意しましょう。

★さやえんどうは煮すぎると色が悪くなるので注意しましょう。

■ Directions

1 Soak the dried shiitake mushrooms in cold water to soften. Chop off the stems, and cut diagonally in half. Reserve 2/5 cup of water used for softening the mushrooms for later use.

2 Cut the devil's tongue into about 1/16-inch bars, and tear into bite-sized pieces by hand. Sprinkle a pinch of salt on the devil's tongue pieces, rub gently with hands and rinse in cold water. Place the devil's tongue and water in a pot, and bring to the boil over a high heat. When it comes to the boil, reduce the heat to medium, simmer for about 5 min and drain on a sieve.

3 Cut the peeled carrot, lotus root and boiled bamboo shoots using the rolling wedges technique.

4 Scrape off the skin of the burdock with the back of a knife, cut using the rolling wedges technique, submerge in water mixed with a small amount of vinegar for 4 to 5 min and rinse in cold water.

5 Remove excess skin and fat from the chicken thigh, and cut into 1 1/5-inch cubes. Pour a small amount of cooking sake over the cubes to eliminate their odor, let stand for 1 to 2 min, transfer to another plate and set aside.

6 Remove the stalks and strings of the snow peas, boil briefly in water mixed with a pinch of salt, rinse in cold water and cut in half.

7 Heat the sesame oil in a pot, add the burdock from step 4, the lotus root from step 3, carrot, devil's tongue from step 2 and bamboo shoots from step 3 in this order, and fry over high heat. When their surfaces have absorbed the oil and glisten, add the shiitake mushrooms from step 1 and chicken from step 5 and continue to fry.

8 When the chicken is heated through, add the water used for softening the mushrooms, which was set aside in 1. above, as well as the stock, and reduce the heat to medium. When it comes to the boil, skim off foam, add the sugar and cooking sake in this order and simmer for 10 min. Add the soy sauce, and cover with a drop-lid to ensure that all the ingredients are seasoned thoroughly.

9 When the simmering liquid is reduced to half or less, turn up the heat to high again and add the mirin sweet cooking sake to make the ingredients glossy. To finish off cooking, add the snow peas prepared in 6. above and mix lightly.

⚠ Tip on Tips

★ Always tear devil's tongues into smaller pieces by hand because this will increase their surface area, facilitating the penetration of seasonings into each piece.

★ If exposed to cooking sake too long, the flavor of chicken thigh will be lost. So, make sure to transfer it to another plate.

★ Don't simmer snow peas too long, otherwise they will be discolored.

Taro Tumbles

里いもの煮っころがし

about **25**min 約25分

121kcal 121キロカロリー

ねっとりとした食感と滋味あふれるおいしさが人気の秋を代表する料理

A popular dish for its chewiness, it represents the wholesome flavor of autumn

■材料（4人分）

里いも	400g
だし汁	1カップ
料理酒	大さじ1と1/2
みりん	大さじ1と1/2
砂糖	大さじ3
しょう油	大さじ1と1/2
黄ゆず	適宜

■ INGREDIENTS (serves 4)

400g Japanese taros
4/5 cup stock (200 ㎖)
1 1/2 Tbsps cooking sake
1 1/2 Tbsps *mirin* sweet cooking sake
3 Tbsps sugar
1 1/2 Tbsps soy sauce
Yellow-colored *yuzu* rind

里いも
Japanese taros

■作り方

1 里いもは、たわしで汚れを取り、水洗いをします。

2 里いもの上下を包丁で適度に切り落とし、六方むきにします。
※六方むきとは、里いもの面を六面にするむき方です。下図参照。

包丁でこのような面を六面作るのが六方向きです。

With a knife, *roppo-muki* turns a taro into a hexagon as pictured.

3 鍋にだし汁、料理酒、みりん、砂糖、しょう油と2の里いもを入れて煮ます。

4 3の里いもが柔らかくなったら、鍋をゆすって里いもをころがしながら煮詰めていきます。
※里いも1個に竹串を刺して、中までスーッと入ったら火の通った証拠です。

5 里いもを器に盛り、黄ゆずの皮をおろし金でおろして上に散らします。

! コツのコツ

★里いもは粒のそろった小粒のものを選ぶと煮崩れしにくいです。

★鍋をゆすり、里いもをころがしながら煮詰めると、全体に味がしみ込みます。

★4の工程で里いもを焦がさないように注意しましょう。

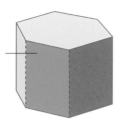

■ Directions

1 Wash the taros using a scrubber in water.

2 Cut off the ends of the taro with a knife then peel it in *roppo-muki* or hexagonal shape.
※ *Roppo-muki* is a way of peeling taros, making six surfaces as a hexagon. See below.

3 Place the stock, cooking sake, mirin, sugar, soy sauce and taros in a pot, and simmer.

4 When the taros in the pot become tender, shake the pot while still simmering so that the taros tumble around.
※ You can tell wether taros have been completely cooked if you can stick a bamboo skewer into them smoothly.

5 Arrange the taros in a bowl, and sprinkle over the grated yellow-colored *yuzu* rind.

! Tip on Tips

★ Choose smaller taros of an equal size size. These types of taros will be more likely to retain their shape while simmering.

★ Let the taros tumble and the stock simmer away while shaking the pot in order that the taros are fully flavored.

★ Take care not to let the taros burn in step 4.

◆ "きぬかつぎ" って何？ ◆

What is *Kinukatsugi*?

◆きぬかつぎとはけっして里いもの種類の名前ではなく、小粒の里いも（石川小芋など）の皮を3分の1を切り取って、蒸した料理のことです。

◆ *Kinukatsugi* is not the name of a taro specirs, but a steamed dish of small taros (*Ishikawa-koimo* and other kinds), with its top 1/3 part peeled.

Braised Meat and Vegetables
肉じゃが

about 25min 約25分

541 kcal 541 キロカロリー

" おふくろ " の味として古くから人気の一品
A traditional and popular dish known as "mother's flavoring"

■材料（4人分）

牛ばら薄切り肉	250g
じゃがいも（男爵）	大 4 個
玉ねぎ	1 個
糸こんにゃく	1/2 玉
あさつき	適宜
七味唐辛子	適宜
サラダ油	大さじ 1
水	1 と 1/2 カップ
砂糖	大さじ 3
料理酒	大さじ 2
しょう油	大さじ 3
みりん	大さじ 1

■ INGREDIENTS (serves 4)

250g beef plate, thinly sliced
4 large *danshakuimo* potatoes
1 onion
1/2 ball *ito-konnyaku* (devil's tongue in "thread" form)
Asatsuki chives
Seven-spice chili mix
1 Tbsp vegetable oil
1 1/4 cups water (300㎖)
3 Tbsps sugar
2 Tbsps cooking sake
3 Tbsps soy sauce
1 Tbsp *mirin* sweet cooking sake

じゃがいも（男爵）
Danshakuimo potato

じゃがいも（メイクイーン）
May queen potato

■ 作り方

1 じゃがいもは皮をむいて4つ割りにし、面取りをして10分くらい水にさらします。

2 玉ねぎは皮をむいてくし形に切ります。牛ばら薄切り肉は4cm幅くらいに切ります。

3 糸こんにゃくは水洗いし、5〜6cmの長さに切ってから熱湯で2〜3分ゆでます。

4 鍋にサラダ油を熱して2の牛ばら薄切り肉を炒め、3の糸こんにゃく、2の玉ねぎ、1のじゃがいもを加え全体に油をなじませます。

5 4の鍋に水を入れ、強火で煮たててアクを取り、弱めの中火にして砂糖、料理酒を入れて5分煮ます。みりん、しょう油を加え、落としぶたをして煮汁がなくなるまで煮詰めます。

6 5を器に盛り、好みで小口切りのあさつき、七味唐辛子をふっていただきます。

❗ コツのコツ

★ 使用する肉は、脂身があった方が旨味が出ておいしく仕上がります。

★ じゃがいもを面取りすることで、煮くずれを防ぎます。

★ 調味料の分量を変えて味を好みの味にしてもよいでしょう。

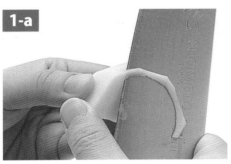

1-a

1-b

2

3

4

5

■ Directions

1 Peel the potatoes, cut lengthwise into four wedges, bevel the edges and soak in cold water for 10 min.

2 Peel the onion, and cut lengthwise into four to six wedges. Cut the beef into 1 1/2-inch pieces.

3 Rinse the *ito-konnyaku* in cold water, cut into 2 to 2 1/3-inch lengths and boil for a few minutes.

4 Heat oil in a pot, and fry the beef. Add the chopped *ito-konnyaku*, onion and potatoes, and fry until their surfaces absorb the oil.

5 Add the water to the pot, bring to the boil over a high heat and skim off foam. Reduce the heat, add the sugar and cooking sake, and simmer for 5 min. Add the *mirin* and soy sauce, cover with a drop-lid and simmer until all the liquid is gone.

6 Transfer the ingredients simmered in step 5 and sprinkle with the edge-cut *asatsuki* chives as well as the seven-spice chili mix if desired.

❗ Tip on Tips

★ Fatty meat will add more flavor to the dish than lean meat.

★ Trimming the potatoes to create beveled edges helps them hold their shape during the cooking process.

★ You may try changing the quantity of seasonings to create your own flavor.

Shiraae, Vegetables Dressed with Ground Tofu and Sesame

白あえ

about **20** min 約20分

143 kcal 143 キロカロリー

体がほっとする伝統のおいしさ
The comforting flavor of traditional Japanese food

■材料（2 人分）

にんじん	……………6cm	三つ葉	……………1/4 束
きくらげ（乾）…	小 4〜5 枚	木綿豆腐	……………1/4 丁
こんにゃく	………1/3 枚	炒りごま（白）	大さじ 2
A 薄口しょう油	…小さじ1/2	白みそ	……………大さじ 1
だし汁	…1/4 カップ	砂糖	……………大さじ 1
砂糖	…大さじ 1/2	塩	……………大さじ 1/8
塩	………小さじ 1/4	料理酒	……………小さじ 1

■作り方

1 こんにゃくは 3cm の長さの拍子きりにし、熱湯でさっとゆがいてアクを取り、水けをきります。にんじんは、皮をむいて 3cm の長さの拍子切りに、きくらげは水で戻して石づきを取り、さっとゆがいてせん切りに、三つ葉は根を切り、さっとゆで冷水に取り 3cm の長さに切ります。

2 鍋に **A** を入れて煮たて、1 のにんじん、こんにゃく、きくらげを入れて汁けがなくなるまで煮て、冷ましておきます。

3 木綿豆腐は半分に切り、熱湯で 2 分くらいゆでて水けをきり、裏ごし器でこします。

4 白ごまを小鍋に入れて焦がさないように炒り、すり鉢に移し、油が出るまでよくすります。

5 3 の裏ごしした豆腐を 4 のすり鉢に入れ、白みそを加えてよくすり、砂糖、塩、料理酒を加えてなめらかになるまですります。2 の具材と、三つ葉をあえて、器に盛ります。

❗ コツのコツ・Tip on Tips

★豆腐の水けをよくきることが大切です。

★4 の工程で白ごまを焦がした場合、最初から作り直しましょう。

★ It's important to completely drain excess water from the tofu.

★ If you let the white sesame burn during step 4, you should try again.

■ INGREDIENTS (serves 2)

2 1/4-inch carrot		1/4 bundle of *mitsuba* (honeywort)
4~5 small dried cloud ear mushroom		1/4 cake "cotton" tofu
1/3 devil's tongue		2 Tbsps white parched sesame
A	1/2 tbsp light soy sauce	1 Tbsp white miso
	1/5 cup stock (50ml)	1 Tbsp sugar
	1/2 Tbsp sugar	1/8 Tbsp shalt
	1/4 tbsp salt	1 tbsp cooking sake

■ Directions

1 Cut devil's tongue into 1 1/4-inch bar rectangles. Blanch briefly in boiling water to remove its harsh taste and drain. Peel carrot and cut into 1 1/4-inch bar rectangles. Soak cloud ear mushrooms in water and remove the stems. Blanch briefly and cut into julienne strips. Cut off the root of mitsuba, blanch briefly and soak in chilled water. Then cut into 1 1/4-inch lengths.

2 Put **A** into a pot and bring to a boil. Add the carrot, devil's tongue and cloud ear mushrooms from step 1 and simmer away the moisture. Set aside to cool.

3 Cut tofu in half and cook in boiling water for about 2 minutes. Drain and strain through a fine sieve.

4 Roast white sesame in a small pot without letting it burn. Transfer to a grinding bowl and grind the sesame well until oily.

5 Add the strained tofu from step 3 and white miso into the grinding bowl and grind well. Put sugar, salt and cooking sake and grind until smooth. Mix the ingredients from step 2 and the *mitsuba* and arrange in a serving dish.

第四章
Chapter 4

Basic Japanese Simmered Dishes
和食の基本・煮もの

和食の定番ともいえる煮もの。体にやさしい野菜の煮もの、おかず、酒肴などに大活躍の豚の角煮、旬の魚を煮ものでいただく。コツを覚えて煮ものをおいしく作りたい。

Simmered dishes are a basic staple of Japanese cooking. Simmered vegetables are good for the body and *Nagasaki*-style braised pork is excellent with both rice and sake. Seasonal fish is best enjoyed in a simmered dish. Get the knack of this Japanese tradition and prepare some delicious simmered dishes.

Simmered Bamboo Shoots
若竹煮

春を代表する野菜のたけのこをいただいて、春の息吹を感じる

Feel the start of spring by enjoying bamboo shoots, one of the favored spring vegetables

■材料 (4人分)

ゆでたけのこ	400g
生わかめ	40g
木の芽	適宜
だし汁	2カップ
料理酒	1/4カップ
砂糖	大さじ1
みりん	大さじ1
薄口しょう油	大さじ1と1/2

※生のたけのこを使う場合には、あまり大きすぎず、ずんぐりとした重みのあるもので、皮につやがあり表面にうぶ毛が生え、穂先が黄色っぽいものを選ぶとよいです。穂先が緑色がかって伸びているものは、育ちすぎている場合が多く、えぐみが強いので避けましょう。

■ INGREDIENTS (serves 4)

400g bamboo shoots, boiled
40g fresh *wakame* seaweed
Kinome (Young leaves of sansho Japanese pepper)
1 2/3 cups stock (400㎖)
1/5 cup cooking sake (50㎖)
1 Tbsp sugar
1 Tbsp *mirin* sweet cooking sake
1 1/2 Tbsps light soy sauce

※ If you are using a raw bamboo shoot, choose the middle-sized stocky one with weight, its husks glossy with downy hair on the surface and its tip colored yellow. Avoid those of which the tips are green since they are overgrown and taste harsh.

■作り方

1 たけのこは穂先5cm くらいのところを切って縦に2〜4つ割りにし、根元は1cm の厚さの半月に切ります。

2 生わかめは湯通しをし、ざく切りにします。

3 鍋に**1**のたけのことだし汁を入れ、落としぶたをして強火にかけ、煮たったら料理酒を入れて弱火にし、15分くらい煮ます。砂糖、みりん、薄口しょう油を加えて30〜40分煮て**2**のわかめを加えて、さっと火を通します。

4 器にたけのことわかめを盛り、煮汁を注ぎ、木の芽をのせます。

❗ コツのコツ

★たけのことわかめの香りを楽しむため、味つけは薄めにしましょう。

★わかめは熱が入りすぎると香り、食感が悪くなるのでさっと火を通す程度にしましょう。

◆生のたけのこのアク抜き

1. たけのこはよく洗い、根元のかたい部分をこそぎます。穂先は斜めに切り落とし、縦の中央に1本（穂先は深く、根元は浅め）切り込みを入れます。

2. 大きな鍋にたけのこ、たっぷりの水、米ぬか2つかみ、赤唐辛子2本を入れて加熱します。煮たったら落としぶたをして弱火で根元に竹串がすっと通るまでゆでます。

3. 火を止めて落としぶたをしたままゆで汁が冷めるまでおきます。水で洗い皮をむきます。

■ Directions

1 Cut the bamboo shoots in half crosswise at about 2 inches from the tip. Cut further in half or quarters lengthwise. Cut the bottom part into 3/8-inch half-moons.

2 Plunge the fresh wakame seaweed into hot water, and cut coarsely.

3 Place the bamboo shoots and stock in a pot, cover with a drop-lid and bring to the boil over a high heat. When it begins to boil, reduce the heat to low and simmer for about 15 min. Add the sugar, *mirin* and light soy sauce, and continue to simmer for 30 to 40 min. Add the *wakame* seaweed, and simmer briefly.

4 Arrange the bamboo shoots and *wakame* seaweed in a bowl, pour in the simmering liquid and place the *kinome* on top of the dish.

❗ Tip on Tips

★ The flavor should be thin so that the aroma of the bamboo shoots and *wakame* seaweed will not be spoilt.

★ When heating *wakame* seaweed, do so briefly to maintain its aroma and texture.

◆ How to remove harshness from uncooked bamboo shoots

1. Wash the bamboo shoots well, and scrape off the hard base part. Chop off the tip diagonally, and make a vertical incision through the center (Deeper in the tip part, and shallower in the base part)

2. Place the bamboo shoots, plenty of water, 2 handfuls of rice bran and 2 red peppers in a large pot, and bring to the boil. When it comes to the boil, cover with a drop-lid and boil over a low heat until the base part of the bamboo shoots becomes tender enough for a bamboo skewer to pierce without difficulty.

3. Remove from the heat, and let stand until the liquid is cool with the drop-lid still placed on top of it. Rinse the bamboo shoots in cold water, and peel the husks.

Taros with Thick Chicken Dressing
里いもの鶏あんかけ

ねっとりとした里いもに甘辛い鶏あんかけがおいしい
Sweet and spicy chicken dressing is nicely paired with chewy taros

■材料（4人分）

里いも …………… 400g

A
┌ だし汁 … 1と1/2カップ
│ 砂糖 ……… 大さじ4
│ 料理酒 …… 大さじ1
└ 薄口しょう油 … 大さじ2

黄ゆず …………… 適宜
鶏ひき肉 ………… 100g

B
┌ だし汁 … 3/4 カップ
│ 砂糖 …… 大さじ2
└ しょう油 … 大さじ2

片栗粉 ……… 大さじ1/2

■ INGREDIENTS (serves 4)

400g taros

A
┌ 1 1/4 cups stock（300 ㎖）
│ 4 Tbsps sugar
│ 1 Tbsp cooking sake
└ 2 Tbsps light soy sauce

Yellow *yuzu* Japanese lime rind
100g ground chicken

B
┌ 3/5 cup stock（150 ㎖）
│ 2 Tbsps sugar
└ 2 Tbsps soy sauce

1/2 Tbsp *katakuriko starch*

■ 作り方

1 里いもは水で洗って、たわしでこすりながら泥をよく落とします。里いもの上下を平らに切り落し、六角むきにします。里いもを水をはったボウルに入れます。

2 1のボウルの水を捨て、塩（分量外）をひとつまみふり入れて手でよくもんでぬめりを取り、水で洗ってざるに上げます。鍋にたっぷりの水と里いもを入れて強火にかけ、煮立ったら火を弱め

て2〜3分ゆでます。ざるに上げてゆで汁をきり、さっと表面のぬめりを水で洗います。

3 鍋にAのだし汁と2の里いもを入れて火にかけ、煮立ったら中火にし、Aの砂糖を入れて落としぶたをして2〜3分煮たら、Aの料理酒、薄口しょう油を加えてアクをすくいながら煮汁が3分の1量になるまで煮ていきます。

4 別の鍋にBのだし汁と砂糖、しょう油を入れて中火で煮立て、鶏ひき肉を入れてよく混ぜます。鶏ひき肉に火が通ったら同量の水（分量外）で溶いた片栗粉を回し入れてあんを作ります。

5 器に3の里いもを入れ、3の煮汁をはり、上から4の鶏あんをかけ、黄ゆずのせん切りをのせていただきます。

■ Directions

1 Wash the taros with water while using a scrubber to remove mud. Cut off the ends of the taros and peel them in *roppo-muki* or hexagonally. Put them in a bowl filled with water.

2 Drain the bowl, sprinkle a pinch of salt (extra quantity) on the taros, and rub them to remove the slime. Rinse the taros, and drain in a sieve. Put the taros and a generous quantity of water in a pot, and heat over a high flame. When it comes to the boil, turn down the heat to low, and boil for about 2 to 3 min. Drain the taros

in a sieve, and quickly rinse off the slime on the surface of the taros.

3 Put the stock of **A** and the taros in a pot, and heat. When it comes to the boil, turn down the heat to medium and add the sugar of A. Place a drop lid on the taros, and simmer for 2 to 3 min. Add the cooking sake, light soy sauce of **A**, and simmer, while skimming off the scum, until the quantity of the liquid is reduced to 1/3.

4 Put all the ingredients of **B** in another pot, and bring it to the

boil over the medium heat. Add the ground chicken, and stir well. When the chicken is cooked, pour in a circular motion a mixture of *katakuriko* starch and the same quantity of water (extra quantity) to thicken the dressing.

5 Arrange the taros in a serving dish, add the simmering liquid of 3, and pour over the thickened dressing of 4. Sprinkle over julienne strips of *yuzu* before serving.

Simmered Pumpkin
かぼちゃの煮もの

about **20**min 約20分

165kcal 165キロカロリー

ほくほくしたかぼちゃの食感と自然な甘味がおいしい

An appetizing dish featuring the natural sweetness and soft texture of steaming-hot pumpkins

■材料（4人分）

かぼちゃ … 1/2 個 (500g)
水…… 1と1/2〜2 カップ
砂糖 ………… 大さじ 3
塩………… 小さじ 1/2
みりん ………… 大さじ 2
しょう油 ……… 大さじ 1

■ INGREDIENTS (serves 4)

1/2 (500g) pumpkin
1 1/4 to 1 2/3 cups water (300〜400 ㎖)
3 Tbsps sugar
1/2 tsp salt
2 Tbsps *mirin* sweet cooking sake
1 Tbsp soy sauce

かぼちゃの煮もの
Simmered pumpkin
(Image photo)

■作り方

1 かぼちゃの種とわたをスプーンで取り、大きめの一口大に切って皮をところどころむき、面取りをして水で洗います。

2 鍋に1のかぼちゃの皮目を下にして入れます。かぶるくらいに水を入れ、強火にかけて煮たってきたらアクを取り、弱めの中火にします。砂糖を入れてひと煮たちさせ、塩を加えて落としぶたをして弱火で煮ます。

3 煮汁が2分の1量くらいになったら、みりん、しょう油を加えて、さらに弱火でことこと煮ます。煮汁が3分の1量くらいになったら火を止め、そのまま粗熱が取れるまでおきます。

❗ コツのコツ

★かぼちゃを切る時や皮をむく時、電子レンジで軽く加熱するとよいでしょう。

★かぼちゃの面取りをすると、煮崩れしにくくなります。

★かぼちゃなどのように柔らかく煮崩れしやすいものは、落としぶたにクッキングシートなど、柔らかい素材のものを使うとよいでしょう。

★火を止めても余熱がかぼちゃに入るので、火を止めるタイミングが遅れないように注意しましょう。

★煮ている途中でかぼちゃを混ぜたり、箸でひっくり返したりすると煮崩れしますので、そのまま煮詰めるのがきれいに仕上げるコツです。

かぼちゃ
pumpkin

■ Directions

1 Remove the pumpkin seeds and the fibers surrounding them with a spoon. Cut the pumpkin into bite-sized (but still as large as possible) pieces, peel roughly and partially, bevel the edges and rinse in cold water.

2 Place the pumpkin with the skin side down in a pot, pour in enough water so that the pumpkin is completely submerged and place over high heat. When it begins to boil, skim off foam and reduce the heat to medium low. Add the sugar, and boil briefly. Add the salt, cover with a drop-lid and simmer over a low heat.

3 When the simmering liquid is reduced to about 1/2, add the *mirin* and soy sauce, and continue to simmer. Remove from the heat when the liquid is reduced to about 1/3. Let rest until cool.

❗ Tip on Tips

★ Heat pumpkins lightly using a microwave prior to cutting and peeling them; such preparation will make things easier.

★ Pumpkins with the edges beveled are more likely to retain their shape while simmering.

★ When simmering pumpkins or other soft ingredients that are prone to lose their shape, use circular baking paper or similar that is soft yet heavy enough to be used as a substitute for a hard drop-lid.

★ Even when the pot is removed from the heat, the pumpkin continues to be heated due to the remaining heat of the liquid. So, pay attention to the timing at which the heat should be turned off, otherwise the pumpkin will be overdone.

★ Don't stir or turn the pumpkin over with chopsticks while simmering. This will cause the pumpkin to lose its shape. Leave the pumpkin intact until the end of simmering.

Giant white radish with White Miso Sauce
ふろふき大根

about **30** min
約30分

176 kcal
176キロカロリー

滋味深い大根と甘いみそがおいしい
Savor the goodness of giant white radish enhanced by sweet miso sauce

大根
Giant white radish

■材料（2人分）

大根（4〜5cm 厚さの輪切り）
・・・・・・・・・・・・・・・・・・・・・・ 2枚
米のとぎ汁 ・・・・・・・・ 適宜
昆布・・・・・・・・・・・・・・・ 10cm
白みそ・・・・・・・・・ 1/4 カップ
みりん ・・・・・・・・ 1/4 カップ
砂糖 ・・・・・・・・・・ 大さじ 1
ゆず皮・・・・・・・・・・・・・ 適宜
ゆず皮（せん切り）・・・ 適宜

■ INGREDIENTS (serves 2)

2 slices giant white radish, 1/6 to 1/8 -inch thick
Water used for washing rice
4 -inch *konbu* kelp
1/5 cup white miso (50 ㎖)
1/5 cup *mirin* sweet cooking sake （50 ㎖ ）
1 Tbsp sugar
Yuzu rind
Shredded *yuzu* rind

■作り方

1 大根は皮をむき、面取りをして大根の片面に十文字の切り込みを入れます。

2 鍋に大根を入れてかぶるくらいの米のとぎ汁を入れて落としぶたをし、強火にかけます。煮たったら弱めの中火で大根が柔らかくなるまで煮ます。

3 2の大根に串を刺して、すっと通るようになったらそのまま湯の中で冷まします。冷めたら取り出し、水で洗います。鍋に昆布と水（大根がかぶるくらいの量）を入れて弱火で加熱し、大根を入れて温めるように煮ます。

4 別鍋に白みそとみりん、砂糖を入れて混ぜながら、弱火にかけます。つやが出てとろりとしたら火から下ろし、ゆずの皮のすりおろしたものを加え、軽く混ぜます。

5 器に3の大根を盛り、4のみそをかけ、ゆず皮のせん切りをのせます。

第四章・和食の基本・煮もの ● Basic Japanese Simmered Dishes

！ コツのコツ

★米のとぎ汁がない時は、米大さじ1をガーゼ（ティーバック）に包んで代用するとよいです。

★大根の皮をむいたら面取りをすることで、煮崩れがなくなります。

★白みそ、みりん、砂糖を鍋で混ぜる時は、弱火にして絶対に焦がさないようにしましょう。もし、焦がしてしまったら、最初から作り直しましょう。

■ Directions

1 Peel the giant white radish slices, bevel the edges and make a cross-shape incision on one end.

2 Place the giant white radish in a pot, and pour in the water in which rice has been washed so that the radish is completely submerged. Cover with a drop-lid, and place over a high heat. When it comes to the boil, reduce the heat to medium low and simmer until tender.

3 Check the tenderness of each radish slice by sticking a skewer into it. When the radish is tender enough for the skewer to go in smoothly, turn off the heat and let stand until cool with the slices still submerged in water. Take the radish out of the pot, and rinse in cold water. Place the konbu kelp in a pot and pour water up to a height just enough to cover the radish. Place over a low heat, add the radish and simmer until the radish becomes sufficiently hot again.

4 Place the white miso, *mirin* and sugar in another pot, and place over a low heat. Stir the mix until it becomes a glossy and thick liquid. Remove from heat, add the grated *yuzu* rind and stir lightly.

5 Arrange the radish in a bowl, pour on the miso sauce and place the shredded *yuzu* rind on top of it.

！ Tip on Tips

★ When the water used for washing rice is not available, put a gauze bag containing 1 Tbsp rice into the pot.

★ Always bevel the edges of giant white radish slices after peeling them. In this way, you can ensure that each slice will keep its shape while simmering.

★ When heating the mix of white miso, *mirin* and sugar in a pot, always do so over a low heat, if it burns, give it another try.

Simmered Mackerel in Miso
さばのみそ煮

about 20min 約20分

300kcal 300キロカロリー

脂ののったさばに、みそがからんでおいしい煮魚料理の定番

A classic and delightful dish of simmered fatty mackerel dressed with miso

■材料（2人分）

さば半身	1枚	みそ	大さじ2
しょうが	1片	みりん	大さじ1
長ねぎ	1本		
白髪ねぎ	適宜		
水	3/4カップ		
料理酒	大さじ2		
砂糖	大さじ1と1/2		
しょう油	大さじ1/2		

※さばと一緒に、ごぼうを大きめのささがきにして酢水にさらしたもの、しいたけ、しめじなどを煮込んでもおいしいです。また、白髪ねぎの代わりに針しょうがを添えると、また違った風味で楽しめます。

■ INGREDIENTS (serves 2)

1 fillet mackerel
1 knob ginger
1 *naga-negi* onion
Fine *naga-negi* onion shreds
3/5 cup water (150 ㎖)
2 Tbsps cooking sake
1 1/2 Tbsps sugar
1/2 Tbsps soy sauce

2 Tbsps miso
1 Tbsp *mirin* sweet cooking sake

※ Burdock cut into largish sasagaki shavings and preliminary exposed to vinegar-added water, shiitake and shimeji mushrooms can be simmered together with mackerel. Enjoy a different flavor by using ginger cut into fine "needle" shreds instead of fine *naga-negi* onion shreds.

■作り方

1 さばは食べやすい大きさに切り、皮目に包丁で切り込みを入れて熱湯にくぐらせ、穴つき玉じゃくしで取り、氷水につけて霜ふりをします。
※この時に残っている血合いや、ぬめりなどを取ります。

2 長ねぎは4cmの長さに切ります。

3 鍋に水、料理酒、砂糖を入れて煮たて、1のさばを皮目を上にして入れ、ひと煮たちさせ、しょう油を入れます。

4 みそとみりんを合わせ、3の鍋の煮汁を少し加えてときのばし、しょうがの薄切りと2の長ねぎを加えます。弱め
の中火で紙の落としぶたをして10分くらい煮ます。
※みそは好みのものや、何種類か合わせるのもよいでしょう。

5 器にさばと長ねぎを盛り煮汁をかけ、白髪ねぎを飾ります。

❗コツのコツ

★さばを熱湯にくぐらせることで、生臭さを取ります。

★煮汁にさばの生臭さが出るので、煮汁が煮たってからさばを入れましょう。

★しょうがは4の工程で加えると、しょうがの香りがつきます。

■ Directions

1 Cut the mackerel into bite-sized pieces. Make a cross-shape incision on the skin surface of each mackerel piece. Blanch the mackerel by first plunging it into hot water, taking it out with a straining ladle and soaking it in chilled water with ice.
※ This process eliminates the remaining blood clots and the slime.

2 Cut the *naga-negi* onion into 1 1/2-inch lengths.

3 Place the water, cooking sake and sugar in a pot, and bring to the boil. Put the mackerel pieces with the skin side facing up into the pot, boil briefly and add the soy sauce.

4 Mix the miso and *mirin* in another pot. Take some liquid out of the pot in which the mackerel was simmered, add to the mixture of miso and *mirin* and stir well. Add the ginger, thinly cut, and the chopped *naga-negi* onion. Place over a medium low heat, cover with a baking paper as a substitute for a drop-lid and simmer for about 10 min.
※ Use your favorite miso or try a blend of several types of miso.

5 Arrange the mackerel and *naga-negi* onion in a bowl, pour over the simmering liquid and garnish with fine *naga-negi* onion shreds.

❗Tip on Tips

★ Plunge the mackerel into hot water before cooking to eliminate the smell.

★ Put mackerel into the simmering liquid only after bringing the liquid to the boil, otherwise, the smell of mackerel will remain in the liquid

★ Add ginger during step 4 in order to enhance the ginger flavor.

Simmered Rockfish (*Mebaru*)
めばるの煮つけ

 about **25**min 約25分   **268**kcal 268キロカロリー

脂ののっためばるの身がほのかに甘くて、おいしい煮つけの定番

A classic dish of simmered fish, the fatty rockfish will please you with its slightly sweet taste

■材料（2人分）

めばる	2 尾
ごぼう	1 本
しょうが（薄切り）	1 片分

A
水	1と1/2 カップ
料理酒	1/4 カップ
砂糖	大さじ 2
しょう油	大さじ 4
みりん	大さじ 4

■ INGREDIENTS (serves 2)

2 whole fresh rockfish
1 burdock
1 knob ginger

A
1 1/4 cups water (300㎖)
1/5 cup sake cooking sake (50㎖)
2 Tbsps sugar
4 Tbsps soy sauce
4 Tbsps *mirin* sweet cooking sake

黒めばる
Black rockfish (*Mebaru*)

めばる
Rockfish (*Mebaru*)

■作り方

1 めばるは包丁などでうろこを取り、割り箸2本をめばるの口に差し込み、えらと内臓をはさんで回転させながら内臓を引き出し(筒ぬき)します。

2 1のめばるに飾り包丁を入れたら、たっぷりの熱湯にくぐらせ、氷水につけうろこや腹の中をよく洗い落として、ペーパータオルで水けを取ります。

3 ごぼうは水洗いし、包丁で皮をこそげて4〜5cmの長さに切り、太ければさらに縦半分に切りさっとゆでておきます。

4 底の広く浅い鍋かフライパンにAを合わせ入れて、煮たたせます。クッキングシートを鍋底に敷き、間隔をあけて

2のめばる、3のごぼうを入れて落としぶたをし、弱めの中火で煮ます。

5 煮汁が半分くらいになったら、薄切りしょうがを入れて、4をさっと煮ます。

6 器にめばるとごぼうを盛りつけます。

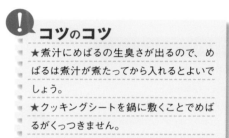

❗ コツのコツ

★煮汁にめばるの生臭さが出るので、めばるは煮汁が煮たってから入れるとよいでしょう。
★クッキングシートを鍋に敷くことでめばるがくっつきません。

◆ 煮つけに適した魚 ◆

Fish suitable for boiled and seasoned fish
◆黒めばる・Black rockfish (*Mebaru*)
◆かさご・Rockfish (*Kasago*)
◆いしもち・White croaker
◆あじ・Horse mackerel
◆いさき・Chiken grunt

かさごの煮つけ /Simmered rockfish (*Kasago*)

1

2-a

2-b

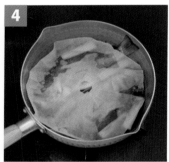
4

■ Directions

1 Scale the rockfish with a knife. Poke a pair of chopsticks into the fish's mouth, twist a few times and pull out the gills and innards.

2 Make a cross-shape incision on one side. Plunge into plenty of boiling water, soak in chilled water with ice and rinse the surface and inside of the fish well. Remove moisture with a paper kitchen towel.

3 Wash the burdock in cold water, scrape off the skin of the burdock with a knife, and cut into a length of 1 1/2 to 2 inches. If the root is too thick, cut it vertically. Briefly boil the burdock.

4 Mix **A** in a large shallow pot or a frying pan, and bring to the boil. Take the liquid out of the pot or pan. Cover the bottom of the pot or pan with a cooking sheet, add the rockfish with some space in between, as well as the burdock and liquid. Place a drop-lid on top of it, and simmer over a medium low heat.

5 When the liquid is reduced to about half, add the thinly sliced ginger and simmer briefly.

6 Arrange the rockfish and burdock in bowls.

❗ Tip on Tips

★ Put rockfish into the simmering liquid only after bringing the liquid to the boil, otherwise, the smell of rockfish will remain in the liquid.
★ Covering the bottom of the pot with a cooking sheet will prevent the rockfish from sticking.

Simmered Prawns
えびの旨煮

84 kcal
84キロカロリー

正月料理や酒肴に最適な目出たい一品
A savory dish for the New Year's menu and best with sake

車えび
Japanese tiger prawn
(*Kuruma* prawn)

■材料（4人分）

有頭えび	8 尾

A
だし汁	250cc
薄口しょう油	大さじ2
みりん	大さじ2
料理酒	大さじ2
砂糖	大さじ1

☐ INGREDIENTS (serves 4)

8 prawns with heads

A
- 1 cup stock (240 mℓ)
- 2 Tbsps light soy sauce
- 2 Tbsps *mirin* sweet cooking sake
- 2 Tbsps cooking sake
- 1 Tbsp sugar

■作り方

1 37ページを参照して、有頭えびの背わたをつまようじか竹串で取ります。頭の先端とひげ、尾の先を包丁で切り落としておきます。

2 鍋に**A**を入れ、火にかけ煮立ったら、1のえびを加えて、強火で3分くらい煮ます。

3 2のえびに火が通ったら、冷水を入れたボウルに煮汁に漬けた鍋のままあてて冷まします。

37ページを参照して

⚠ コツのコツ

★生きている新鮮なえび（車えび）を使用しましょう。

★えびを煮すぎると、身がかたくなるので注意しましょう。

★冷めるまで煮汁に漬け、えびに味をふくませましょう。

◆ えびの縁起 ◆
A bit about prawns

◆えびがまるで腰が曲がっているように見えることから老人を連想させ、長寿を祈願して、正月に食べられます。

◆ Japanese people eat prawns for New Year's celebration because they are a symbol of longevity. This derives from the prawns' round shape — it is reminiscent of elderly people's crooked backs.

1-a

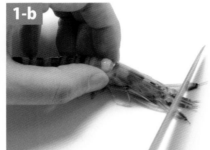
1-b

1-c

2-a

2-b

3

■ Directions

1 Refer to p.37 and de-vein the prawns. Remove the entrails of the prawns with a toothpick or a bamboo skewer. Devein the prawns. Cut off the tips of the heads, filaments, and tails.

2 Put the ingredients of **A** in a pot, and heat. When it comes to the boil, add the prawns, and cook over a high heat for about 3 min.

3 When the prawns are cooked, put cold water in a bowl and the pot while everything is still in to cool the prawns and the liquid.

Refer to p.37

⚠ Tip on Tips

★ Use fresh shrimp (prawns).

★ Don't cook live shrimp too long or the meat will get hard.

★ Leave the prawns in the liquid until cool to allow the seasonings to seep into the prawns.

◆ えびの種類 ◆
Kind of the prawn

◆車えび・Japanese tiger prawn (*Kuruma* prawn)
◆大正えび・Fleshy prawn
◆芝えび・*Shiba* shrimp
◆ボタンえび・*Botan* shrimp
◆トヤマえび・Corn stripe shrimp
◆甘えび（ホッコク甘えび）・Northern shrimp
◆伊勢えび・Japanese spiny lobster

甘えび（ホッコク甘えび）
Northern shrimp

Nagasaki-style Braised Pork
豚の角煮

about 150 min 約150分

638 kcal 638キロカロリー

豚肉がホロホロと柔らかく旨味が口いっぱいに広がる
The tender and succulent pork will melt in your mouth

■材料（4人分）

豚ばら肉（塊） … 600g
下ゆで用おから … 2カップ
さやえんどう …… 12枚
下ゆで用塩 ……… 少々
練り辛子 …………… 適宜
水……… 1と1/4カップ
料理酒 …… 1/4カップ
砂糖 ………… 大さじ4

しょう油 … 大さじ2と1/2
みりん ………… 大さじ1

※豚肉は薄紅色でツヤがあり引き締まっていて、脂肪が白くかたいものを選びましょう。肉にハリがなく、脂肪が黄色っぽいものは避けましょう。また、産地名が明確に表記されている信頼できるものを使うようにしましょう。

■ INGREDIENTS (serves 4)

600g slab pork belly
1 2/3 cups *okara* tofu lees (for preparing pork) (400㎖)
12 snow peas Pinch salt (for preparing pork)
Mustard
1 cup water (240 ㎖)
1/5 cup cooking sake (50 ㎖)
4 Tbsps sugar

2 1/2 Tbsps soy sauce
1 Tbsp *mirin* sweet cooking sake

※ Choose firm pork meat that has glossy pale pink color and its fat firm and white. Avoid the one without firmness and its fat turned yellow. It is recommended to use those of which are specified the area of production on the package.

■作り方

1 豚ばら肉とおからを鍋に入れ、たっぷりの水（分量外）で下ゆでします。沸騰したら、弱めの中火にし、水を足しながら竹串がすっと刺さる柔らかさになるまで2時間くらいゆでて、そのまま冷まします。

2 1が冷めたら水洗いし、汚れや余分な脂身を取り、一口大に切ります。

3 鍋に水、料理酒、砂糖、2の豚ばら肉を入れて火にかけ、煮たったらしょう油を入れて落としぶたをし、煮汁が半分くらいになるまで煮詰め、強火にして、みりんを回し入れます。

4 さやえんどうは筋を取り、さっと塩ゆでにします。

5 器に3の豚ばら肉を盛り、4のさやえんどうと練り辛子を添えます。

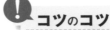

コツのコツ

★豚ばら肉が煮崩れしないように、たこ糸で結んでからゆでてもよいでしょう。

★おからで煮ることで豚ばら肉の臭みが取れ、柔らかくなります。

★おからで煮込んだ豚ばら肉は、柔らかくなり壊れやすくなっていますので丁寧に扱いましょう。

★みりんを入れることで、豚ばら肉に照りがでます。

1-a

1-b

3-a

3-b

■ Directions

1 Place the pork and tofu lees in a pot, fill the pot full of water (except quantity) and bring to the boil. When it comes to the boil, reduce the heat to medium low, and continue to boil for about 2 hours while occasionally adding water until the pork becomes tender enough for a bamboo skewer to pierce without difficulty.

2 Let stand until cool. When cool, rinse the pork in cold water, eliminate any unclean parts and excess fat and cut into bite-sized pieces

3 Place the water, cooking sake, sugar and pork in a pot, and bring to the boil. When it comes to the boil, add the soy sauce and cover with a drop-lid. When the liquid is reduced to about half, turn up the heat to high, and pour in the *mirin* in a circulating motion.

4 String the snow peas, boil briefly in salted water and cut into julienne strips.

5 Arrange the pork from step 3 in a bowl, and garnish with the snow peas from step 4 and mustard.

Tip on Tips

★You can bind pork with a kite string before boiling it to keep its shape.

★ Boiling the pork with tofu lees removes the smell of pork and also tenderizes the meat.

★Handle pork with care after boiling it with tofu lees as it is very tender and crumbles easily.

★ The *mirin* glazes the surface of the pork.

Lotus Root Kimpira

れんこんのきんぴら

about **10** min
約10分

79 kcal
79キロカロリー

シャクシャクした食感がおいしいれんこんのきんぴら
Crispy Lotus root kimpira is fun and delicious to eat

■材料（4人分）

れんこん ……… 200g	しょう油　大さじ1と1/2
赤唐辛子………… 1本	みりん ……大さじ 1/2
ごま油……… 大さじ1	〈下ごしらえ用〉
料理酒 …… 大さじ1	酢……………… 適宜
砂糖……… 大さじ 1/2	

■ INGREDIENTS (serves 4)

200g lotus root
1 red pepper
1 Tbsp sesame oil
1 Tbsp cooking sake
1/2 Tbsp sugar
1 1/2 Tbsps soy sauce
1/2 Tbsp *mirin* sweet
cooking sake

〈**For preliminary prepa-rations**〉
Vinegar

■作り方

1 れんこんは皮をむいて薄い半月形に切り、酢を少々加えた水にさらしてアクを抜き、水けをきります。

2 赤唐辛子はへたを切り、種を取って輪切りにしておきます。

3 鍋にごま油を熱して1のれんこんを炒め、れんこんに透明感が出てきたら2の赤唐辛子、料理酒、砂糖、しょう油、みりんを加え煮汁がなくなるまで炒め煮します。

■ Directions

1 Peel the lotus root and cut thinly into half-moons. Soak in vinegar-added water to remove the bitterness and wipe dry.

2 Remove the stalk and seeds of the red pepper, and cut thinly.

3 Heat the sesame oil in a pot, and fry the lotus root. When the lotus root gets translucent color, add the red pepper, cooking sake, sugar, soy sauce, and *mirin*. Simmer until all the liquid is gone.

❗ コツのコツ・Tip on Tips

★れんこんはアクが強いので、酢水につけてアクを抜きましょう。

★れんこんの皮は厚めにむきましょう。

★ Soak lotus root in vinegar-added water to remove the strong bitterness of the lotus root.

★ Peel off the skin of lotus root thickly.

1

3-a

3-b

第五章
Chapter 5

Basic Japanese Grilled and Pan-Fried Dishes
和食の基本・焼きもの

おかずはもちろんのこと、酒肴、弁当のおかずなどにも最適な焼きもの。体にやさしい魚の焼きものから、ボリュームのある肉類の焼きもの、お好み焼きなどをおいしく作りたい。

Grilled dishes are best suited as a main dish, but are also great with sake or in your lunch box. Cook and serve healthy grilled fish dishes, satisfying dishes of grilled meat and "As-you-like-it" pancakes.

Rolled Omelet
だし巻き卵

ふわふわ感と卵の旨味が楽しめて、おかず、酒のつまみ、弁当に最適

Enjoy the velvety texture and pleasant flavor of eggs. It goes well with rice, sake or your lunchbox

■材料（4人分）

卵………………… 5個

A
┌ だし汁 … 1/4 カップ
│ 砂糖 …… 大さじ 3
│ 塩……… 小さじ 1/4
└ しょう油 … 小さじ 1

サラダ油………… 適宜
大根おろし ……… 少々
かいわれ大根……… 少々

※だし巻き卵に使う卵は、パックの日付けが新しく、殻の色がきれいで光沢があり、ヒビの入っていないものを選びましょう。また、卵を割ってみて、卵黄にハリがなく、白身が少ないものは、古いものなので使わないようにしましょう。

■ INGREDIENTS (serves 4)

5 eggs

A
┌ 1/5 cup stock (50 ㎖)
│ 3 Tbsps sugar
│ 1/4 tsp salt
└ 1 tsp soy sauce

Vegetable oil
Small quantity of grated giant white radish
Small quantity of young giant white radish shoots

※ It is recommended to select eggs of which the package shows recent dates of production and the eggshells are clean and sheen without any crack. When opening eggs, check if the yolk is lacking firmness and the white is less in volume. Do not use these since they are not fresh.

■作り方

1 Aを合わせて鍋に入れ、火にかけて冷ましておきます。

2 卵をボウルに割り入れカラザを取り、泡だたないように溶ほぐし、**1**を混ぜ合わせて卵液を作ります。

3 卵焼き鍋を熱し、サラダ油を卵焼き鍋の四隅、側面まで塗ります。菜箸に卵液をつけて、卵焼き鍋につけるとジュッと音がするくらいの中火にしておきます。

4 卵焼き鍋に**2**の卵液の2分の1量くらい流し入れ、表面が半熟になってきたら菜箸で卵の端を持って折り畳み、卵焼き鍋のあいた部分に油を塗り、卵焼きを向こう側にずらします。残りの卵液の半量を入れ、菜箸で持ち上げながら焼けている卵焼きの下にも流し入れます。この作業を卵液がなくなるまでくり返します。

5 焼き上がったら巻きすで巻いて形を整え、食べやすい大きさに切り、大根おろしとかいわれ大根を添えます。

！ コツのコツ
★卵焼き専用の鍋（フライパン）を使用し、よく熱して油をなじませてから使用すると卵がくっつきません。

■ Directions

1 Mix **A** in a pot, bring to the boil and let stand until cool.

2 Drop the eggs into a bowl, and remove the chalaza. Beat the eggs lightly so that the yolks and whites are roughly mixed (Don't froth). Add the liquid prepared in 1. above to make the "egg mixture."

3 Heat a square omelet pan, and coat all the surface of the pan, including the four corners and inner sides, with the vegetable oil. Test the pan to see whether it is hot enough for frying by placing a drop of the egg mixture into the center of the pan with cooking chopsticks. It should sizzle. Maintain this temperature over a medium heat.

4 Pour 1/2 of the egg mixture for one roll into the pan, and tilt so that it spreads over the bottom. When the surface of the egg sheet is half cooked, hold the far end of the sheet with cooking chopsticks and fold towards you. Oil the pan surface not covered by the omelet, and push the omelet to the just-oiled-part of the pan. Pour in 1/2 of the remaining egg mixture, and lift the edge of the rolled omelet so that the raw egg mixture flows under it too. Repeat the folding and oiling operation, and pour in all the remaining egg mixture. Repeat the process until the egg mixture is gone.

5 When cooked, wrap in a bamboo mat to adjust the shape. Slice crosswise into bite-sized pieces. Garnish with the grated giant white radish and young giant white radish shoots.

！ Tip on Tips
★ Use a special pan designed for frying omelets, and coat with oil thoroughly before cooking to prevent the eggs from sticking to the pan.

Fried Dumplings
焼きギョウザ

about **30** min
約30分

66 kcal
66キロカロリー

皮がパリッとして、中がジューシーなギョウザはみんな大好き

Crispy outside and juicy inside. Everyone loves fried dumplings

■材料 (15 個分)

ギョウザの皮 ……	15 枚
豚ひき肉 ………	200g
長ねぎ …………	1/4 本
しょうが ………	1 かけ
にら …………	1/2 束
キャベツ ………	2 枚
塩 ……………	小さじ 1/2
サラダ油 ………	大さじ 1

A
こしょう ………	少々
料理酒 ………	大さじ 1
しょう油 ……	大さじ 1/2
ごま油 ……	大さじ 1

【つけダレ】
しょう油 …………	適宜
酢 ……………	適宜
ラー油 …………	適宜

■ INGREDIENTS (makes 15 dumplings)

15 dumpling wrappers
200g minced pork
1/4 *naga-negi* onion
1 small piece ginger
1/2 bundle leek
2 cabbage leaves
1/2 tbsp salt
1 Tbsp vegetable oil

A
Pinch pepper
1 Tbsp cooking sake
1/2 Tbsp soy sauce
1 Tbsp sesame oil

〈**For preparing dipping sauce**〉
Soy sauce
Vinegar
Hot sesame oil

■作り方

1 キャベツは水洗いし、熱湯でさっとゆでて、みじん切りにし水けをふきんなどでよく絞ります。

2 長ねぎ、しょうがはみじん切りにし、にらは水洗いして、長さ1cmに切ります。

3 ボウルに豚ひき肉と塩を入れ、ねばりが出るまでよく練り、Aを加えてさらに練ります。

4 3に1のキャベツと2の長ねぎ、しょうが、にらを入れ、混ぜ合わせてひとまとめにします。これであんの完成です。

5 手のひらにギョウザの皮をのせ、中央に4のあんを大さじ1強のせ、皮を半分に折り、縁をくっつけたら端からひだを作りながら、生地と生地を止めて包んでいきます。

6 フライパンにサラダ油を入れて強火で熱し、5のギョウザを並べ、水（分量外）をさっと回し入れ、ふたをして弱火で蒸し焼きにします。

7 6のふたを取り、水分がなくなったら、中火にしてこんがりと焼き色がつくように焼き上げます。

8 焼き上がったら、焼き色を上にして皿に盛り、つけダレを添えていただきます。

❗ コツのコツ

★ キャベツを軽くゆでたら、みじん切りにし、よく水けを絞りましょう。きっちりと水けをしぼらないと水っぽいあんになってしまいます。

★ 豚ひき肉と他の具材をよく練り合わせると、焼き上がりがとてもジューシーになります。

★ 7の工程で水分がなくなり、皮がパリッとするまで焼きましょう。

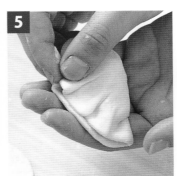

■ Directions

1 Wash the cabbage in water, cook quickly in boiling water, chop and squeeze out the water with a cloth.

2 Chop the *naga-negi* onion and ginger finely. Wash the leek in water and cut into 3/8-inch length.

3 Put the pork and salt into a bowl. Knead them well into gruel. Add **A** and knead some more.

4 Add the cabbage from step 1, the *naga-negi* onion, ginger and leek from step 2 into step 3. Mix them well and make a lump. This is your dumpling filling.

5 Place a dumping wrapper on your palm. Put 1 Tbsp of the filling from step 4 in the center of the wrap. Fold it in half as to make a semicircle. Fold the layers to wrap the filling and crimp the edges.

6 Put the vegetable oil in a frying pan and place over high heat. Line up the dumplings side by side and pour some extra water over them. Maintaining a low heat, place a lid over the pan to steam and fry the dumplings.

7 Remove the lid so the water evaporates. Turn the heat to medium and fry the dumplings until golden brown.

8 After the dumplings fry, transfer them to a plate with their brown side up. Serve with the dipping sauce.

❗ Tip on Tips

★ Remember to squeeze out the excess water from the lightly boiled cabbage. If this isn't done well, the filling will become watery.

★ Knead the pork well with other ingredients. It makes the filling very juicy.

★ Fry the dumplings until the water is evaporated and the wraps become crispy during step 7.

"As-You-Like-It" Pancake (*Okonomiyaki*)
お好み焼き

about 20 min 約20分

608 kcal 608キロカロリー

週末に家族や仲間で楽しみたいお好み焼きパーティー

Enjoy an "As-You-Like-It" Pancake party on weekends with your family and friends

■材料（2人分）

〈生 地〉

薄力粉	75g
長いも	25g
だし汁（かつおだし）	100cc

〈具 材〉

卵	1個
豚ばら肉（薄切りのもの2枚）	約100g
キャベツ	約100g
青ねぎ	適宜
天かす	適宜
紅しょうが	適宜
かつお節	適宜
青のり	適宜
お好みソース	適宜
マヨネーズ	適宜
サラダ油	適宜

■ INGREDIENTS (serves 2)

〈For making batter〉

75g *hakurikiko* flour
25g Chinese yam
100cc stock (dried bonito)

〈Fillings〉

1 egg
2 thin slices (100g) pork belly
100g cabbage
Ao-negi onion
Bits of deep-fried tempura batter
Beni-shoga red pickled ginger
Dried bonito flakes
Green laver
Okonomi sauce (Thick Japanese-style Worcester sauce)
Mayonnaise
Vegetable oil

■作り方

1 キャベツ、青ねぎを水洗いし、キャベツはせん切りに、青ねぎは小口切りにします。長いもは皮をむいてすりおろしします。紅しょうがをみじん切りにします。豚ばら肉1枚を2cm幅に切り分けます。

2 ボウルに薄力粉、だし汁、**1**の長いもを入れ、よく混ぜ合わせて生地を作ります。

3 **2**に**1**のキャベツ、青ねぎ、紅しょうが、豚ばら肉と天かす、卵を割り入れてよく混ぜます。

4 ホットプレートを200℃に熱してサラダ油をひき、**3**を流し入れ円にします。その上に豚ばら肉1枚、かつお節をのせ、3分ほど焼きます。

5 **4**をへら（鉄製）で裏返して5分ほど焼き、さらに裏返して5分、再び裏返して3分ほど焼き、さらに裏返します。

6 **5**にお好み焼きソースをまんべんなく塗り、お好みでマヨネーズをかけ、青のりをふりかけていただきます。

！コツのコツ

★生地と具材を混ぜ合わせる時は、空気をよく含ませるようにすると焼き上がりがふんわりとします。

★焼いている時は、形がくずれるのであまりいじらないようにしましょう。

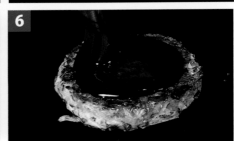

■ Directions

1 Rinse the cabbage and *ao-negi* onion in cold water, and cut the former into julienne strips, and the latter using the edge cut technique. Peel the Chinese yam, and grate. Chop the *beni-shoga* finely. Cut one of the pork belly slices into 1/16-inch wide pieces.

2 Place the flour, stock and grated Chinese yam in a bowl, and mix well to make batter.

3 Add the cabbage, *ao-negi* onion, *beni-shoga*, pork, bits of deep-fried tempura batter and egg to the bowl, and mix well.

4 Heat the hot plate to 400°F and add some vegetable oil. Pour the batter mixture prepared in step 3 above in a circular shape onto the plate, place the other slice of pork on top of it and sprinkle on the dried bonito flakes. Above onto the plate, place the other slice of pork on top of it and sprinkle on the dried bonito flakes. Heat for about 3 min.

5 Turn over the pancake from step 4 with an iron spatula, and heat about 5 min. Reverse again, and heat for about 5 min. Reverse again, and heat for about 3 min. Reverse again.

6 Spread the *okonomi* sauce all over the surface of the pancake from step 5. Put on some mayonnaise and sprinkle on the green laver if desired.

！Tip on Tips

★ When mixing the batter and fillings, blend well with air so that the pancake becomes full and plump.

★ Do not to touch the pancake too much while frying or it gets deformed.

Salt-grilled Horse Mackerel
あじの塩焼き

焼き魚の定番 "あじの塩焼き" をおいしく作りたい

Delicious "Salt-grilled Horse Mackerel" is a standard for grilled fish

■材料（2人分）

あじ（真あじ）	……… 2尾
塩	……………… 大さじ1
大根おろし	……… 少々
レモン	………… 4切れ

■ INGREDIENTS (serves 2)

2 whole horse mackerels
1 Tbsp salt
Small quantity of grated giant white radish
4 slices lemon

◆塩焼きに適した魚◆

Fish suited for salt-grill

◆いさき・Chieken grunt
◆いわし・Sardine
◆さんま・Pacific saury
◆いしもち・White croaker
◆あゆ・Sweetfish 〈ayu〉

いさき
Chieken grunt

■作り方

1 あじはゼイゴ（ゼンゴ）と呼ばれる、尾のつけ根にあるかたいうろこを包丁でそぎ取ります。うろこを包丁の刃で取り、えらぶたに包丁の刃先を入れ、つけ根に切り込みを入れて引っぱり出します。

2 盛りつける時に下になる側に切れ目を入れて、内臓をかき出します。腹の中に残っている内臓や血合いなどをきれいに洗い落とします。

3 焼く直前に2のあじに塩をふります。尾、胸びれ、背びれに塩をまぶして化粧塩をします。

4 グリルをよく熱し盛りつける方から焼きます。あじに6割火が通ったら、裏返して焼きます。

5 器に4のあじを盛り、大根おろし、レモンを添えていただきます。

！ コツのコツ

★尾、胸びれ、背びれに化粧塩をすることで焦げずに形よく焼き上がります。

★網をよく焼いておくか、網に刷毛で油を少し塗ると魚がくっつきにくくなります。

★焼き魚は盛りつけて表になる方を強火で焼き、裏側は最初強火で仕上げを中火でじっくり焼くとよいでしょう。

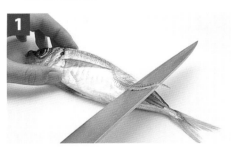

■ Directions

1 Scrape off the hard scales (known as zeigo) of the horse mackerel at the joint of the tail with a knife. Scrape off the hard scales at the joint of the tail with a knife. Scrape the scales of the other parts away in short strokes. Insert the tip of the knife behind the gill cover, cut the base of the gills and pull the gills out.

2 Make a slit on the side that will face down when served, and scoop out the innards with your hands. Wash away any remaining innards and blood in the belly with cold water.

3 Sprinkle salt on the fish immediately before grilling. Coat the tail, pectoral fins and dorsal fins heavily with salt (decorative salting).

4 Heat a cooking grill well, and grill the fish. Always grill first the side of fish that will face up when served. When the whole fish is about 60% done, turn it over and grill the other side.

5 Arrange the fish on a plate, and garnish with the grated giant white radish and lemon slices.

！ Tip on Tips

★ The decorative salting will prevent the fins from scorching and help them retain their shape.

★ Either preheat the grill well or coat it with oil using a brush to prevent fish from sticking to the grill.

★ Grill the presentation side of the fish over high heat. For the other side, grill over a high heat at first and then slowly grill over a medium heat until it's cooked through.

Grilled Spanish Mackerel, *Saikyo*-Style
さわらの西京焼き

about **20** min 約20分

249 kcal 249キロカロリー

西京みそが"さわら"にしみ込んでおいしさが倍増
The flavor of *Saikyo*-style miso soaks into Spanish mackerel and enhances its tastiness

■材料（2人分）

さわらの切り身	…2切れ
塩	小さじ1
西京みそ	300g
料理酒	大さじ2
みりん	大さじ2

■ INGREDIENTS (serves 2)

2 fillets Spanish mackerel
1 tsp salt
300g *Saikyo* miso
2 Tbsps cooking sake
2 Tbsps *mirin* sweet cooking sake

◆西京焼きに適した魚◆
Fish suited for *Saikyo*-style miso grilling

◆さけ・Chum salmon
◆まながつお・Butter fish
◆めだい・Japanese gnomefish
◆甘だい・Japanese branquillo
◆金目だい・Alfonsino(golden eye bream)
◆あこうだい・Matsubara's red rock fish

■作り方

1 さわらを盆ザルにのせ塩をふって10分おき、表面に出てきた水分をふき取ります。

2 西京みそ、料理酒、みりんを混ぜ合わせてみそ床を作り、密閉容器に半量敷いて平にならします。水で濡らしてかたく絞った清潔なガーゼを敷いて**1**のさわらを並べます。ガーゼをかぶせて残りのみそ床を平らにのせて、2～3日冷蔵庫で寝かしておきます。

3 **2**のみそ床からさわらを取り出し、身についている余分なみそを取り、弱火で焼きます。

4 焼き上がったら器に盛っていただきます。

1-a

1-b

2-a

2-b

2-c

3

■ Directions

1 Place the Spanish mackerels on a flat basket and sprinkle the salt. Leave for 10 min and wipe off moisture on the surface.

2 Stir the *Saikyo* miso, cooking sake, *mirin* and make miso paste. Put half of the miso paste flatly into an airtight container. On top of the paste, spread a clean gauze after moistening it with water and wringing out hard. Place the Spanish mackerels side by side and cover with another wringed gauze. Fill the container with the rest of the miso paste flatly on top of the gauze, and let the container rest in a refrigerator for 2 to 3 days.

3 Bring the Spanish mackerel from Step 2 out from the miso paste, remove excess miso from the fish and grill over a low heat.

4 When grilled thoroughly, arrange them on a plate.

！ Tip on Tips

★ Sprinkle salt on fish and eliminate moisture so that odors of the fish can be removed.

★ Placing fish on gauze spread on the miso paste before resting in a refrigerator will prevent taking excess miso paste when taking the fish out.

★ Remember to grill over a low heat otherwise only the miso paste will be scorched.

Japanese Amberjack (Yellowtail) Teriyaki
ぶりの照焼き

about **20**min / 約20分

354 kcal / 354キロカロリー

しょう油がからんだぶりが食欲をそそる

Japanese amberjack (yellowtail) coated with soy sauce will stimulate your appetite

■材料（2人分）

ぶりの切り身 ······ 2切れ

A
┌ 料理酒 ··· 大さじ1
└ しょう油 ··· 小さじ2

酢どりしょうが ······ 2本

サラダ油 ········ 小さじ1

B
┌ 砂糖 ······ 小さじ1
├ しょう油 ··· 大さじ1と1/2
└ みりん ····· 大さじ2

※ぶりの切り身を買う時は、血合いの色が鮮やかな赤色で、身にはりがあり、パックに血がにじみ出ていないものを選ぶとよいでしょう。血合いの色が茶色く、身割れしているものは鮮度が悪いものなので選ばないようにしましょう。

■ INGREDIENTS (serves 2)

2 fillets Japanese amberjack (yellowtail)

A
┌ 1 Tbsp cooking sake
└ 2 tsps soy sauce

2 vinegar-pickled ginger shoots

1 tsp vegetable oil

B
┌ 1 tsp sugar
├ 1 1/2 Tbsps soy sauce
└ 2 Tbsps *mirin* sweet cooking sake

※ When purchasing fillets of Japanese amberjack, check if their dark flesh has bright red color. Choose resilient ones, and avoid those of which the blood is leaked in a package and the flesh is separated into parts.

■作り方

1 ぶりの切り身を器に入れ、**A**の調味料を入れて約10分おき、味をなじませます。10分たったら汁けをペーパータオルでふき取ります。

2 フライパンにサラダ油を入れ熱し、盛りつける時に上になる方から焼きます。焼き色がついたら裏返してふたをし、弱火で蒸し焼きにします。

3 **B**の調味料を混ぜ合わせてタレを作ります。

4 2のフライパンの余分な油をペーパータオルでふき取り、3のタレを入れてぶりにからめながら汁を煮詰めます。

5 器に**4**のぶりを盛り、酢どりしょうがを添えます。

> **！ コツのコツ**
> ★魚から脂が出てくるのでサラダ油は多く入れすぎないようにしましょう。
> ★フライパンの余分な油をきっちりとペーパータオルでふき取らないと、油っぽくなるので注意しましょう。

■ Directions

1 Soak the Japanese amberjack (yellowtail) fillets in the **A** mixture for about 10 minutes to let the fish absorb the flavor. After 10 minutes, wipe off the moisture with a paper towel.

2 Heat the vegetable oil in a frying pan, and fry the fillets. Always cook first the side of fish that will face up when served. When browned, turn over, cover the pan and fry the other side over a low heat.

3 Mix the ingredients of **B** to make the teriyaki sauce.

4 Remove excess oil from the frying pan used in 2. above with a paper kitchen towel. Put the sauce into the pan, and simmer the sauce while coating the fish with the sauce thoroughly.

5 Arrange the fillets on plates, and garnish with vinegar-pickled ginger shoots.

> **！ Tip on Tips**
> ★ Use only a small amount of vegetable oil because fat will exude from the fish.
> ★ Remember to remove the excess oil from your frying pan with a paper towel. This will save your fish from becoming too greasy.

Ginger Pork Saute
豚肉のしょうが焼き

しょがしょう油がからんだ豚肉が食欲をそそる

A temping dish of pork glistened with ginger soy sauce

■材料（4人分）

豚ロース薄切り肉…　200g	
A ┌ しょうがの絞り汁…小さじ1	B ┌ 料理酒　…　大さじ1
└ 料理酒　…　小さじ2	│ 砂糖　…　大さじ1/2
サラダ菜…………　4 枚	│ しょう油　…　小さじ2
キャベツ（せん切り）…適宜	│ みりん　…　大さじ1/2
プチトマト…………　4 個	│ しょうが（すりおろし）
サラダ油………　大さじ1	└ 　　…　大さじ1/2

※その他のつけ合わせとして、レタス、大根のせん切り、かいわれ大根、
クレソンなどの野菜を好みでつけ合わせてもよいでしょう。

■ INGREDIENTS (serves 4)

200g pork loin, thinly sliced	
A ┌ 1 tsp fresh ginger juice	B ┌ 1 Tbsp cooking sake
└ 2 tsps cooking sake	│ 1/2 Tbsp sugar
4 *saradana* leaves	│ 2 tsps soy sauce
Cabbage, cut into julienne strips	│ 1/2 Tbsp *mirin* sweet cooking sake
4 cherry tomatoes	└ 1/2 Tbsp grated ginger
1 Tbsp vegetable oil	

※ Refreshing vegetables such as lettuce, julienne-strip giant white radish, young giant white radish shoots, and watercress can be arranged as garnishes.

■作り方

1 豚ロース薄切り肉は、広げて食べやすい大きさに切ります。切った肉はバットに入れて、**A** をふりかけ５分くらいおき、ペーパータオルなどで汁けをふき取ります。

2 **B** の調味料をボウルに混ぜ合わせておきます。

3 フライパンにサラダ油を入れて熱し、**1** の豚ロース薄切り肉を広げるように入れて中火で焼きます。肉が焼けたら **2** のタレを入れてからめます。

4 器に **3** の豚ロース薄切り肉を盛り、サラダ菜、キャベツのせん切り、プチトマトを添えます。

！ コツのコツ

★ 豚肉は料理酒としょうが汁につけ込むと柔らかくなり、臭みも取れます。

★ 豚肉にあまり火を通しすぎると、身がかたくなるので注意しましょう。

1-a

1-b

1-c

2

3-a

3-b

■ Directions

1 Spread out each pork loin slice fully, and cut into bite-sized pieces. Place the pork in a rectangle tray, pour in the **A** mixture, and let stand for about 5 min. Wipe off the moisture with a paper towel.

2 Mix the ingredients of **B** in a bowl to make the sauce.

3 Heat the vegetable oil in a frying pan, and lay the pork slices within. Make sure that each slice is fully spread out in the pan. Fry the pork over a medium heat. When heated through, pour the sauce prepared in 2. above, and coat the pork with the sauce thoroughly.

4 Arrange the pork on plates, and garnish with the *saradana* leaves, shredded cabbage and cherry tomatoes.

！ Tip on Tips

★ Soaking pork in cooking sake and ginger juice will eliminate the odor of the meat.

★ Be careful not to overheat the pork, otherwise, the meat will become tough.

Chicken Saute
鶏肉のつけ焼き

about **25**min
約25分

581kcal
581キロカロリー

甘辛いタレと鶏肉がからんでご飯や酒のつまみ、弁当に最高
This sweet and spicy glazed chicken is best with rice, sake and in your lunchbox

■材料（2人分）

鶏もも肉 ·············· 2枚	砂糖 ·········· 大さじ2
大葉 ··············· 2枚	
大根 ··············· 5cm	※その他のつけ合わせとして、キャ
ラディッシュ ········· 2個	ベツのせん切り、サラダ菜、クレ
かいわれ大根 ···1/4パック	ソン、パセリなど、さっぱりとした
サラダ油········· 大さじ1	味で、シャキシャキとした歯触りの
A ┌ 料理酒 ··· 大さじ2	ものを好みでつけ合わせても よい
│ みりん ····· 大さじ2	でしょう。
└ しょう油··· 大さじ1と1/2	

■ INGREDIENTS (serves 2)

2 chicken thighs
2 leaves green perilla
2 inches giant white radish
2 radishes
1/4 package young giant white radish shoots
1 Tbsp vegetable oil

A ┌ 2 Tbsps cooking sake
　 │ 2 Tbsps *mirin* sweet cooking sake
　 └ 1 1/2 Tbsp soy sauce

2 Tbsps sugar

※ Vegetables of refreshing taste and crispy texture like julienne-strip cabbage, sarada-na greens, watercress, and parsley can be good accompaniments.

■作り方

1 鶏もも肉は余分な皮や脂肪を取り除き、フォークで突き刺して穴をあけて一口大に切り、ボウルに入れます。そこに**A**を混ぜ合わせ、鶏もも肉にかけて10分くらいおいたら、鶏もも肉の汁けをペーパータオルなどでふき取ります。漬け汁はそのまま取っておきます。

2 大根とラディッシュはせん切りにして水にさらし、3cmの長さに切ったかいわれ大根と合わせておきます。

3 フライパンにサラダ油を入れて熱し、1の鶏もも肉を焼きます。余分な油は

ペーパータオルでふき、ふたをして弱火にし、蒸し焼きにします。

4 1の漬け汁と砂糖を3のフライパンに入れて、フライパンをゆすりながら鶏もも肉に煮からめます。

5 器に4の鶏もも肉、水洗いし水けをふき取った大葉と、2の野菜を盛り合わせます。

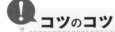
コツのコツ

★鶏もも肉はフォークで突き刺し、漬け汁をしみやすくします。

★鶏もも肉は最初、強火で両面に少し焦げ目がつく程度に焼いて、旨味を閉じ込め、次に弱火でじっくりと肉に火を通します。

★余分な油をきっちりふき取りましょう。

第五章・和食の基本・焼きもの ● Basic Japanese Grilled and Pan-Fried Dishes

■ Directions

1 Remove the excess skin and fat from the chicken thighs, pierce a few times with a fork and cut into bite-sized pieces. Place the chicken in a bowl, pour in the **A** mixture, let stand for 10 min and remove the moisture from the chicken with a paper towel.

2 Cut the giant white radish and radishes into julienne strips, and rinse in cold water. Add the young giant white radish shoots, cut into 1 1/5-inch lengths and mix.

3 Heat the vegetable oil in a frying pan, and fry the chicken. Eliminate the excess oil, cover the pan, reduce the heat to low and continue to fry.

4 Add the liquid set aside in step 1 and the sugar, and let the sauce get soaked in to the chicken as you shake the pan.

5 Arrange the chicken in a bowl, and garnish with the green perilla leaves, rinsed in cold water drained, and the vegetables prepared in 2. above.

Tip on Tips

★ Pierce chicken thighs with a fork so that the meat soaks up the sauce.

★ First, fry both sides of the chicken thighs over a high heat until slightly scorched. This will keep the flavor in the meat. Then reduce the heat to low and fry slowly until they are heated through.

★ Wipe off the excess oil completely.

123

Yakitori
やき鶏

about **35**min
約00分

555kcal
555キロカロリー

子どもも大人も大好きな、おいしいやき鶏を自宅で作りたい

Both children and adults love homemade juicy *yakitori*

■材料（3〜4人分）

鶏もも肉 … 2枚（約400g）	〈タレの材料〉
鶏手羽先 …… 9〜12本	しょう油 …… 2/5 カップ
長ねぎ ……………… 1本	みりん ……… 1/4 カップ
レモン（くし形）… 3〜4個	料理酒 ……… 大さじ2
塩・こしょう ……… 適量	ざらめ ……… 大さじ3
料理酒 …………… 少々	※タレの材料は好みによって調節
サラダ油 …………… 適量	しましょう。
※竹串 12〜16本	

■ INGREDIENTS (serves 3 or 4)

2 chicken thighs (about 400g)	〈for preparing sauce〉
9 to 12 chicken wings	1/3 cup soy sauce (80 ㎖)
1 *naga-negi* onion	1/5 cup *mirin* sweet cooking
3 to 4 wedge-cut lemons	sake (50 ㎖)
salt and pepper	2 Tbsps cooking sake
a small amount cooking sake	3 Tbsps coarse sugar
vegetable oil	※ Adjust each amount of sauce
※ 12 to 16 bamboo skewers	ingredients to accommodate to your taste.

■作り方

1 最初にタレを作ります。しょう油、みりん、料理酒、ざらめを合わせ中火から弱火で約1〜2割ほど量が減るまで煮つめます。

2 鶏もも肉を包丁で食べやすい大きさに切ります。長ねぎを約2〜3cmの長さに切ります。竹串に鶏もも肉、長ねぎの順に刺していき、塩、こしょうをします。

3 鶏手羽先の先を包丁で切り落とし、中骨にそって骨の間に真横に包丁を入れて開きます。細い方の骨の関節部分を包丁を入れて切り取ります。

4 3の鶏手羽先を竹串に刺します。竹串1本に鶏手羽先2〜3本が目安です。

5 フライパンにサラダ油を入れ、2の鶏もも肉の両面を焼きます。鶏もも肉に火が通ったら、1のタレを入れ、からめて出来あがりです。

6 4の鶏手羽先全体に酒（分量外）をきり吹きで吹き、塩、こしょうをして、あらかじめ熱しておいた魚焼きグリルで両面を焼きます。

7 5と6を皿に盛り、レモンを添えます。鶏手羽先にレモンを絞りかけていただきます。

コツのコツ

★タレを作る時に強火で煮て焦がすと、やき鶏が焦げくさくなるので、焦がさないように注意しましょう。

★フライパンで作るやき鶏は油が多いと油っぽくなってしまいますので、油を少なくしましょう。

★魚焼きグリルをあらかじめ熱しておくか、ハケで薄く油を塗ると鶏手羽先がくっつきにくくなります。

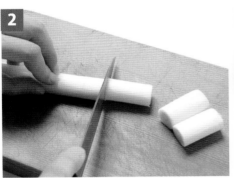 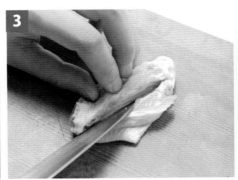 

■ Directions

1 Prepare the sauce first. Combine the soy sauce, *mirin*, cooking sake and coarse sugar and bring the mixture to a boil over medium low heat until the sauce thickens and reduces by ten to twenty percent.

2 Cut the chicken thighs into bite-size pieces. Cut the *naga-negi* onion into about an inch long pieces. Thread a piece of chicken onto the bamboo skewer first and a *naga-negi* onion next and repeat in this order. Sprinkle with salt and pepper.

3 Cut off the tips of the chicken wings. Insert your knife perpendicularly between the bones along the big bone to open the wings. Cut off the joint on the smaller piece with your knife.

4 Thread the chicken wings from step 3 onto the other skewer. Two or three pieces per one skewer should be plenty.

5 Put the vegetable oil in a frying pan and fry both sides of the chicken thighs from step 2. When the chicken is cooked, dress them with the sauce from step 1.

6 Drizzle extra cooking sake evenly on the chicken wings from step 4 and sprinkle with salt and pepper. Grill both sides of the chicken wings on a preheated grill.

7 Transfer the chickens from step 5 and 6 to a serving plate and garnish with the lemon wedges. Squeeze the lemon wedge over the chicken wings before you eat them.

Tip on Tips

★ Be careful not to let the sauce burn over high heat or the whole meal will taste burnt.

★ For *yakitori* made on a frying pan, remember to reduce the amount of oil. If you use a lot of oil, the chicken will be greasy.

★ Preheating your grill or brushing oil thinly on the wire rack will prevent the chicken wings from sticking.

第五章・和食の基本・焼きもの ● Basic Japanese Grilled and Pan-Fried Dishes

全国の麺・麺料理

Noodles and Noodle Dishes of Japan

　各都道府県に数多くの麺・麺料理があります。ここでは古くから伝わるそば、うどん、そうめんをはじめ B 級グルメでも人気のご当地ラーメン、焼きそばなど、特徴ある麺・麺料理を紹介します。また、日本三大といわれる麺・麺料理、麺処がありますのでそちらも紹介します。

　日本三大うどんは、秋田の稲庭うどん、群馬の水沢うどん、香川の讃岐うどん、日本三大そばは、岩手のわんこそば、長野の戸隠そば、島根の出雲そば、日本三大そうめんは、奈良の三輪そうめん、兵庫の揖保乃糸、香川の小豆島そうめんになります。日本三大ラーメン処は、北海道の札幌、福島の喜多方、福岡の博多になります。

There are many kinds of noodles and noodle dishes in every Japanese prefecture. In this column, we introduce a variety of distinct noodles and noodle dishes that use traditional buckwheat, *udon* and *somen* noodles, as well as local ramen and *yakisoba* noodles that are very popular as grade B food. We also introduce the three major noodle dishes and shops.
The three major *udon* noodles in Japan are Inaniwa *udon* of Akita, Mizusawa of Gunma and Sanuki of Kagawa prefecture.
The three major buckwheat noodles are Wanko *soba* of Iwate, Togakushi of Nagano and Izumo of Shimane prefecture.
The three major *somen* noodles are Miwa somen of Nara, *Ibono-ito* of Hyogo and Shodoshima of Kagawa prefecture. The three major ramen shops are Sapporo ramen of Hokkaido, Kitakata of Fukushima and Hakata of Fukuoka.

伊勢うどん（三重）Ise *Udon* (Mie)

札幌ラーメン（北海道）
Sapporo Ramen (Hokkaido)

旭川ラーメン（北海道）
Asahikawa Ramen (Hokkaido)

稲庭うどん、横手の焼きそば（秋田）
Inaniwa *Udon*, Yokote chow mein (Akita)

へぎそば（新潟）
Hegi *Soba* (Nigata)

小豆島そうめん（香川）
Shidoshima *Somen* (kagawa)

戸隠そば（長野）
Togakushi *Soba* (Nagano)

函館ラーメン（北海道）
Hakodate Ramen (Hokkaido)

氷見うどん（富山）
Himi *Udon* (Toyama)

わんこそば（岩手）
Wanko *Soba* (Iwate)

久留米ラーメン（福岡）
Kurume Ramen (Fukuoka)

越前そば（福井）
Echizen *Soba* (Fukui)

白石温麺（宮城）
Shiroishi *Umen* (Miyagi)

にしんそば（京都）
Nishin *Soba* (kyoto)

喜多方ラーメン（福島）
Kitakata Ramen (Fukushima)

博多ラーメン（福岡）
Hakata Ramen (Fukuoka)

出石皿そば（兵庫）
Izushi Sara-*Soba* (Hyogo)

水沢うどん、上州太田焼きそば（群馬）
Mizusawa *Udon*, Joshu Ota chow mein (Gunma)

出雲そば（島根）
Izumo *Soba* (Shimane)

ほうとう（山梨）
Hoto (Yamanashi)

武蔵野うどん（埼玉・東京）
Musashino *Udon* (Saitama and Tokyo)

五島うどん（長崎）
Goto *Udon* (Nagasaki)

吉田うどん（山梨）
Yoshida *Udon* (Yamanashi)

富士宮焼きそば（静岡）
Fjinomiya chow mein (Shizuoka)

三輪そうめん（奈良）
Miwa Somen (Nara)

きしめん、みそ煮込みうどん（愛知）
Kishimen, Miso-nikomi *Udon* (Aichi)

熊本ラーメン（熊本）
Kumamoto Ramen (Kumamoto)

讃岐うどん（香川）
Sanuki *Udon* (Kagawa)

伊勢うどん（三重）
Ise *Udon* (Mie)

沖縄そば（沖縄）
Okinawa *Soba* (Okinawa)

※上記の麺・麺料理は代表的なものとなり、各地にさまざまな麺・麺料理がある
※ The above shown are only representative noodles and noodle dishes. There are a variety of noodles and noodle dishes in each region.

第六章
Chapter 6

Basic Japanese Deep-Fried Dishes
和食の基本・揚げもの

衣をつけて油で揚げるだけで食材の旨味が倍増。揚げものを代表する天ぷら、フライ、コロッケ、とんかつなどを紹介。季節の食材をうまく利用しましょう。

The flavors of your ingredients will be enhanced simply by deep-frying with batter. In this chapter, we introduce deep-fried dishes such as tempura, croquette, pork cutlet and other deep-fried favorites. Make good use of fresh, seasonal ingredients.

Assorted Tempura
天ぷらの盛り合わせ

about 25 min 約25分 | 599 kcal 599キロカロリー

サクッと揚がった衣の食感とぎゅっと旨味が詰まった食材がおいしい
Crunchy outside and delicious inside, all the ingredients become more relishing

■材料（2人分）

えび	4 本
いか	1/4 本
なす	1 本
さつまいも	1/4 本
大葉	4 枚
大根おろし	少々
おろししょうが	少々
揚げ油	適宜

〈天つゆの材料〉

水	1/2 カップ
薄口しょう油	大さじ 3
みりん	大さじ 3
削りがつお	1/2 カップ

〈衣の材料〉

卵黄1個+冷水	3/4 カップ
薄力粉	3/4 カップ

■ INGREDIENTS (serves 2)

4 shrimps
1/4 squid
1 eggplant
1/4 sweet potato
4 leaves green perilla
Small quantity of grated giant white radish
Small quantity of grated ginger
Oil for deep-frying

〈For preparing dipping sauce〉
2/5 cup water (100 ㎖)
3 Tbsps light soy sauce
3 Tbsps *mirin* sweet cooking sake
2/5 cup dried bonito flakes (100㎖)

〈For preparing batter〉
1 egg yolk + chilled water to make
3/5 cup (150 ㎖)
3/5 cup *hakurikiko* flour (150 ㎖)

■作り方

1 えびは頭と背わたを取り、尾のひと節を残して殻をむきます。油はねしないように尾の先端を重ねて切り落とし包丁の刃先でこそげて水分を出します。腹を上にし、胴に3本の包丁目を入れて手で折るように切れ目を開きます。

2 いかは食べやすい大きさに切り、両面に浅く斜めに切り込みを数本入れます。

3 なすは縦4つに切り、横半分に切り、端を末広に切ります。水につけてアクを抜き、水けをよくふき取ります。

4 さつまいもはよく洗って皮つきのまま輪切りにし、水に4～5分放してアクを抜き、水けをしっかりとふき取ります。大葉は水洗いし、水けをふき取ります。

5 天つゆを作ります。水2分の1カップ、薄口しょう油大さじ3、みりん大さじ3、削りがつお2分の1カップを鍋に入れて、ひと煮たちさせたら火を止め、その

まま2～3分おいたらこし器でこします。

6 天ぷらの衣を作ります。薄力粉をふるっておきます。卵黄と冷水を合わせて4分の3カップになるように冷水で調整しながら混ぜ、薄力粉の粘りが出ないように手早く混ぜます。

7 大葉以外の材料に、それぞれ揚げる直前に薄力粉（分量外）を薄くはたきつけます。揚げ油を熱し、天ぷらの衣を材料につけて揚げていきます。野菜は160℃で、魚介類は170℃で揚げます。途中揚げかすを丁寧に取ります。揚がった天ぷらを皿に盛り合わせます。

! ## コツのコツ

★衣を作る時は冷やした卵、冷水を使用します。冷えていない場合は氷を2～3個入れてもよいです。

★衣はさっと軽くまぜる程度にします。だまの状態がベストです。

★材料は油に臭いが移らない野菜（かたいものから）から揚げていきます。

★いかは水分が残っていると油はねをするので、よく薄力粉をまぶすようにしましょう。

■ Directions

1 Remove the heads of the shrimps, devein and shell, but leave the tails attached. Chop off the tips of the shrimp tails and gently press out the moisture from the shrimps with the flat blade of the knife tip (If moisture remains in the tail, it will cause the oil to sputter). To prevent the shrimps from curling, make 3 incisions across the belly, and open each of the cuts with your hands to straighten the body.

2 Cut the squid into bite-sized pieces. Score each side in a shallow diamond pattern.

3 Cut the eggplant into quarters lengthwise, and then cut each piece in half crosswise. Make a few cuts at one end of each piece and spread out so that its shape is like a fan. Soak in cold water to eliminate bitterness, and wipe moisture away thoroughly.

4 Wash the sweet potato well, and cut into rounds without peeling.

Soak in cold water for 4 to 5 min to eliminate bitterness, and wipe moisture away thoroughly. Rince the greenperilla leaves in cold water and remove excess water.

5 To prepare the dipping sauce: Place 2/5 cup water, 3 Tbsps light soy sauce, 3 Tbsps *mirin* and 2/5 cup dried bonito flakes in a pot, boil briefly and turn off the heat. Let stand for a few minutes, and strain.

6 To prepare the batter: Sift the flour. In a mixing bowl, lightly beat the egg yolk and pour in chilled water to make 2/5 cup. Add the sifted flour, and stir briefly. Don't over-mix; otherwise, the batter will become sticky.

7 Dust each of the ingredients to be fried with flour(except quantity) except for the green perilla leaves. Heat oil, and start deep-frying while coating each material with batter. The oil temperature should

be 320°F, for vegetables and 340°F, for fish. Remove any frying remnants from the oil while deep-frying. Transfer the deep-fried ingredients to a platter.

! ## Tip on Tips

★ When preparing batter, always use cooled eggs and ice water. If the water is not chilled, you can put in a few pieces of ice.

★ Don't mix the batter too much. It should be lumpy.

★ Hard-to-cook vegetables that are less likely to leave odor in the oil should be put into the pan and fried first.

★ Any moisture remaining on the squid will cause the oil to spatter. Remember to coat well with flour.

Mixed *Tempura*
かき揚げ

about **25**min
約25分

498kcal
498キロカロリー

野菜のサクッとした食感とえびの甘味がおいしい

Battered sweet shrimp and crunchy vegetables are a treat to share

■材料（2 人分）

むきえび …………	100g
三つ葉 …………	小 2 束
長ねぎ …………	1/2 本
大根おろし ………	少々
おろししょうが …	少々
レモン …………	少々
揚げ油 …………	適宜

〈衣の材料〉

卵黄 1 個＋冷水 …	1/2 カップ
薄力粉 …………	1/2 カップ

〈天つゆの材料〉

水 …………	1/2 カップ
薄口しょう油 …	大さじ 3
みりん …………	大さじ 3
削りがつお …	1/2 カップ

■ INGREDIENTS (serves 2)

100g peeled shrimp
2 small bundles of *mitsuba* (honeywort)
1/2 *naga-negi* onion
Small quantity of grated *daikon* radish
Small quantity of grated ginger
Small quantity of lemon
Oil for deep-frying

〈**Ingredients for batter**〉
2/5 cup mixture of egg yolk and chilled water (100㎖)
2/5 cup flour (100㎖)

〈**Ingredients for dipping sauce**〉
2/5 water (100㎖)
3 Tbsps light soy sauce
3 Tbsps *mirin* sweet cooking sake
2/5 cup dried bonito flakes (100㎖)

■作り方

1 むきえびは背わたを取りザルに入れ、水でふり洗いします。三つ葉は 2cm の長さに切ります。長ねぎは 1cm の小口切りにします。

2 天つゆを作ります。水 2 分の 1 カップ、薄口しょう油大さじ 3、みりん大さじ 3、削りがつおカップ 2 分の 1 を鍋に入れてひと煮たちさせたら火を止め、そのまま 2 ～ 3 分おいてこします。

3 天ぷらの衣を作ります。薄力粉はふるっておきます。卵黄と冷水を合わせてカップ 2 分の 1 になるように冷水で調整してよく混ぜ、薄力粉を粘らないように手早く回数を少なめに混ぜ合わせます。粉の粒（だま）が残っている状態にします。

4 **1** の材料の水けをペーパータオルでよくふき取り、ボウルに入れて薄力粉大さじ 1（分量外）をふりかけて軽く混ぜ合わせ、**2** の天ぷらの衣に入れます。

5 揚げ油を 170℃くらいに熱し、**3** を小さめの玉じゃくしなどですくい、鍋の縁から静かに落とし入れ、菜箸で軽く押さえて形を整えます。周囲がかたまったら裏返し、中まで火が通るように何回かひっくり返して揚げます。

6 揚げバットで油をきり、器に盛って大根おろし、おろししょうが、レモン、天つゆを添えていただきます。

■ Directions

1 Remove the entrails from the shrimp and put them in a strainer. Wash them with water while shaking your strainer. Cut the *mitsuba* (honeywort) into 2cm length. Cut the *naga-negi* onion finely.

2 Prepare the dipping sauce. Combine water, light soy sauce, *mirin* and dried bonito flakes in a pot and bring the mixture to a boil. Remove from the heat. Set aside for a few minutes and drain.

3 Prepare the batter. Sift the flour. Mix the egg yolk and chilled water. Adjust the amount of the mixture to be 2/5 cup with chilled water and mix well. Whisk the mixture until combined but the batter should remain lumpy.

4 Pat dry the ingredients from Step 1 well with paper towels. Put them in a bowl and sprinkle on 1 Tbsp of extra flour and stir lightly. Transfer them into the batter of Step 2.

5 Heat the frying oil to reach around 340°F. Scoop up the mixture from step 4 with a small ladle and tip it gently into the oil from the edge of your pan. Hold the fritter lightly with cooking chopsticks to arrange the shape. Turn it over when the edges of the fritter are cooked. Flip it repeatedly until thoroughly cooked.

6 Drain excess oil on a wire rack. Transfer the fritters to a serving plate and serve with grated daikon, grated ginger, lemons and dipping sauce.

Japanese Whiting Tempura
きすの天ぷら

about **15** min
約15分

389 kcal
389キロカロリー

きすの身がほろっとほどけ、旨味が口いっぱいに広がる
The succulent meat of Japanese Whiting is a pleasure in your mouth

■材料（2人分）

きす（天ぷら用開き身）… 4〜6枚
小麦粉 …………… 適量
大葉 …………… 4枚

〈天つゆの材料〉
水…………… 1/2 カップ
薄口しょう油 … 大さじ 3
みりん ………… 大さじ 3
削りがつお … 1/2 カップ

〈衣の材料〉
薄力粉…… 3/10 カップ
卵黄 1 個＋冷水
…… 合わせて 3/5 カップ
揚げ油（サラダ油） … 適量
大根おろし ………… 適量
レモン（くし形切り）… 2 切れ

■ INGREDIENTS (serves 2)

4-6 Japanese whiting (cut open for tempura)
Flour
4 green perilla leaves

〈**For preparing dipping sauce**〉
2/5 cup water (100 ㎖)
3 Tbsps light soy sauce
3 Tbsps *mirin* sweet cooking sake
2/5 cup dried bonito flakes (100㎖)

〈**For preparing batter**〉
1/4 cup flour (60 ㎖)
1/2 cup mixture of 1 egg yolk and chilled water (120㎖)
Vegetable oil for frying
Grated *daikon* giant white radish
2 lemon wedges

■作り方

1 きすの水けをペーパータオルなどでよくふき取ります。大葉は水洗いし、ペーパータオルなどで水けをふき取ります。

2 天つゆを作ります。水2分の1カップ、薄口しょう油大さじ3、みりん大さじ3、削りがつお2分の1カップを鍋に入れて、ひと煮たちさせたら火を止め、そのまま2～3分おいたらこし器でこします。

3 天ぷら衣を作ります。薄力粉をふるっておきます。卵黄と冷水を合わせて混ぜ、薄力粉の粘りが出ないように手早く混ぜます。

4 鍋に揚げ油を入れて熱し、適温にします。1のきすに薄く小麦粉をはたき、2

の天ぷら衣を薄くつけ、170℃の揚げ油に入れてカラリと揚げます。

5 大葉は表側に薄く小麦粉（分量外）をはたき、小麦粉をはたいた面のみに天ぷら衣を薄くつけ、カラッと揚げます。器に盛り、大根おろしとレモンを添え、温めた天つゆを添えます。

※きすの天ぷらは、塩をつけていただいてもおいしいです。

！ コツのコツ

★天ぷら衣を作る際、水が冷えていない場合には、衣に氷を1～2個落とすとよいです。

★衣は粘りが出ないようにさっくりと混ぜるのがコツです。

★きすは身が薄いですから、比較的火の通りが早いです。揚げすぎに注意しましょう。

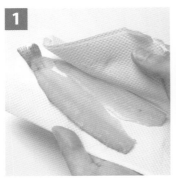 1
 2
 3
 4

■ Directions

1 Dry the Japanese whiting well with kitchen paper. Rinse the green perilla leaves, and paper-dry.

2 To prepare the dipping sauce: Place 2/5 cup water, 3 Tbsps light soy sauce, 3 Tbsps *mirin* and 2/5 cup dried bonito flakes in a pot, boil briefly and turn off the heat. Let stand for a few minutes, and strain.

3 Prepare the batter. Sift the flour. Combine the egg yolk and chilled water with the flour and whisk quickly to form a lumpy batter without making it smooth.

4 Put the vegetable oil in a pot and heat. Dust the fish prepared in step 1 with the flour, thinly coat with the batter prepared in step 2 and deep-fry at 340°F until crisp.

5 Dust the top surface of the green perilla leaves with extra flour, coat only the flour-dusted side with the batter and deep-fry until crisp. Arrange the tempura on a serving plate and garnish with lemon wedges and grated *daikon*. Serve with warmed tempura sauce.

※ The Japanese whiting tempura is also good with salt.

！ Tip on Tips

★ When preparing the batter, put one or two ice cubes into the batter if the water isn't chilled.

★ Prepare the batter lightly and leave lumps for best results.

★ The meat of Japanese Whiting is thin so it cooks quickly. Be careful not to deep-fry too long.

Deep-fried Horse Mackerel
あじフライ

about **40**min 約40分 **693**kcal 693キロカロリー

サクッと揚がったあじフライは、ご飯のおかず、酒のつまみに最高
Crispy deep-fried horse mackerel goes great with rice or sake

■材料（2人分）

あじ（中）…………	2尾
キャベツ（せん切り）…	適宜
パセリ ………………	適宜
レモン（くし形）……	2個
ホースラディッシュ …	適宜
卵…………………	1個
パン粉…	1と1/4カップ
揚げ油 ……………	適宜
塩・こしょう ……	各少々
中濃ソース ………	適宜

■ INGREDIENTS (serves 2)

2 medium size horse mackerels
Cabbage, cut into julienne strips
Parsley
2 lemon wedges
Horseradish
1 egg
1 cups dried bread crumbs
Oil for deep-frying
Pinch salt and pepper
Semi-thick Worcester sauce

◆ フライに適した魚◆
Fish suited for deep-frying

◆いわし・Sardine
◆ます・Trout
◆さけ・Chum salmon
◆いか・Squid

いわし
Sardine

■ 作り方

1 34 ページを参照してあじの頭を切り落とし、36 ページを参照して背開きにします。あじの腹骨を包丁ですき取り、血合い骨を骨抜きで取ります。
※大型のあじは、三枚おろしにするとよいでしょう。

2 1 のあじの身側に塩、こしょうを均一に少々振ります。10 分ほどおいて、出てきた水分をペーパータオルなどで押さえるように取ります。

3 卵を割りほぐし、バット（平たい皿）などに入れます。薄力粉、パン粉を別々のバット（平たい皿）に入れます。

4 2 のあじに 3 の薄力粉を均一にまぶし、全体に粉をつけます。よけいな粉を手で軽くはたいて落とし、次に 3 の卵に全体をつけ、パン粉をつけます。パン粉は両手であじにしっかりとつけます。

5 揚げ油を 170℃ に熱し、4 の衣をつけたあじをひっくり返しながら、きつね色になるまで揚げます。揚がったら油を鍋（フライパン）の上で、振りきり、バットにあげます。
※揚げすぎ（焦がしすぎ）に注意しましょう。

6 皿にせん切りキャベツを盛り、5 のあじをのせ、パセリ、レモン、ホースラディッシュを添え、お好みで中濃ソースをかけていただきます。
※タルタルソースもよく合います。タルタルソースの材料、作り方は 136・137 ページを参照してください。

! コツのコツ

★時間がたつと衣がはがれてしまいますので、あじに衣をつけたらすぐに揚げるようにしましょう。

★衣を焦がしてしまうと、焦げくさいあじフライになるので、揚げすぎには注意しましょう。

■ Directions

1 Refer to P.34 to cut off the head of the horse mackerel and to p.36 to split open along the back. Remove the bones around the stomach using your knife. Remove the bloody bones with tweezers.
※ A large size horse mackerel can be made into three fillets.

2 Sprinkle on the salt and pepper evenly on the meat side of the horse mackerel. Set aside for about 10 min. Pat dry with paper towels.

3 Beat the egg on a rectangular tray (or a flat plate.) Put the flour and the bread crumbs into rectangular trays (or flat plates) separately.

4 Dust the flour from step 3 onto the horse mackerel from step 2 evenly. Lightly beat off the excess flour with your hands. Drench the horse mackerel in the egg from step 3 and coat with the bread crumbs firmly using both hands.

5 Heat the frying oil to reach 340°F. Deep-fry the coated horse mackerel and turn over until brown. After frying, drain the excess oil over the pot (or frying pan) and place in a rectangular tray.
※ Be careful not to deep-fry them too long.

6 Arrange the shredded cabbage and set the horse mackerel from Step 5 onto it. Garnish with the parsley, lemon wedges, horseradish, and serve with semi-thick Worcester sauce if desired.
※ It's also good with tartar sauce. See P. 136 and 137 for preparations.

! Tip on Tips

★ Do not set aside the coated horse mackerel too long or the coating will come off. Deep-fry as soon as the horse mackerel is coated.

★ If you fry the coating for too long, the horse mackerel will taste burnt. Be careful not to deep-fry too long.

Deep-fried Oyster
かきフライ

栄養たっぷりの "かき" をジューシーなフライでいただく
Enjoy juicy deep-fried oysters that are rich in nutrients

■材料（4人分）

かき	16 個	レモン（くし形）	適宜
塩・こしょう	各少々	パセリ	適宜
〈衣の材料〉		クレソン	適宜
小麦粉	適宜	ウスターソース	適宜
A 卵	2 個	〈タルタルソース〉	
A 小麦粉	50g	ゆで卵	2 個
A 水	1/2 カップ	マヨネーズ	1 カップ
パン粉	適宜	パセリのみじん切り	大さじ 2
揚げ油	適宜	ピクルスのみじん切り	大さじ 2
〈つけ合わせ〉		レモン汁	大さじ 1
キャベツ（せん切り）	適宜	牛乳	小さじ 1
ラディッシュ（輪切り）	適宜	塩・こしょう	各少々

■ INGREDIENTS (serves 4)

16 oysters	Parsley
Pinch salt and pepper	Watercress
〈**For preparing batter**〉	Japanese-style Worcestershire sauce
Flour	
A 2 eggs	〈**For preparing tartar sauce**〉
A 50g flour	2 boiled eggs
A 2/5 cup water (100 ㎖)	4/5 cup mayonnaise (200 ㎖)
Dried breadcrumbs	2 Tbsps parsley, chopped finely
Oil for deep-frying	2 Tbsps pickles, chopped finely
〈**For garnishing**〉	1 Tbsp fresh lemon juice
Cabbage, cut into julienne strips	1 tsp milk
Radish, cut into rounds	Pinch salt and pepper
Lemon wedges	

■ 作り方

1 タルタルソースを作ります。みじん切りにしたゆで卵、パセリ、ピクルス、マヨネーズ、レモン汁、牛乳をボウルに入れてよく混ぜ合わせ、塩、こしょうをして味を調えたら、冷蔵庫で約20分冷やします。

2 かきは流水で1粒ずつ洗い、水けをふき取り、塩、こしょうを全体にふりかけます。

3 バットに小麦粉、パン粉をそれぞれ広げます。ボウルに **A** を入れて泡立てないように混ぜ合わせ、卵液を作ります。

4 揚げ油を中火で熱し、170℃に温めておきます。

5 2 のかきを小麦粉、3 の卵液、パン粉の順につけていきます。

6 5 を170℃の油の中に入れ、衣がかたまってきたら時々軽くかき混ぜます。全体的にきつね色になって表面に浮き上がってきたら揚げバットに取り上げて油をきっておきます。

7 皿にキャベツのせん切り、ラディッシュの輪切り、パセリ、クレソン、レモン（くし形）を添え、6 のかきフライを盛りつけ、1 のタルタルソース、または好みでウスターソースにつけていただきます。

■ Directions

1 Prepare the tartar sauce. Place the finely chopped boiled eggs, parsley and pickles, as well as the mayonnaise, lemon juice and milk, in a bowl, and mix well. Adjust the flavor with salt and pepper. Let cool for about 20 min in a fridge.

2 Wash each oyster, one by one, in running cold water, wipe dry and sprinkle on salt and pepper.

3 Spread the flour and breadcrumbs on separate trays. Place all the ingredients of **A** in a bowl, and mix (Don't froth).

4 Preheat oil over a medium heat to 340°F.

5 Coat the oysters with the flour from step 2, the egg mixture from step 3 and the bread crumbs in this order.

6 Place the oysters from step 5 into oil preheated to 340°F. When the batter around the oysters hardens, stir gently occasionally. When the batter turns completely light brown, and the fried oysters float up to the oil surface, retrieve and drain on a tray.

7 Arrange the shredded cabbage, sliced radish, parsley, watercress and lemon wedges on plates. Place the fried oysters from step 6 on the plate. Dip in either tartar sauce from step 1 or Japanese-style Worcestershire sauce, and eat.

Potato Croquette
コロッケ

じゃがいものホクホク感とほのかな甘さがみんな大好き
Everyone loves the steaming hot fried potatoes and its slight sweetness

■材料（4人分）

じゃがいも	4~5 個
バター	大さじ1
玉ねぎ	1/2 個
ローリエ	1 枚
牛ひき肉	150g
塩・こしょう	各少々
白ワイン	大さじ1
牛乳	大さじ3
サラダ油	少々
揚げ油	適量

〈衣の材料〉

小麦粉	適宜
溶き卵	適宜
生パン粉（または普通のパン粉）	適宜

〈つけ合わせ〉

キャベツ（せん切り）	適宜
かいわれ大根	適宜
トマト	適宜

■ INGREDIENTS (serves 4)

4 or 5 potatoes
1 Tbsp butter
1/2 onion
1 laurel leaf
150g minced beef
Pinch salt and pepper
1 Tbsp white wine
3 Tbsps milk
Small quantity of vegetable oil
Oil for deep-frying

〈**For preparing batter**〉
Flour
Beaten egg
Fresh or dried bread crumbs

〈**For garnishing**〉
Cabbage, cut into julienne strips
Young giant white radish shoots
Tomatoes, cut into wedges

■作り方

1 玉ねぎはみじん切りにし、フライパンにサラダ油を入れ、玉ねぎがしんなりするまで炒め、ローリエと牛ひき肉を加えて肉がぽろぽろになるまで炒めます。塩、こしょう、白ワイン大さじ1を加えて2～3分炒めて火を止め、ローリエを取り除きます。

2 じゃがいもは丸ごと（皮つき）水からゆで、竹串を刺してスーッと通るくらいまで柔らかくゆでたら皮をむきます。

3 2のじゃがいもは湯を捨てた鍋に入れ、弱火にかけて水分を飛ばしながら木ベラで切るように潰します。

4 3に1を入れて混ぜ合わせ、牛乳を加えてしっとりとなるように混ぜ、バットに広げて粗熱を取り、冷めたら8等分にします。

5 小麦粉、溶き卵、パン粉をそれぞれバットに入れておきます。手にサラダ油少々（分量外）をつけて4のたねを1個分ずつ取り、厚さ1.5～2cmの小判型に整えます。

6 5を小麦粉、溶き卵、パン粉の順に衣をつけていきます。

7 175℃に熱した油の中に6のたねを入れます。表面がかたまってきたら揚げ箸でゆっくりと混ぜながら、時々コロッケをひっくり返しながら揚げます。

8 7のコロッケがカラッときつね色になったら、揚げバットに上げて油をきります。

9 皿に8のコロッケを盛り、キャベツのせん切りとかいわれ大根、くし形に切ったトマトを添えます。ウスターソース、デミグラスソースなど、好みのソースをかけていただきます。

! コツのコツ

★じゃがいもは冷めてしまうとかたくなって潰しづらくなりますので、ゆで上がったら素早く潰しましょう。

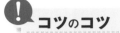

■ Directions

1 Chop the onion finely. Place the vegetable oil in a frying pan, and fry the chopped onion until tender. Add the laurel leaf and minced beef, and fry until the meat becomes dry and crumbles. Add the salt, pepper and 1 Tbsp white wine, and continue to fry for a few minutes. Turn off the heat, and remove the laurel leaf.

2 Place the potatoes with skin in a pot filled with water, and bring to the boil. When the potatoes are tender enough for a bamboo skewer to pierce without difficulty, discard the hot water and peel the potatoes.

3 Place the peeled potatoes from step 2 in the same pot, and mash with a wooden spatula while evaporating the moisture remaining in the pot over a low heat.

4 Add the meat mixture prepared in 1. above, and mix. Add the milk, and mix until the whole mixture becomes thick and soft. Spread the mixture on a tray, and let stand until cool. When cool, divide into 8 equal portions.

5 Prepare three trays each containing one of either the flour, beaten egg or breadcrumbs. Moisten your hands with a small amount of vegetable oil (except quantity), take one of the 8 portions of the mixture from step 4 and a 1/2 to 3/4-inch thick oval shape. Repeat this operation for all the remaining portions.

6 Coat each of the oval portions with the flour, beaten egg and breadcrumbs in this order.

7 Place the oval portions from step 6 in oil at 350°F. When the batter hardens in the oil, turn each croquette over occasionally while stirring gently with cooking chopsticks.

8 When the batter from step 7 is crispy and turns light brown, retrieve the croquettes and drain on a tray.

9 Arrange the croquettes from step 8, and garnish with the shredded cabbage, young giant white radish shoots and tomato wedges. Pour on Japanese-style Worcestershire sauce, demiglace sauce or any other sauce you like.

! Tip on Tips

★ Because potatoes become hard when they are cooled, mash them as soon as possible after boiling them.

Deep-fried Sole (*Karei* Flounder)
かれいの唐揚げ

about 10 min 約10分

198 kcal 198キロカロリー

カラッと揚がったかれいの身が甘くておいしい

Sweet and delicious crispy fried Sole (*Karei* Flounder)

■材料（約2人分）

かれい（約20cm）	… 2尾
しし唐	4〜6本
レモン	1/3個
塩・こしょう	少々
片栗粉	適宜
揚げ油	適宜

■ INGREDIENTS (serves 2)

2 (8-inch) Sole (*Karei* flounders)

4 to 6 *shishito* sweet green peppers

1/3 lemon

Pinch salt and pepper

Katakuriko starch

Oil for deep-frying

◆唐揚げに適した魚◆

Other fish suited to deep-frying

◆かさご・Rockfish (*Kasago*)
◆めばる・Rockfish (*Mebaru*)
◆黒めばる・Black rockfish (*Mebaru*)
◆かわはぎ・File fish
◆あじ・Horse mackerel
◆いわし・Sardine

かさご
Rockfish (*Kasago*)

■作り方

1 かれいは包丁で、両面のうろこやぬめりをこそげ落とし、皮の白い裏側の胸びれの下に切り込みを入れて腹わたを出し、よく洗います。表の中央に飾り包丁を入れ、両側にはひれにそって切り目を入れます。

2 1のかれいに塩、こしょうをし、片栗粉をはたきつけて170℃の油でじっくり揚げます。片栗粉がかたまったら

時々裏返し、全体がカラッと揚がったら揚げバットに上げて油をきります。

3 しし唐は縦に切り込みを1本入れ、30秒ほど揚げたらバットに上げて塩をふります。

4 皿に2のかれいを盛り、3のしし唐、レモンを添えていただきます。

コツのコツ

★かれいのうろこは小さく、びっしりついているので、両面を包丁で丁寧に取りましょう。

★しし唐はつまようじや竹串で数か所に穴を開けるとよいでしょう。

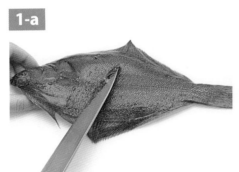
1-a

1-b

2-a

2-b

3-a

3-b

■ Directions

1 Scrape the scales and slippery coating away on the both sides with a knife. Make a slit behind the pectoral fin on the reverse white skin side to pull out the innards, and wash well. On the top brown side of the fish, make a cross-shaped incision at the center, and run the knife along the dorsal and anal fins.

2 After sprinkling on salt and pepper, dust the flounders with *katakuriko* starch and deep-fry in oil at 340°F. When the starch hardens, turn the

fish over occasionally while frying. When the whole surface is crispy, retrieve the fish and drain on a tray.

3 Make a vertical incision on the surface of each *shishito* sweet green pepper. Deep-fry the *shishito* for about 30 sec, drain on a tray and salt.

4 Arrange the flounder from step 2 on plates, and garnish with lemon and the fried *shishito* from step 3.

Tip on Tips

★ Because the scales of Sole (*Karei* flounders) are small and dense, special effort is required to remove them from both sides of the fish with a knife.

★ Pierce *shishito* sweet green peppers with a toothpick or bamboo skewer to make a few holes before cooking.

Deep-fried Marinated Chicken
鶏肉の竜田揚げ

about **18** min
約18分

315 kcal
315キロカロリー

しょう油風味が食欲をそそる和風唐揚げ
Tempting Japanese-style fried chicken with soy sauce flavor

■材料（2人分）

鶏むね肉	1枚	片栗粉	適宜
フリルレタス	1枚	揚げ油	適宜
にんじん	4cm		
大根	4cm		
黄ピーマン	少々		
しょうが汁	小さじ1		
しょう油	大さじ1		
みりん	小さじ1		

※その他のつけ合わせとして、キャベツのせん切り、ラディッシュの薄切り、クレソン、かいわれ大根、そばの芽などを添えてもよいでしょう。

■ INGREDIENTS (serves 2)

1 chicken breast
1 curly lettuce
1 1/2 -inch carrot
1 1/2 -inch giant white radish
1 small yellow pepper
1 tsp fresh ginger juice
1 Tbsp soy sauce
1 tsp *mirin* sweet cooking sake

Katakuriko starch
Oil for deep-frying

※ Julienne-strip cabbage, thinly-sliced radish, watercress, young giant white radish shoots, or soba buckwheat sprouts can also be used as a garnish. Squeeze lemon if you'd like.

■作り方

1 鶏むね肉は余分な皮や脂肪を取り、皮目にフォークで数カ所に穴をあけ、一口大のそぎ切りにしボウルに入れます。そこにしょうが汁、しょう油、みりんを入れて、手でもみ込み 10 分くらいおきます。

2 皮をむいたにんじんと大根、黄ピーマンはせん切りにし水にさらします。

3 1 の鶏むね肉の余分な汁けをふき取り、まんべんなく片栗粉をまぶし、170℃〜180℃の油で揚げます。

4 器に 3 の鶏むね肉を盛り、フリルレタス、2 のせん切り野菜の水けをきったものを添えます。

！コツのコツ

★鶏むね肉を漬け込んだ後に、水けをきっちりとふき取ってから片栗粉をまぶさないと、カラッと揚がらなくなってしまうので注意しましたう。

★フォークで鶏むね肉の皮目に何カ所かに穴をあけることで、タレが中までしみ込みます。

さばの立田揚げ

Deep-fried Marinated Mackerel

■材料（2人分）	■ INGREDIENTS (serves 2)
さば………… 半身	Half mackerel
サラダ菜……2〜3 枚	2 to 3 saradana leaves
レモン……… 1/3 個	1/3 lemon
しょうが汁 … 小さじ 1	1 tbsp ginger juice
酒（料理酒）… 小さじ 1	1 tbsp sake
しょう油 … 大さじ 1/2	1/2 Tbsp soy sauce
みりん …… 小さじ 1	1 tbsp *mirin* sweet cooking sake
片栗粉……… 適宜	*Katakuriko* starch
揚げ油……… 適宜	Oil for deep-frying

■作り方

※さばは背身と脂身を分けるように包丁を入れ、一口大のそぎ切りにします。次からの工程は、鶏肉の竜田揚げと同じになります。

■ Directions

※ Using you knife, cut the mackerel into bite-size pieces as though you were separating the back-side and fatty meats away from the mackerel. The following steps are the same with the deep-fried marinated chicken.

1-a

1-b

3

■ Directions

1 Remove any excess skin and fat from the chicken, pierce the remaining skin with a fork to make several holes, cut diagonally into bite-sized pieces and place in a bowl. Add the ginger juice, soy sauce and *mirin*, and rub the chicken with your hands to make it absorb the seasonings. Let stand for about 10 min.

2 Peel the carrot, giant white radish and yellow pepper, cut into julienne strips and rinse in cold water.

3 Wipe excess moisture away from the chicken, coat every part of the chicken with *katakuriko* starch and deep-fry in oil at 340 to 360 °F.

4 Arrange the chicken on plates and garnish with curly lettuce. Remove excess moisture from the shredded vegetables prepared in step 2 and arrange to garnish.

！Tip on Tips

★ After marinating the chicken, thoroughly remove moisture from the chicken before coating with *katakuriko* starch, otherwise, the results will not be crispy.

★ Pierce the remaining skin with a fork so the seasonings soak into the chicken.

Fried Chicken
鶏肉の唐揚げ

ご飯のおかず、酒のつまみ、弁当と大活躍の"鶏の唐揚げ"

A very popular accompaniment to rice or sake and goes great in your lunch box

■材料（2人分）

		〈衣の材料〉	
鶏もも肉	2枚	小麦粉	100g
塩・こしょう	少々	にんにく（おろし）	適宜
小麦粉	適宜	水	少々
揚げ油	適宜	料理酒	1/2 カップ
レモンの輪切り	適宜	塩	少々
クレソン	適宜	黒こしょう（粗挽）	適宜

■ INGREDIENTS (serves 2)

	〈**Ingredients for coating**〉
2 boneless chicken thighs	100g flour
Small quantity of salt and pepper	Grated garlic
Flour	Small quantity of water
Frying oil	2/5 cup cooking sake (100 ㎖)
Sliced lemon	Small quantity of salt
Watercress	Black pepper (coarsely ground)

■作り方

1 ボウルに小麦粉、にんにく（おろし）、水、料理酒を入れ、泡立て器でゆっくりと泡立てないようにかき混ぜます。泡立て器を持ち上げて上から衣がとぎれないように、スルスルッと落ちるまでなめらかになったら衣の完成です。塩、黒こしょうを加えてさっと混ぜ合わせます。

2 鶏もも肉は、余分な脂身を取り除き、1枚を8等分に切ります。

3 2の鶏もも肉全体に塩、こしょうをふりかけ、下味をつけます。

4 バットに小麦粉を広げ、下味をつけた3の鶏もも肉を押しつけるように表面にしっかりとつけ、余分な粉ははたき落とします。

5 揚げ油を中火で熱し、170～180℃に温めておきます。

6 4の鶏もも肉を、1の衣にくぐらせ衣が均一につくようにし、5に入れます。一度に入れる量は3～4個が目安です。中火にし、時々揚げ箸で鶏肉を持ち上げてひっくり返しながら火が中まで通るまでじっくり揚げていきます。

7 6がきつね色に揚がり、鶏肉全体が浮いてきたら火が通った証拠です。箸で持ち上げて振り、油をきり、揚げバットに取り上げて油をきっておきます。

8 7を器に盛り、クレソン、レモンの輪切りを添えていただきます。

！コツのコツ

★中火にして揚げないと周りの衣だけが焦げ、肉の中まで火が通らないので注意しましょう。

★揚げている時に鶏もも肉からでる気泡が小さくなったら、火が通った証拠です。

★箸で油をきる時に揚げ油に唐揚げを落とさないよう注意しましょう。

■ Directions

1 Put in a bowl the flour, grated garlic, water, and cooking sake, and mix with a whisk. Move the whisk carefully so that bubbles are not formed. Lift the whisk to see if the batter is smooth enough to fall unbroken. If so, the batter is ready. Add the salt and black pepper, and lightly mix.

2 Remove excess fat from the boneless chicken thighs, and cut each thigh into 8 equal pieces.

3 Sprinkle the entire surface of the chicken with the salt and pepper for preliminary seasoning.

4 Spread the flour on a cooking tray, press the chicken to cover the entire surface with the flour, and dust off excess flour.

5 Heat the frying oil over a medium flame from 340 to 360°F.

6 Dip the chicken from step 4 in the batter from step 1 to evenly coat the chicken and put it in the oil from step 5. Put 3 to 4 pieces in the oil at a time. Fry the chicken thoroughly over a medium heat until fully cooked, while occasionally lifting and turning the chicken with heat resistant chopsticks.

7 When the chicken is fried brown and begins to float in the oil, it's fully cooked. Lift the chicken with the chopsticks and shake off excess oil. Place on a draining tray.

8 Arrange the fried chicken on a serving dish, garnishing with the watercress and sliced lemon.

！Tip on Tips

★ Make sure the flame is medium. Otherwise, the coating will burn before the chicken is fully cooked.

★ When deep-frying, you can tell if the chicken is fully cooked when the bubbles rising from the chicken become small.

★ When shaking off excess oil with the chopsticks, be careful not to drop the fried chicken in the frying oil.

Pork Cutlet
とんかつ

about **35**min 約35分

295kcal 295 キロカロリー

サクッと揚がった衣とジューシーな豚ロース肉がおいしい
A delicious dish of crispy batter and juicy pork loin

■材料 (4人分)

豚ロース肉 …………	2 枚
塩・こしょう ………	少々
溶き卵 …………	1 個分
薄力粉 …………	適宜
パン粉 …………	適宜
キャベツ …………	1/4 個
サラダ菜 …………	4 枚
プチトマト …………	4 個
レモン …………	1/2 個
パセリのみじん切り …	1 枝分
とんかつソース ……	適宜
練り辛子 …………	適宜
揚げ油 …………	適宜

※キャベツのせん切りに、きゅうりのせん切りやラディッシュの薄切り、大葉のせん切り、紫キャベツなどを混ぜると彩りもよくなります。また、クレソンやパセリなどを添えてもよいでしょう。

■ INGREDIENTS (serves 4)

2 slices pork loin
Pinch salt and pepper
1 egg, beaten
Hakurikiko flour
Dried breadcrumbs
1/4 cabbage
4 *saradana* leaves
4 cherry tomatoes
1/2 lemon

1 branch parsley, chopped finely
Commercially prepared *tonkatsu* pork cutlet sauce
Mustard paste
Oil for deep-frying

※ Mixing julienne-strip cucumber, green perilla leaves, red cabbage and thinly-sliced radish with julienne-strip cabbage will make the dish more colorful. Watercress and parsley can also be arranged on the side.

■作り方

1 キャベツはせん切りにして水にさらし、水けをきり、パセリのみじん切りを混ぜます。レモンは絞りやすい大きさに切ります。プチトマト、サラダ菜は水洗いします。

2 豚ロース肉は、脂身と赤身の間の筋に、包丁で数か所の切り込みを入れます。

3 包丁の背で豚ロース肉全体をたたき、肉を柔らかくし、塩、こしょうを両面にふります。

4 薄力粉、溶き卵、パン粉、バットなどを準備し、**3** の豚ロース肉に薄力粉をまんべんなくつけ、余分な薄力粉は払い落としておきます。

5 **4** の豚ロース肉に溶き卵をつけ、パン粉の上におき、豚ロース肉の上からパン粉をかけて軽く手で押さえるようにしてつけます。余分なパン粉はふり落とします。

6 170℃に熱した油に、**5** の豚ロース肉を鍋肌から静かに入れます。表面がかたまってきつね色になってきたら、箸で裏返し全体を揚げます。

7 揚げ油の泡が小さくなってきて、**6** のとんかつがきつね色になったら揚げバットに上げて油をきります。

8 皿に **1** のサラダ菜、せん切りキャベツ、レモン、プチトマトを添え、**7** のとんかつを食べやすいように包丁で切ったものを盛り、練り辛子、とんかつソースを添えていただきます。

！ コツのコツ

★豚ロース肉の脂身と赤身の筋に包丁で切り込みを入れることで、揚げた時の縮みを防ぎます。

★包丁の背で豚ロース肉をたたくことによって柔らかくなります。

■ Directions

1 Cut the cabbage into julienne strips, rinse in cold water and drain. Mix the shredded cabbage and chopped parsley. Cut the lemon into wedges the size of which can be easily squeezed with two fingers. Rinse the cherry tomatoes and *saradana* leaves in cold water.

2 In a few places, slash the sinew running between the fat and lean tissue with a knife.

3 Strike the entire surfaces of the pork slices with the back of a knife to soften the meat. Sprinkle salt and pepper on both sides.

4 Prepare three trays or bowls with each containing one of either the flour, beaten egg or breadcrumbs. Coat the pork with the flour thoroughly, and shake off excess flour.

5 Dip the pork in the beaten egg, and then place on the top of the breadcrumbs. Put some breadcrumbs over the meat, and press lightly with your hands. Shake off excess breadcrumbs.

6 Preheat oil to 340°F, and from the rim of the pan let the pork slide gently into the oil. When the surface of the pork hardens and becomes light brown, flip with chopsticks to fry the meat thoroughly.

7 When the bubbles of oil become small, and the pork cutlet turns light brown completely, retrieve and drain on a tray.

8 Arrange the *saradana* leaves, shredded cabbage, lemon wedges and cherry tomatoes on plates. Cut the pork cutlet into several pieces and put them on the plate. Garnish with mustard. Pour on the *tonkatsu* sauce.

！ Tip on Tips

★ Making a few cuts in the sinew running between the fatty and lean parts of the pork loin prevents the meat from shrinking.

★ Pound the pork loin with the back of your knife to tenderize the meat.

江戸時代のファーストフードだった "天ぷら"

"Tempura," the Edo Period's Fast Food

天ぷらは、もともとは日本のものではなく、室町時代の長崎に西洋人が伝えたといわれています。天ぷらの語源は、ポルトガル語の「テンポラ（tempero・調理を意味）」や、スペイン語の「テンペロ（templo・魚肉の揚げものを食べる日の意味）」などの説があります。

当初、天ぷらは高級品でしたが、江戸時代に入ると立ち食いの屋台が登場し、手軽に食べられる庶民のファーストフードになりました。

当時の天ぷらは、芝えび、小柱、小肌、いかなどを一口大に切り、串に刺したものに衣をつけ油で揚げ、それをどんぶり鉢に入った天つゆにつけて食べるものでした。

Tempura isn't originally a Japanese food. It's believed to have been introduced by Westerners to Nagasaki during the Muromachi period. There are several views about the word's origin; "tempero," a Portuguese word meaning "to watch how to season" and a Spanish word "templo," meaning a day to eat deep-fried fish.

Initially tempura was expensive, but street stands started appearing from the Edo period and it became a common fast food.

Tempura of that time was prepared as follows: ingredients such as *Shiba* shrimp (prawn), small scallops, spotted shad and squid were cut into bite-size pieces. They were skewered, battered and deep-fried. People enjoyed them with tempura sauce poured in domburi bowls.

江戸時代のファーストフードとして庶民に人気だった屋台の天ぷら
鍬形蕙斎作「近世職人尽絵詞」（東京国立博物館所蔵・複製禁止）
Image:TNM Image Archives Source:http://TnmArchives.jp/
The *Edo* period's popular fast food, tempura, used to be served at stands.
"Kinsei Shokunin-zukushi Ekotoba" by Kuwagata Keisai (by Tokyo National Museum, all rights reserved.)

Basic Japanese Packed Lunch
和食の基本・お弁当

弁当箱に愛情たっぷりの和食がいっぱい。今や弁当は、アメリカやフランスでも大人気。ここでは子ども弁当、大人弁当、キャラ弁当、行楽弁当を紹介。おいしいお弁当にチャレンジしてみて…。

Lunch boxes filled with hearty Japanese food are now very popular in the United States and France. In this chapter, we introduce you to the preparation of fun packed lunches for kids and adults, lunches with character designs and for picnics. Try preparing a tasty packed lunch!

日の丸弁当
"Hinomaru," the rising sun
flag packed lunch

Variety of Lunch Boxes and Accessories
お弁当箱・小物コレクション

いろんなお弁当箱と小物でお弁当作りを楽しみましょう
A packed lunch is even more fun when it comes in these intesting lunch boxes and accessories

おかずがたくさん入りそうな男の子用弁当箱。
A spacious lunch box for boys.

花柄がおしゃれな女の子用の弁当箱。
A flower-print lunch box for girls.

カエル顔がかわいい幼稚園児むけの弁当箱。
A cute frog-face lunch box for kinder-gardeners.

がっつり食べたいサラリーマンや男子学生に最適な大きめの弁当箱。
A large lunch box for male corporate workers and students.

体育会系男子やガテン系男子に最適。伝統的なアルミ弁当の"ドカ弁"。
A classic aluminum lunch box called *"doka-ben,"* best for athletic men and blue-collar workers.

OLや女子学生に最適なおしゃれな、おかずとご飯が別の2段式弁当箱。
A stylish two-stage lunch box with separate containers for rice and side dishes, for female office workers and students.

大きなおにぎりが1個入る、とても便利なおにぎりケース。
A container for a large rice ball.

竹で編んだ昔ながらの弁当籠。ちょっとした行楽時に最適。
A traditional lunch basket woven with bamboo, suitable for a picnic.

おにぎりを包む竹皮。日本初の駅弁がおにぎりとたくあんだった。
A bamboo leaf for wrapping rice balls. The first *"ekiben,"* or lunch sold at train stations, was rice balls and *"takuan"* pickles.

おにぎりやご飯にアクセントをつける "のりパンチ（星型）"。

Use a star-shaped seaweed puncher for rice and rice balls.

おにぎりに顔をつけられる "のりパンチ（笑顔）"。

This seaweed puncher will put a smiley face on your rice balls.

おにぎりをくまの顔に型抜きできるすぐれものステンレスごはん型。

A useful stainless bear-face-shaped rice ball maker.

ハム、チーズなどのおかずやフルーツを型抜きできる型抜き。

Cutters in various shapes for ham, cheese and fruit.

魚の形をしたアルミ用おかずケース。おかずもおしゃれに演出。

Amuse yourself with a fish-shaped aluminum side dish case.

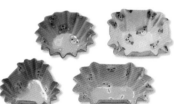

さまざまな形があるアルミ用おかずケース。用途に合わせて使いわけたい。

Cases for side dishes come in various shapes. Choose a case depending on the intended use.

スタンダードなアルミおかずケース。汁けの多いおかずに最適。

Standard aluminum side dish cases, suitable for moist side dishes.

食べやすいように、おかずやフルーツに刺すお弁当用ピック。

Picks designed to include in your lunch box to use with side dishes and fruit.

★弁当作りの注意点・Tips on Preparing Packed Lunches

弁当作りには注意しなくてはいけないことが、何点かありますので紹介します。

There are several points to remember when packing a lunch.

①生ものは絶対に入れない
　魚介類の生ものは食中毒の原因などになりますので、絶対に入れてはいけません。

②汁け、油けはよくきる
　余分な汁け、油けは汁もれや味移りの原因になるため、キッチンペーパーなどでよくふき取りましょう。

③汁けのあるおかずの詰め方
　アルミ用おかずケースを使用しましょう。

④おかずは素手でさわらない
　弁当箱におかずを詰める時は、食中毒の原因になるため、極力箸やフォークなどを使用し、素手でさわらないようにしてください。

⑤冷ましてからふたをする
　おかずは冷ましてから弁当に詰めましょう。温かいままふたをすると傷みの原因になります。また、ご飯は温かいうちに弁当に詰めても、冷めた頃合いをみておかずを詰めるとよいでしょう。

⑥清潔なものを使用する
　弁当箱、包丁、まな板など使用するものは、すべて清潔なものを使用しましょう。

① **Never use raw seafood ingredients**
Don't use raw seafood as it can cause food poisoning.

② **Remove the moisture and oil**
Remove any excess moisture and oil with paper towels before packing in order to prevent messy leaking and mixing of flavors.

③ **How to pack moist ingredients**
Use aluminum side dish cases.

④ **Don't touch side dishes with hands**
Remember not to touch side dishes with hands as it can cause food poisoning when packing. Use chopsticks or forks as much as possible.

⑤ **Cover after cool**
Pack side dishes after cool. If covered while warm, they spoil more rapidly. You can pack rice while warm, but pack side dishes after the rice is cooled.

⑥ **Use clean tools**
Use only clean lunch boxes, knives and cutting boards.

Rice Ball
おにぎり

Rice balls are hearty because they are lovingly made by hand

愛情こめて手でにぎるからおいしい "おにぎり"

■材料（5〜6人分）

温かいご飯‥‥‥‥ 2合分
〈具 材〉
梅干し‥‥‥‥‥‥‥‥ 適宜
さけ（焼いてほぐしたもの）
‥‥‥‥‥‥‥‥‥‥‥‥ 適宜
昆布の佃煮‥‥‥‥‥ 適宜
塩‥‥‥‥‥‥‥‥‥‥ 少々
焼きのり‥‥‥‥‥‥ 適宜

■ INGREDIENTS (serves 5~6)

360g warm boiled rice
〈**Stuffing**〉
Pickled plums
Chum salmon, grilled and torn
into small pieces
Konbu kelp salt-sweet preserves
(Tsukudani)And various others
Pinch salt
Toasted *nori* seaweed sheets

◆ おにぎりに適した具材◆

Other ingredients suited to rice ball stuffing
◆めんたいこ・*Mentaiko* (seasoned cod roe)
※焼いてもおいしいです
※ Cooked mentaiko is also good.
◆辛子めんたいこ・Spicy mentaiko (spicy seasoned cod roe)
◆高菜漬け・*Takana-duke* (pickled takana leaf mustard)
◆のりの佃煮・Boiled seaweed in soy sauce
◆じゃこの佃煮・Boiled baby sardines in soy sauce

■作り方

1 茶碗に軽くご飯をよそい、ご飯の中心を少しくぼませ、その上に好みの具をのせて、その上で軽くご飯をのせます。

2 手を少し濡らし、塩をほんの少量手のひらにつけます。

3 1の茶碗のご飯を手のひらに移し、具が中心にいくようにボール形に軽くまとめます。

4 左手にご飯をのせた状態で右手は山形にし、手前に回すようにしながら三角形に整えて、のりを巻いて、おにぎりの完成です。

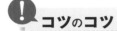

❗ コツのコツ

★ 入れる具によって、手につける塩を加減しましょう。

★ のりには裏表があるので注意しましょう。ざらざらした方（裏面）が中側にくるように巻きます。

★ ご飯をきつくにぎると、かたくなってしまうので注意しましょう。

1

2

3-a

3-b

4-a

4-b

■ Directions

1 Put a handful of boiled rice lightly into a rice bowl, make an indentation at the center of the rice, tuck in whichever stuffing you prefer and put some more rice on top to cover the stuffing.

2 Moisten your hands, and spread a small amount of salt over the palms.

3 Transfer the rice in the bowl from Step 1 to your palm, and form into a ball lightly while rolling in both hands. Make sure that the position of the stuffing comes to the center.

4 To make a triangle rice roll, follow this processe–Transfer the rice in the bowl to the palm of the left hand, and angle the right palm. Roll the rice counterclockwise in both hands while maintaining the angle of the right palm to make it into a triangle. Wrap the roll with a *nori* seaweed sheet.

❗ Tip on Tips

★ Adjust the quantity of salt depending on the type of stuffing.

★ Pay attention to the side of the nori seaweed sheets. Place the sheet around the rice ball so that the coarse side is on the inside.

★ Don't roll the ball too tightly. Otherwise, the rice ball will be too hard.

おにぎり（P152）
Rice ball

おにぎり＋焼きさけ（P152）
Rice ball ＋ Chum salmon(grilled)

サラダ菜
Saradana leaves

鶏肉の唐揚げ（P144）
Fried Chicken

プチトマト
Cherry Tomatoes

ひじきの煮もの（P75）
Simmered *Hijiki* Seaweed

カニウインナー（ゆで）
Boiled crab-shaped sausage
※作り方は下参照
See below for the directions

★バリエーション・Variations

ミートボール
Meatball

※市販品
Commercial item

だし巻き卵
Rolled Omelet

P108 参照
See P.108

カニウインナー
Crab-shaped sausage

ウインナー（ゆで）
Vienna sausage (boiled)

※市販品
Commercial item

きんぴらごぼう
Burdock Kimpira

P80 参照
See P.80

■作り方
ゆでたウインナーを横に切ります（**A**）。**B**の順番に包丁で切り込みをしていきます。

■ **Directions**
Cut a boiled sausage in half lengthwise(**A**). Make cuts in the order illustrated in **B** below.

A

B

A Packed Lunch for Kids
子ども弁当

A tasty and cute packed lunch for girls, it's colorful and balanced nutrition

彩りと栄養を考えたおしゃれでおいしい女の子弁当

プチトマト
Cherry Tomatoes

ポテトサラダ（P218）
Potato Salad

キウイフルーツ
Kiwi

ブロッコリー（ゆで）
Broccoli (boiled)

ご飯＋ふりかけ
Rice + "Furikake" toppings

ぶりの照焼き（P118）
Japanese Amberjack
(Yellowtail) Teriyaki

だし巻き卵（P108）
Rolled Omelet

ウインナー（ゆで）
Vienna sausage (boiled)

第七章・和食の基本・お弁当●Basic Japanese Packed Lunch

★バリエーション・Variations

鶏肉の唐揚げ
Fried Chicken

P144 参照
See P.144

きんぴらごぼう
Burdock Kimpira

P80 参照
See P.80

うずらの卵（水煮）
Boiled quail eggs

※市販品
Commercial item

鶏肉のつけ焼き
Chicken Saute

P122 参照
See P.122

ちくわ＋きゅうり、チーズ、ハム
Chikuwa fish sausage +
cucumber, cheese and ham

バターコーン
Buttered sweet corn

A Character Packed Lunch

キャラ弁当

An entertaining packed lunch will make your child smile

ふたをあけた子どもの笑顔が思い浮かぶ、楽しいキャラ弁

きゅうり（雲形）
Cucumber (cloud-shaped)

サラダ菜
Saradana leaves

ハム（音符形）
Ham (musical note-shaped)

ハム（音符形）
Ham (musical note-shaped)

だし巻き卵（P108）
Rolled Omelet

ウインナー（ゆで）
Vienna sausage (boiled)

おにぎり
Rice ball

ハム（花形）
Ham (flower-shaped)
※作り方は下参照
See below for the directions

はんぺん（花形）
Hampen white boiled fish paste
(flower-shaped)

★バリエーション・Variations

ブロッコリー（ゆで）
Broccoli (boiled)

たこウインナー
Octopus-shaped sausage

ミートボール
Meatball

※市販品
Commercial item

うずらの卵（水煮）
Boiled quail eggs

※市販品
Commercial item

プチトマト
Cherry Tomatoes

えび焼売
Shrimp dim sum

※市販品
Commercial item

★使用する道具・Useful tools

ハム（花形、音符形）、
きゅうり（雲形）
Cutters for flower and
musical note ham and
cloud cucumbers

P151 参照
See P.151

のりパンチ
Seaweed puncher

P151 参照
See P.151

顔型 Face shape

星型 Star shape

156

A Character Packed Lunch
A packed lunch full of adorable animals is almost too cute to eat

キャラ弁当
食べるのがもったいない、かわいらしい動物たちが入ったお弁当

パンダおにぎり
Panda rice ball
※作り方は下参照
See below for the directions

ブタさんおにぎり
Pig rice ball
※作り方は下参照
See below for the directions

パセリ
Parsley

ライオンおにぎり
Lion rice ball
※作り方は下参照
See below for the directions

うずらの卵（ゆで）
Boiled quail eggs

★動物おにぎりの作り方・How to make animal rice balls

パンダおにぎり
Panda rice ball

■ 作り方
1. P151のクマのステンレスご飯型で、ご飯を型抜きします。
2. 耳の部分に合わせてハサミなどで、のりを切ります。目、鼻も切ります。口はP156ののりパンチを使用します。

■ Directions
1. Make a bear-shaped rice ball by using a stainless bear-face-shaped rice ball maker.
2. Cut seaweed to make ears of the panda with scissors. Also cut out eyes and a nose. Use a seaweed puncher shown on P.156 to make a mouth.

ライオンおにぎり
Lion rice ball

■ 作り方
1. ゆでたロングウインナーに包丁で切り込みを入れます。
2. 温かいご飯に少量の塩とカレー粉を加え味を調え、写真の形にします。
3. 耳はチーズを、鼻の部分はチーズとハムを切り、目はのりを切ります。鼻はマヨネーズで貼りつけます。

■ Directions
1. Make a number of cuts on a long sausage.
2. Add a little salt and curry powder in warm rice and make the shape as shown in the picture.
3. Use cheese for ears, cheese and ham for a nose and seaweed for eyes. Attach the nose with mayonnaise.

ブタさんおにぎり
Pig rice ball

■ 作り方
1. P151のクマのステンレスご飯型で、少量のケチャップと塩で味を調えたご飯を型抜きします。
2. ソーセージを耳に合わせて半月切りにします。鼻はソーセージを輪切りにし、穴2つをストローで抜きます。目はのりをハサミなどで切ります。ほっぺはさくらデンブになります。耳と鼻はマヨネーズで貼りつけます。
3. 足はソーセージを2分の1に切り、写真のように切り込みを入れます。

■ Directions
1. Season rice with a little salt and ketchup. Make a bear-face-shaped rice ball by using a stainless bear-face-shape rice ball maker listed on P.151.
2. Cut a sliced sausage in half to make ears. Use a round cut sausage for a nose and make two holes with a straw. Cut seaweed to make eyes. Use sakura-dembu (flaked fish meat colored in pink) for cheeks. Attach ears and a nose with mayonnaise.
3. Cut a sausage in half sidewise and make cuts as shown in the picture to make legs.

157

A Packed Lunch for Adults

A satisfying lunch for fathers and male students

大人弁当

お父さんや男子学生のための満腹、満足弁当

キャベツ（千切り）
Cabbage, cut into julienne strips

さやいんげん
String bean

コロッケ（P138）
Potato Croquette

きんぴらごぼう（P80）
Burdock Kimpira

ブロッコリー（ゆで）
Broccoli (boiled)

鶏肉のつけ焼き（P122）
Chicken Saute

たくあん（漬けもの）
Takuan pickled giant white radish

ご飯＋塩ごま
Rice + sesami and salt

★バリエーション・Variations

ぶりの照焼き
Japanese Amberjack (Yellowtall) Teriyaki

P118 参照
See P.118

さわらの西京焼き
Grilled Spanish Mackerel, *Saikyo*-Style

P116 参照
See P.116

豚肉のしょうが焼き
Ginger Pork Saute

P120 参照
See P.120

鶏肉の唐揚げ
Fried Chicken

P144 参照
See P.144

切り干し大根煮
Simmered *Kiriboshi-daikon*

P76 参照
See P.76

プチトマト
Cherry Tomatoes

158

A Packed Lunch for Adults
大人弁当

A healthy and balanced packed lunch for women
栄養を考えた女性のためのヘルシー弁当

ご飯＋しらす＋グリーンピース
Rice + dried whitebait + green peas

さわらの西京焼き（**P116**）
Grilled Spanish Mackerel,
Saikyo-Style

ひじきの煮もの（**P75**）
Simmered Hijiki Seaweed

切り干し大根煮（**P76**）
Simmered kiriboshi-daikon

ポテトサラダ（**P218**）
Potato Salad

★バリエーション・Variations

鶏肉の唐揚げ
Fried Chicken

P144 参照
See P.144

ぶりの照焼き
Japanese Amberjack
(Yellowtall) Teriyaki

P118 参照
See P.118

えび焼売
Shrimp dim sum

※市販品
Commercial item

だし巻き卵
Rolled Omelet

P108 参照
See P.108

ちくわ＋きゅうり、チーズ、ハム
Chikuwa fish sausage +
cucumber, cheese and ham

ブロッコリー（ゆで）
Broccoli (boiled)

159

キャベツ
Cabbage

とんかつ（P146）
Pork Cutlet

プチトマト
Cherry tomatoes

ピーマン炒め
Fry-up of the green pepper

白飯
Boiled rice

だし巻き卵（P108）
Rolled Omelet

豚肉のしょうが焼き（P120）
Ginger Pork Saute

たくあん
Takuan pickled giant white radish

★バリエーション・Variations

鶏肉の唐揚げ
Fried Chicken

P144 参照
See P.144

さわらの西京焼き
Grilled Spanish Mackerel, *Saikyo*-Style

P116 参照
See P.116

きんぴらごぼう
Burdock Kimpira

P80 参照
See P.80

鶏肉のつけ焼き
Chicken Saute

P122 参照
See P.122

ミートボール
Meatball

※市販品
Commercial item

ブロッコリー（ゆで）
Broccoli (boiled)

A Packed Lunch for Picnics
行楽弁当

A packed lunch for two is good to bring on a short trip
二人でちょっとしたおでかけに最適なお弁当

レタス
Lettuce

おにぎり（**P152**）
Rice Ball

鶏肉の唐揚げ（**P144**）
Fried Chicken

おにぎり＋焼きさけ（**P152**）
Rice ball ＋ Chum salmon
(grilled)

大根ときゅうりの浅漬け
Lightly pickled daikon
radish and cucumber

レモン
Lemon

おからの炒り煮（**P78**）
Simmered *Okara* Tofu Lees

★バリエーション・**Variations**

だし巻き卵
Rolled Omelet

P108 参照
See P.108

きんぴらごぼう
Burdock Kimpira

P80 参照
See P.80

鶏肉のつけ焼き
Chicken Saute

P122 参照
See P.122

筑前煮
Chicken and Vegetables.
Chikuzen-Style

P82 参照
See P.82

さわらの西京焼き
Grilled Spanish Mackerel,
Saikyo-Style

P116 参照
See P.116

たくあん（漬け物）
Takuan pickled giant
white radish

※市販品
Commercial item

A Packed Lunch for Picnics

A packed lunch filled with rice balls and sushi pockets is perfect for a fun day out admiring the cherry blossoms or enjoying sports festivals

行楽弁当

花見や運動会などに重宝するおにぎりといなり寿しの行楽弁当

だし巻き卵 (**P108**)
Rolled Omelet

筑前煮 (**P82**)
Chicken and Vegetables.
Chikuzen-Style

おにぎり＋梅 (**P152**)
Rice Ball ＋ Pickled plums

いなり寿し (**P196**)
Sushi Pockets

★バリエーション・**Variations**

巻き寿し
Sushi Roll

P184 参照
See P.184

鶏肉のつけ焼き
Chicken Saute

P122 参照
See P.122

切り干し大根煮
Simmered *Kiriboshi-daikon*

P76 参照
See P.76

鶏肉の唐揚げ
Fried Chicken

P144 参照
See P.144

さわらの西京焼き
Grilled Spanish Mackerel,
Saikyo-Style

P116 参照
See P.116

きんぴらごぼう
Burdock Kimpira

P80 参照
See P.80

第八章
Chapter 8

Basic Japanese Steamed Dishes
和食の基本・蒸しもの

食材の旨味をぎゅっと閉じ込めた蒸しもの料理。一口食べるとほっとする茶わん蒸しや、あさり
の旨味をあますことなく楽しめるあさりの酒蒸しから豪華な金目だいの姿蒸しを紹介。

Steamed dishes are rich in taste as the ingredients' flavors are enhanced by steaming. We
introduce a number of steamed dishes including a soothing steamed cup custard, delicious
sake-steamed short-necked clams and a gorgeous steamed whole alfonsino.

Steamed Whole Alfonsino (Golden Eye Bream)
金目だいの姿蒸し

ちょっとしたパーティや祝いごとに最適な豪華な姿蒸し

This is a sumptuous main dish for parties and festive occasions

■材料（3〜4人分）

金目だい（約25cm〜30cm）
……………………… 1尾
しょうが ………… 2かけ
長ねぎの白い部分… 2本分
長ねぎの青い部分… 1本分
赤ピーマン ……… 1/4個
香菜………………… 適宜
料理酒 ………… 大さじ1
サラダ油…… 1/4カップ

〈タレ用調味料〉
しょう油 ……… 小さじ2
塩………… 小さじ1/4
こしょう ………… 少々

■ INGREDIENTS (serves 3〜4)

1 (10 to 12-inch) whole Alfonsino (golden eye bream)
2 knobs ginger
White parts of 2 *naga-negi* onions
Green part of 1 *naga-negi* onion
1/4 red pepper
Coriander

1 Tbsp cooking sake
1/5 cup vegetable oil（50㎖）

〈**For preparing sauce**〉
2 tsps soy sauce
1/4 tsp salt
Small quantity of pepper

■作り方

1 金目だいはうろこを取り、水洗いしてうろこをよく落とします。えらぶたをあけて、包丁の刃先でつけ根を切り、えらを取りはずします。腹に切り目を入れ、内臓をかき出して水洗いします。

2 1の金目だいの背から腹に、包丁で斜めに1本中骨のところまで切り込みを入れます。

3 長ねぎは水洗いし、長さ4～5cmの白髪ねぎをつくります。しょうがは水洗いして針しょうがにします。

4 赤ピーマンは水洗いし、へたと種を取りせん切りに、香菜は水洗いし食べやすい大きさに切ります。

5 蒸し器に水を入れ、火にかけます。

6 バットに長ねぎの青い部分を敷き、2の金目だいを頭が左側になるようにのせ、料理酒をふりかけ、湯気のたった蒸し器に入れ、強火で約15分くらい蒸します。

7 6の金目だいを皿に盛り、3の白髪ねぎと針しょうが、4の赤ピーマンをのせます。

8 7でバットに残った蒸し汁をこし器でこし、小鍋に入れて火にかけ、タレ用調味料を加えて煮たたせタレを作ります。

9 別の小鍋、または中華鍋にサラダ油4分の1カップを入れて火にかけ、煙りが出るくらいまで高温に熱し、2の白髪ねぎ、針しょうが、赤ピーマンの部分に回しかけ、香りと香ばしさを出したら、8のタレをかけ、4の香菜を散らしていただきます。

❗ コツのコツ

★金目だいはあまり蒸しすぎると、身がかたくなるので注意しましょう。

★油は煮えたぎるほど熱く熱したものをかけることで、食べた時に油っぽさが口に残りません。

■ Directions

1 Scale the alfonsino (golden eye bream). Wash well in cold water to thoroughly remove any remaining scales.Hold a gill slit open, insert the tip of a knife and cut the base of the gills to remove them. Make a slit along the underbelly, scoop out the innards with your hands and wash in cold water.

2 Make a diagonal incision on one side of the fish from step 1.

3 Rinse the white parts of *naga-negi* onions, and cut into 1 1/2 to 2-inch long fine strips. Rinse the ginger in cold water, and cut into "needle" shreds.

4 Rinse the red pepper in cold water, remove the stalk and seeds, and cut into julienne strips. Rinse the coriander in cold water, and cut into bite-sized pieces.

5 Pour water in a steam cooker and heat it.

6 Lay the green part of a *naga-negi* onion on a tray. Place the fish from step 2 on top of the onion so that the head is on your left, and sprinkle on the cooking sake. Put the tray into a preheated steamer, and steam over a high heat for about 15 min.

7 Arrange the fish from step 6 on a plate. Place the shredded white parts of *naga-negi* onions from step 3, "needle" ginger and red pepper from step 4 on top of the fish.

8 Strain the liquid left in the tray from step 7 after steaming the fish, and heat the strained liquid in a small pot. Add all the sauce ingredients, and bring to the boil.

9 Place 1/5 cup vegetable oil in another small pot or wok, and heat to a high temperature. When the oil is so hot that it almost begins to smoke, pour the oil onto the shredded white parts of *naga-negi* onions from step 2 and the "needle" ginger and red pepper in a circular motion to add a nice aroma and flavor to the dish. Pour on the sauce from step 8. Scatter the chopped coriander from step 4 and serve.

❗ Tip on Tips

★ Be careful not to steam alfonsino(golden eye bream) too much, otherwise, the flesh will become hard.

★ The oil should be heated to a very high temperature to prevent the dish from becoming oily.

Chawan-mushi Savory Cup Custard

茶碗蒸し

約20分 about 20min

155kcal 155キロカロリー

温かいうちに食べたい具だくさんの茶碗蒸し

This savory custard is packed with goodness and best while it's hot

■材料（2人分）

小えび	…………	4 尾
鶏ささ身	…………	1 本
にんじん	…………	少々
しいたけ	…………	1 枚
ぎんなん	…………	4 個
三つ葉	…………	5~6 本
かまぼこ	…………	2 枚
卵（小）	…………	2 個

A
だし汁	…	1と1/2 カップ
塩	………	小さじ 1/2
薄口しょう油	…	小さじ 1
みりん	…	小さじ 1/2

料理酒	…………	適宜
塩	…………	適宜

■ INGREDIENTS (serves 2)

4 small shrimps
1 fillet chicken breast
Small quantity of carrot
1 shiitake mushroom
4 ginkgo nuts
5 or 6 stalks trefoil
2 slices *kamaboko* fish paste
2 small eggs

A
1 1/4 cups stock (300㎖)
1/2 tsp salt
1 tsp light soy sauce
1/2 tsp *mirin* sweet cooking sake

Cooking sake
Salt

■作り方

1 小えびは背わたを取って小鍋に入れ、料理酒（大さじ1）、水（大さじ2）と塩を少々を入れて炒り煮をし、殻を取ります。ぎんなんは殻をむき、ひたひたのお湯に塩を少々入れてゆでて薄皮をむきます。

2 にんじんは2〜3mmの厚さに切り、型抜きで抜きさっと塩ゆでにします。しいたけは軸を取り薄切りにします。鶏ささ身は薄皮と筋を取ってそぎ切りにし、塩と料理酒を少々ふりかけます。

3 卵をボウルに割り入れ、泡立てないように溶きます。**A**を入れてよく混ぜ、卵液をこしてなめらかにします。

4 蒸し器に水を入れ、火にかけておきます。
※蒸し器の使い方は、66ページを参照してください。

5 器に2の鶏ささ身を入れて、3の卵液を6〜7分目まで静かに注ぎ入れます。湯気の立っている蒸し器に入れ、ふたを少しずらして1分ほど強火で蒸し、弱火にして6〜7分蒸らします。

6 5の表面がかたまったら2のしいたけ、かまぼこ、1のえび、ぎんなん、2のにんじんをのせて残りの卵液を器の8〜9分目までたします。ふたをずらし1分程強火で蒸し、弱火で6〜7分蒸します。

7 3cmの長さに切った三ツ葉を飾っていただきます。

！ コツのコツ

★強火で、長い時間蒸すとすがたつので注意しましょう。

★竹串を刺してみて、透明なだし汁が出てくれば蒸し上がりの証拠です。

1-a

1-b

2

4

■ Directions

1 De-vein the small shrimps, and put into a small pot. Add 1 Tbsp cooking sake, 2 Tbsps water and a pinch of salt, and simmer while stirring until all the liquid is gone. Skin the shrimps. Remove the shells of the ginkgo nuts, and put into a small pot. Add just enough water to cover the gingko nuts, as well as a pinch of salt, and boil. Remove the thin film around the nuts. Cut the carrot crosswise into about 1/16-inch pieces, and stamp out into a flower shape.

2 Boil the carrot in salted water briefly. Chop the stem off the shiitake mushroom, and cut thinly. Remove the skin and sinew from the chicken fillet, cut diagonally and sprinkle on a small amount of salt and cooking sake.

3 Beat the eggs in a bowl (Don't froth). Add all the ingredients of **A**, and mix well. Strain this egg stock mixture.

4 Pour water into your steam cooker and heat it.
※ See P.66 for the directions to use a steam cooker.

5 Place the chicken in serving cups, and gently pour in the egg stock mixture until 60 to 70% full. Transfer the cups to a preheated steamer. Steam over a high heat for about 1 min with the lid slightly askew. Then steam over a low heat for 6 to 7 min with the steamer completely covered.

6 When the surface of the custard is set, place the shiitake mushroom, *kamaboko*, shrimps, gingko nuts and carrot on top of it and pour in the remaining egg stock mixture until 80 to 90% full. Steam over a high heat for about 1 min with the lid slightly askew. Then steam over a low heat for 6 to 7 min with the steamer completely covered.

7 Remove the cups from the steamer, and garnish with the trefoil stalks, cut into 1 1/5-inch lengths.

！ Tip on Tips

★ Don't steam *chawan-mushi* over a high heat for a long time, otherwise it will become spongy.

★ To see whether or not *chawan-mushi* is done, insert a bamboo skewer into the center. When it comes out clean, it means that the *chawan-mushi* is ready for serving.

Sake-steamed Short-Necked Clams
あさりの酒蒸し

春からおいしくなる "あさり" の旨さをあますことなくいただく

Short-necked clams are best enjoyed when spring comes

あさり
Short-necked clams

■材料（2人分）

あさり	300g
水	1 カップ
料理酒	1/2 カップ
昆布（5×10cm のもの）	1枚
しょう油	少々
塩	適宜
万能ねぎ（小口切り）	適宜

■ INGREDIENTS (serves 2)

300g short-necked clams
4/5 cup water (200 ㎖)
2/5 cup cooking sake (100 ㎖)
1 (2 × 4 inch) *konbu* kelp
Small quantity of soy sauce
Salt
Edge-cut *bannou-negi* onion

■作り方

1 あさりは、水1カップに対して塩小さじ1弱の割合の塩水（分量外）に30分くらいつけて、暗い場所におくか、新聞紙をかぶせて暗くし、砂を吐かせます。
※暗くするとあさりがよく砂を吐くといわれています。

2 あさりの殻と殻をこすり合わせてよく洗い、ぬめりや汚れを取ります。
※この時点で殻だけのものや、われているものは取り除きます。

3 鍋に水1カップ、料理酒2分の1カップ、昆布、しょう油少々と、**2**のあさりを入れて中火にかけ、ふたをします。

4 **3**を5〜6分煮て、あさりの殻が完全に開いたら、あさりを皿に盛り、煮汁をかけ、小口切りの万能ねぎを散らしていただきます。
※殻が開いていないものは死んでいるものですから、食べないようにしましょう。もしくは、身の入っていないものになります。

❗ コツのコツ

★あさりの砂が残っていると食感が悪くなりますので、きっちりと砂抜きをしましょう。

★砂抜きされたものが売っていますので、使用すると便利です。

★熱を通しすぎると、身がかたくなるので注意しましょう。

1-a

1-b

3

4

■ Directions

1 Soak the short-necked clams in salted water (slightly less than 1 tsp salt per 4/5 cup of water, except quantity) for about 30 min. Set aside in a dark place or cover with newspaper to let them spit their sand out.
※ It's said that clams will spit out sand in the dark.

2 Wash the clams well by rubbing them together.
※ Remove empty shells and those with cracks.

3 Put 4/5 cup water, 2/5 cup cooking sake, *konbu* kelp, a small amount of soy sauce and the clams into a pot, and place over a medium heat. Cover the pot.

4 Simmer for 5 to 6 min. When the shells have fully opened, arrange the clams in a bowl and pour on the simmered liquid and sprinkle edge-cut *bannou-negi* onion.
※ Don't eat the any clams that don't open because they were no longer alive or might not have meat inside.

❗ Tip on Tips

★ Ensure that the short-necked clams have thoroughly expelled the sand. Sand remaining in short-necked clams is unpleasant on the tongue.

★ Try to use short-necked clams that were already flushed of sand if available at stores.

★ Don't overcook the short-necked clams or they get hard.

Aluminum Foil-Steamed Cod
たらのホイル蒸し

たらと野菜のおいしさを蒸して、あますことなくいただく

Enjoy the delicate flavor of steamed whole cod and vegetables

■材料（2 人分）

たら（切り身）………	2 切れ
玉ねぎ………………	1/8 個
れんこん……………	約 2cm
えのきだけ…………	1/2 束
赤ピーマン…………	1/10 個
バター………………	大さじ 1
料理酒………………	大さじ 2

A
- 白すりごま … 大さじ 1
- しょう油 …… 大さじ 2
- 砂糖 …… 小さじ 1/2
- 万能ねぎ（小口切り）… 2 本分

スナップえんどう …… 2 個
塩・こしょう ……… 適量

■ INGREDIENTS (serves 2)

2 fillets cod
1/8 onion
About 3/4-inch lotus root
1/2 bundle *enokidake* mushrooms
1/10 red bell pepper
1 Tbsp butter
2 Tbsps cooking sake

A
- 1 Tbsp ground white sesame seeds
- 2 Tbsps soy sauce
- 1/2 tsp sugar
- 2 *bannou-negi* onions (cut into small rounds)

2 pods snap peas
Salt and pepper

■作り方

1 玉ねぎはへたを切り取り、皮をむいて約 7 〜 8mm の厚さの輪切りに、れんこんは皮をむいて約 1cm の厚さの輪切りに、えのきは根もとを切り取り、小房に分けます。赤ピーマンは短冊切りにします。スナップえんどうを塩（分量外）ゆでにします。Aを合わせてタレを作ります。

2 アルミホイルにたらをのせ、軽く塩、こしょうをします。

3 2 の上に 1 の玉ねぎ、れんこん、えのき、赤ピーマンの順にのせ、バターをおいて料理酒をふってアルミホイルを閉じます。グリルかオーブントースターで約 10 分焼きます。

4 3 を器に盛り、彩りに 1 のスナップえんどうをあしらい、1 のタレを添えます。

■ Directions

1 Cut off the root of the onion, peel, and cut into about 1/3-inch thick round slices. Peel the lotus root, and cut into 3/8-inch thick rounds. Chop off the base of the *enokidake* mushrooms, and separate into small portions. Cut the red bell pepper into rectangles. Boil the snap peas in salty water (extra quantity salt). Mix the ingredients of **A** to make the sauce.

2 Place the cod on aluminum foil sheets, and lightly sprinkle with salt and pepper.

3 Put on the ingredients in the order of onion, lotus root, *enokidake*, and red pepper. Add butter, and sprinkle with cooking sake. Close the foil wrap, and grill in a griller or toaster oven for about 10 min.

4 Place on a serving dish, open the foil, and garnish with the snap peas, and serve with the sauce.

Aluminum Foil-Steamed Oyster
かきのホイル蒸し

かきとみその相性が抜群で、酒のつまみに最適
The exceptional chemistry between oysters and miso perfectly suits sake

■材料（2人分）

生かき	6〜8粒
長ねぎ	1本
あさつき	1〜2本
みそ	大さじ2
砂糖	大さじ1
牛乳	大さじ1

■ INGREDIENTS (serves 2)

6 or 8 oysters
1 *naga-negi* onion
1 or 2 leaves *asatsuki* chive
2 Tbsps miso
1 Tbsp sugar
1 Tbsp milk

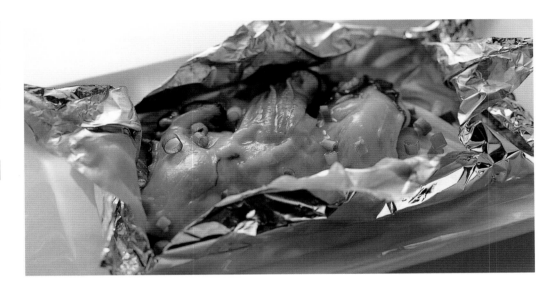

■作り方

1 生かきをザルに入れ、塩（分量外）を全体に軽くまぶし入れ、冷水でふり洗いをし、ぬめりと汚れを取った後、ペーパータオルなどで水けをふき取ります。

2 長ねぎは斜め切り、あさつきは小口切りにします。

3 器にみそと砂糖を入れてよく混ぜ、牛乳を入れてよく練り合わせます。

4 アルミホイルに2の長ねぎを最初に入れ、その上に1のかきをのせ、3のみそをかけて、アルミホイルの四方をたたみオーブントースターで10〜15分くらい焼き、2のあさつきをかけていただきます。

■ Directions

1 Place the oysters on a sieve and sprinkle salt (except quantity) lightly and wholly on the oysters. Wash the oysters while shaking together with the sieve in cold water and wipe dry.

2 Cut the *naga-negi* onion diagonally and *asatsuki* chives by using the edge cut technique.

3 Combine the sugar and the miso well. Add the milk and mix up thoroughly.

4 Place the *naga-negi* onion and oysters. Pour on the miso sauce prepared in 3. above and close the foil by folding all sides. Bake in an oven toaster for 10 to 15 min. Sprinkle on the *asatsuki* chives before serving.

❗ コツのコツ・Tip on Tips

★かきに塩を軽くまぶして、冷水でふり洗いをして、ぬめりと汚れを取ります。

★かきは、あまり火を通しすぎるとかたくなるので注意しましょう。

★ Remove sliminess and dirt from oysters by sprinkling salt lightly and shaking with a sieve in cold water.

★ Pay attention not to over-cook oysters otherwise they become hard.

Aluminum Foil-Steamed Chum Salmon
さけのホイル蒸し

about 20 min / 約20分

140 kcal / 140キロカロリー

脂がのったさけにみそダレがよくあい、ご飯やお酒がすすむ一品
Fatty chum salmon and miso sauce make a tasty combination, especially when paired with rice and sake

■ 材料 (4 人分)

さけの切り身	4 切れ	プチトマト	4 個
料理酒	小さじ2	〈みそダレの材料〉	
しょうがの絞り汁	小さじ1	みそ	大さじ3
キャベツ	2 枚	料理酒	大さじ1
玉ねぎ	1/2 個	みりん	大さじ2
しいたけ	2 枚	長ねぎ (みじんぎり)	1/3 本分
しめじ	1/2 パック	炒りごま (白)	小さじ1

■ INGREDIENTS (serves 4)

4 fillets chum salmon
2 tsp cooking sake
1 tsp fresh ginger juice
2 leaves cabbage
1/2 onion
2 shiitake mushrooms
1/2 packet *shimeji* mushrooms
4 cherry tomatoes

〈**For preparing miso sauce**〉
3 Tbsps miso
1 Tbsp cooking sake
2 Tbsps *mirin* sweet cooking sake
1/3 *naga-negi* onion, chopped finely
1 tsp white parched sesame

■ 作り方

1 さけの切り身に料理酒、しょうがの絞り汁をふりかけて10 分おきます。

2 キャベツは1 ～ 2cm の角切り、玉ねぎは薄切り、しめじは石づきを切り取り小房にわけます。しいたけは石づきを切り取り4 つに割ります。

3 みそに料理酒、みりんをよく練り混ぜみじん切りの長ねぎ、炒りごま (白) を加えてよく混ぜます。

4 アルミホイルに2 のキャベツ、玉ねぎ、しめじ、しいたけ、プチトマト、汁けをふいた1 のさけの切り身をのせ、3 のみそダレをかけて包み、オーブントースターで15 ～ 20 分焼きます。

5 焼き上がったらアルミホイルを開いていただきます。

■ Directions

1 Sprinkle the cooking sake and fresh ginger juice on the chum salmon fillets, and let stand for 10 min.

2 Cut the cabbage leaf into 3/8 to 3/4-inch squares. Slice the onion thinly. Chop off the hard tips of the stems of the *shimeji* mashrooms,and divide into small portions.Chop off the stem of the shiitake mushroom, and cut into quarters.

3 Mix the cooking sake, *mirin* and miso, and stir well. Add the chopped *naga-negi* onion and white parched sesame, and mix well.

4 Place the cabbage leaf, onion, *shimeji* mushrooms, shiitake mushroom, cherry tomatoes and fish (wiped dry) on aluminum foil, pour on the miso sauce prepared in 3. above and close the foil. Bake in an oven toaster for 15 to 20 min.

5 Open the foil, and eat.

❗ コツのコツ・Tip on Tips

★ 熱を通しすぎるとさけの身がパサパサになるので注意しましょう。

★ Be careful not to heat the fish too much, otherwise, the flesh will become dry and tasteless.

Basic Japanese Sashimi and Sushi Dishes

和食の基本・刺し身・寿し

一年で１番おいしい旬の魚介類を刺し身と寿しでいただく。和食の技と知恵が冴えわたる。祝いごとやおもてなし料理としても最適。そんな刺し身と寿しは、世界各国で大人気。

Enjoy the most delicious fresh fish and seafood in season in the freshest way—use the indicated techniques and pointers to make wonderful sashimi and sushi. Now popular around the world, these dishes are best for festive occasions and welcoming guests.

Thinly-Sliced *Madai* Red Sea Bream
真だいの薄造り

about 8 min / 約8分　113 kcal / 113キロカロリー

日本人の大好きなめでたい真だいをおいしくいただく

Enjoy an auspicious fish, *Madai* Red Seam Bream, a Japanese love

■材料（1人分）

真だい（刺身用さく）
………… 約4〜5cm
万能ねぎ …………… 2本
大根 ……… 約5〜6cm
鷹の爪（赤唐辛子）… 1本
ぽん酢しょう油 …… 適量

■ INGREDIENTS (serves 1)

1 1/2 to 2 inch block *madai* red sea bream (for sashimi)
2 *bannou-negi* onions
About 2 inches giant white radish
1 red chili pepper (red pepper)
Ponzu soy sauce (citrus-juice-mixed soy sauce)

◆薄造りに適した魚◆

Other fish suited to thin slices
◆かれい（まこがれい）・Sole (*karei* flounder)
◆ひらめ・Bastard halibut
◆すずき・Japanese sea bass perch
◆かわはぎ・File fish
◆まごち・Bartailed flathead

■ 作り方

1 大根は皮をむき、箸で穴をあけ、鷹の爪（赤唐辛子）のへたを切ったものを刺し、そのままおろし金でおろし、もみじおろしを作ります。

※大根が大きい場合は使用する鷹の爪の本数を増やすとよいでしょう。

2 万能ねぎは水洗いし、水けをふき取り約4cmの長さに切ります。

3 真だいのさくを薄造りにします。

4 器に3の真だいの薄造り、1のもみじおろし、2の万能ねぎをバランスよく盛ります。真だいの薄造りに万能ねぎを2〜3本のせて巻き、1のもみじおろしを適量身にのせて、ぽん酢しょう油でいただきます。

※しょう油とおろしわさびでもおいしいです。

1-a

1-b

1-c

1-d

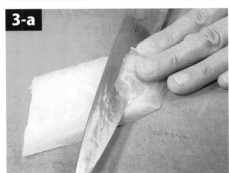

3-a

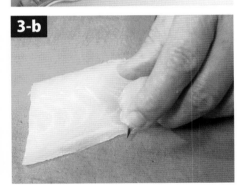

3-b

■ Directions

1 Peel the giant white radish. Dig a hole with a chopstick, and insert the red chili pepper (the calyx removed). Grate the giant white radish with a grater to make *momiji-oroshi*.

※ For a large *daikon*, use more cone peppers.

2 Wash the *bannou-negi* onions, and cut into a length of 1 1/2 inches.

3 Thinly slice the *madai* block.

4 Arrange the sliced *madai*, *momiji-oroshi*, and the *bannou-negi* onion on a plate beautifully. When you eat, place two to three pieces of the *bannou-negi* onions on a slice of *madai* then roll. Put some of the *momiji-oroshi* onto it and dip in *ponzu* soy sauce.

※ They are also delicious with soy sauce and grated wasabi.

!) **Tip on Tips**

★ Use a sharp knife when making thin slices of *madai* sashimi fillet.

★ When making thin slices of *madai*, use the whole blade of the knife.

Sliced Fresh Raw Tuna
まぐろの刺し身

ご飯のおかず、酒のつまみとして大人気の刺し身

A very popular delicacy, sashimi goes well with rice or sake

黒まぐろ（中トロ）
Bluefin tuna(Medium fatty tuna)

黒まぐろ（大トロ）
Bluefin tuna (Fatty tuna)

■材料（1人分）

まぐろ（刺し身用さく）
‥‥‥‥‥ 5～6cm
きゅうり ‥‥‥‥‥ 適量
大葉 ‥‥‥‥‥ 2枚
すりわさび ‥‥‥‥ 適量
しょう油 ‥‥‥‥‥ 適量

■ INGREDIENTS (serves 1)

5-6 cm long sashimi fillet of raw tuna
Cucumber
2 green perilla leaves
Grated *wasabi*
Soy sauce

■作り方

1 きゅうりは皮をむき、かつらむきにし、端から細く切りつまを作ります。大葉は水洗いして、水けをペーパータオルでふきとっておきます。

2 まぐろの刺し身用さくを横に置き、包丁の刃元を身の角に当て、包丁を引くようにしながら、刃の全体を使い、端から約1cmの厚さに切っていきます。

3 器に 1 の大葉をしき、その上に 2 のまぐろをおき、1 のきゅうりのつま、すりわさびを添えます。しょう油でいただきます。
※すりわさびをしょう油に入れて、そこにまぐろの刺し身をつけてもいいですし、まぐろの刺し身の上にすりわさびをのせ、まぐろの刺し身をしょう油につけていただいてもよいでしょう。

コツのコツ

★よく切れる包丁を使用しましょう。

★まぐろのさくを切る場合は、包丁の刃元から包丁の全体を使うように切りましょう。

★きゅうりの代わりに、大根のかつらむきや薄いいちょう切りでもよくあいます。

◆ まぐろの種類 ◆
Tuna species
◆黒まぐろ (本まぐろ)・bluefin tuna
※黒まぐろ (本まぐろ) は、まぐろの中の最高峰になります。
※ Bluefin tuna is considered to be the finest among the tunas.
◆南まぐろ (インドまぐろ) southern bluefin
◆目ばちまぐろ・bigeye tuna
◆黄はだまぐろ (わだまぐろ)・yellowfin tuna
◆びんながまぐろ (びんちょうまぐろ)・albacore

黒まぐろ
bluefin tuna

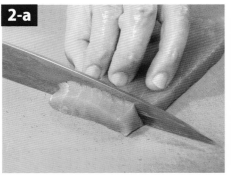

2-a

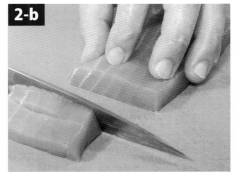

2-b

2-c

■ Directions

1 Prepare your garnish. Peel the cucumber and cut it thinly lengthwise while rotating the cucumber (*katsura-muki* cutting technique.) Cut the thin slice of cucumber into julienne strips from the edge. Wash the perilla leaves in water and pat dry with paper towels.

2 Place the sashimi fillet of raw tuna sideways. Place the bottom of your knife at the edge of the fillet and slice into 3/8-inch thick pieces by using the whole blade of your knife in a pulling motion.

3 Arrange the perilla leaves from step 1 on a plate. Place the tuna from step 2 onto them. Garnish with the cucumber from step 1 and grated *wasabi*. Serve with soy sauce.
※ When you eat, you can dissolve *wasabi* in soy sauce first and then dip your slice of tuna or you can place some *wasabi* on the tuna and then dip into soy sauce.

Tip on Tips

★ Use a very sharp knife.

★ When slicing the tuna fillet, use the whole blade of your knife.

★ Instead of cucumber, *daikon* radish cut by using the *katsura-muki* technique or cut in quarter-rounds also makes excellent garnish.

◆ まぐろの刺し身の切り方
Sliced fresh raw tuna cutting techniques

角造り・*Kaku-zukuri*

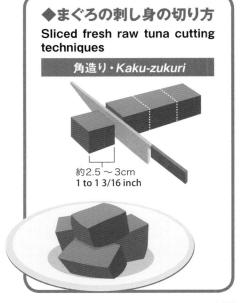

約2.5〜3cm
1 to 1 3/16 inch

Sliced Fresh Raw Horse Mackerel
あじの刺し身

about 20 min 約20分 | 138 kcal 138キロカロリー

脂ののったあじをおいしくいただく刺し身の定番

Fresh fatty horse mackerel is a standard dish among sashimi varieties

■材料（2〜3人分）

あじ（中）	3〜4尾
大根のつま	適量
大葉	1〜2枚
パセリ	適宜
あさつき（小口切り）	適宜
しょうが（おろし）	適宜
しょう油	適量

※大根のつまがなければ、大根の皮をむき、約2mmほどの厚さのいちょう切りを使用してもよいでしょう。

■ INGREDIENTS (serves 2〜3)

3 to 4 medium-size horse mackerels
Garnish made of giant white radish
1 to 2 perilla leaves
Parsley
Asatsuki-onion, edge-cut
Grated ginger
Soy sauce

※ If prepared garnish isn't available, you can make it by peeling the *daikon* and cutting into about 1/12-inch thick quarter rounds.

■作り方

1 35 ページを参照してあじを三枚におろします。あじの腹骨を包丁ですき取り、血合い骨を骨抜きで取ります。
※血合い骨は指でさわって探しましょう。

2 1のあじの皮目を下にして、頭側の端から手で皮を少し引っ張って少しむき、その皮をつまみ包丁のみね（背の部分）で尾の方向に皮目をしごくようにして、皮をはいでいきます。

3 2のあじの皮目を下にし、身の上に左手を軽く添え、包丁を斜めに当てて刃全体を使うようにして、好みの大きさに切ります。

4 皿に大根のつまを盛り、水洗いし水けをふき取った大葉をひいて、3のあじの刺し身をおき、上にパセリを飾ります。小皿にあさつき（小口切り）、しょうが（おろし）を入れ、添えます。しょう油にあさつき、しょうがを入れ、あじの刺し身をつけていただきます。

❗ コツのコツ

★あじは新鮮なもので、必ず刺し身用のものを使用しましょう。

★あじに手の温もりをつたえないよう短時間でさばきましょう。

★あじの皮を包丁のみねではぐ時は、皮をひっぱってはぐのがコツです。

★よく切れる包丁を使用し、刃全体を使うようにして、あじを切りましょう。

1-a

1-b

1-c

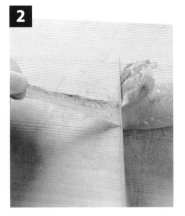

2

■ Directions

1 Referring to P. 35, fillet the horse mackerel into three. Slice off the bones around the stomach with your knife. Pick the bloody bones out of the meat with tweezers.
※ Find the bloody bones by feeling with your fingers.

2 Place the skin side of the horse mackerel from step 1 down. From the edge of the head side, peel the skin a little bit with your hands. Hold the skin with your fingers and insert the dull side of your knife between the skin and meat. Peel the skin toward the tail as though you are rubbing down on the skin with your knife.

3 Place the skin side of the horse mackerel from step 2 down. Place your left hand lightly and your knife diagonally on the fillet. Slice into the desired sizes by using the whole blade.

4 Arrange the giant white radish garnish and the washed and pat-dried perilla leaves on a plate. Place the horse mackerel from step 3 on the garnish. Serve with the edge-cut *asatsuki*-onions and grated ginger in a small plate. When you eat, put some *asatsuki*-onions and grated ginger in soy sauce and dip the horse mackerel.

❗ Tip on Tips

★ Use only fresh horse mackerel for sashimi.

★ Prepare the horse mackerel quickly in order not to warm the fish with your hands.

★ When you skin the horse mackerel with the dull side of your knife, pull the skin with your hand while peeling.

★ Use a very sharp knife and the whole blade of your knife when you slice the horse mackerel.

Bonito *Tataki* with an Array of Condiments
かつおのたたき

滋味あふれるかつおを薬味たっぷりでおいしくいただく
Enjoy a wholesome bonito delicacy with an array of garnish

■材料（2人分）

かつお（刺身用おろし身・皮つき）……… 1/2 節	塩……………………… 適量
しょうが …………… 1 片	ぽん酢しょう油 ……… 適量
にんにく …………… 1 片	※薬味には、玉ねぎのスライスなどもよくあいます。
万能ねぎ……………… 2 本	
みょうが …………… 1 個	
大葉 …………… 2 枚	
ピーマン ……… 1/4 個	

■ INGREDIENTS (serves 2)

1/2 block bonito (prepared for sashimi with skin)	Salt
1 knob ginger	*Ponzu* soy sauce (citrus-juice-mixed soy sauce)
1 clove garlic	※ Thin slices of onion are also good as garnish.
2 *bannou-negi* onions	
1 *mioga*	
2 green perilla leaves	
1/4 green sweet pepper	

■作り方

1 しょうがは皮をむき、すりおろします。にんにくは皮をむき、薄切りにします。万能ねぎは水洗いして、水けをよくふき取り小口切りにします。みょうがは根の部分を切り落とし、薄い輪切りにします。大葉は水洗いをし、水けをよくふき取りせん切りにします。ピーマンは水洗いをし、水けをよくふき取りへたと種を切り取り、せん切りにします。

2 かつおは熱したフライパンで全体の表面をさっと焼き、氷水（分量外）を入れたボウルに入れさっと冷まし、水けをペーパータオルなどでふき取ります。

3 2のかつおを、約1cmの厚さに切り、切り口に軽く塩をふり約20～30分おきます。

4 3のかつおを器に盛り、1の薬味をあしらい、ぽん酢しょう油をかけて、かつおを薬味とともにいただきます。

※かつおのたたきの本場は高知県です。ぽん酢しょう油をかけて、かつおの身になじむように手でたたいたのが、"かつおのたたき"の名の由来の一つともいわれています。

1 / 2-a / 2-b / 3

■ Directions

1 Peel the ginger, and grate. Skin the garlic, and slice thinly. Rinse the *bannou-negi* onion, pat-dry well and cut into small rounds. Cut off the root part of the *mioga*, and slice thinly into rounds. Rinse the green perilla leaves, pat-dry well and cut into thin strips. Wash the green sweet pepper, wipe off the moisture well, remove the stem and seeds and cut into thin strips.

2 Quickly fry the surface of the bonito in a heated frying pan, chill in iced water (extra amount), and paper-dry.

3 Cut the bonito into 3/8 inch-thick slices, and sprinkle salt on the cross section of the slices. Leave them for 20 to 30 min.

4 Arrange the sliced bonito on a serving dish, garnished with the condiments prepared in 1, and pour over the *ponzu* soy sauce. Eat the bonito with the prepared condiments.

※ The birthplace of bonito *tataki* is Kochi prefecture. The name tataki means "to strike or pat" and is believed to derive from the local tradition of patting down the sliced bonito after pouring the *ponzu* soy sauce on it so the flavor would soak into the meat.

How to Prepare Vinegared Rice
寿し飯の作り方

about **130**min 約130分

484kcal 484キロカロリー

ちらし寿しや巻き寿しなどに大活躍の寿し飯をきっちり作りたい

Master the preparation of perfect sushi rice, the base for garnished sushi, sushi rolls and others sushi dishes

■材料（2～3人分）

米	2 カップ
水	2 カップ
昆布	10cm
酢	1/4 カップ
砂糖	大さじ 2
塩	小さじ 1/2
酢＋水	適宜

■ INGREDIENTS (serves 2 ～ 3)

1 1/2 cups rice (360 ㎖)
1 2/3 cups water (400 ㎖)
4 -inch *konbu* kelp
1/5 cup vinegar (50 ㎖)
2 Tbsps sugar
1/2 tsp salt
Vinegar-added water

寿し飯を使用したちらし寿し
Garnished sushi prepared by
using the vinegared rice

■ 作り方

1 水に昆布を1時間くらい漬けてだしを取ります。米は炊く30分前にとぎ、ザルに上げておきます。

2 酢、砂糖、塩を小鍋に入れて溶かす程度に温めて、合わせ酢を作ります。

3 炊飯器に**1**の米とだし汁を入れて炊き上げ、約10分蒸らします。

4 酢水で湿らせた飯台にご飯をあけ、しゃもじでご飯を軽く広げます。そこに**2**の合わせ酢を回しかけ、うちわであおぎながらしゃもじで切るようにご飯を混ぜます。酢水で濡らした清潔なふきんをかけておきます。

※しゃもじで切るように合わせ酢をご飯に混ぜるのがポイントです。しゃもじでご飯をつぶさないようにしましょう。

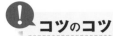

コツのコツ

★ご飯に合わせ酢を混ぜる時は、必ず切るように混ぜましょう。押しつぶすとご飯がつぶれてしまい、べたついた寿し飯になってしまいます。

★家庭に扇風機がある場合には、扇風機を微風にして首ふりにし、酢飯にやさしく風が当たるようにしながらしゃもじでご飯を混ぜると、簡単に冷ますことができ、つやのある寿し飯に仕上がります。

■ Directions

1 Soak the *konbu* kelp in the water for about one hour to make stock. Wash the rice 30 min prior to cooking, and drain on a sieve.

2 Put the vinegar, sugar and salt into a small pot, and heat slightly until dissolved. This completes the vinegar dressing.

3 Place the rice from step 1 and stock into a rice cooker, and cook. When cooking is finished, keep the cooker covered and let it stand for about 10 min until the grains are settled.

4 With a rice paddle, lightly spread the rice. Transfer the rice to a wooden sushi bowl moistened with vinegar-added water. Sprinkle the vinegar dressing all over the rice. Using a flat wooden spoon, toss the rice with horizontal, cutting strokes while cooling the rice with a hand-fan. When tossing is completed, cover the rice with a clean cloth moistened with vinegar-added water.

※ The key is to mix vinegar dressing with rice as if you are cutting the rice with the rice paddle. Be careful not to crush the rice with the paddle.

Tip on Tips

★ Wooden sushi bowls eliminate the excess moisture of cooked rice, and keep the grains firm.

★ Use an electric fan if any at home, and set the current of air low and let it swing in order to let the rice exposed to the breeze while mixing the rice. It will facilitate cooling off the rice and result in making tasty and glossy vinegared rice.

Sushi Roll
巻き寿し

行楽やお祝いごとにおすすめの "巻き寿し" を作りたい

Prepare sushi rolls for picnics or festive occasions

■材料 (2人分)

寿し飯 …… 米2カップ分	山ごぼうの漬けもの
焼きのり ………… 2枚	…………… 4〜6本
酢水 ……………… 適宜	でんぶ …… 大さじ 4〜5
卵焼き ……… 卵5個分	
かんぴょう (乾) …… 10g	
干ししいたけ ……… 4枚	
ほうれん草 ……… 4株	

■ INGREDIENTS (serves 2)

Vinegared rice, cooked with
1 1/2 cups (360㎖) rice
2 sheets toasted *nori* seaweed
Vinegar-added water
Omelet, cooked with 5 eggs
10g dried gourd strip
4 dried shiitake mushrooms

4 whole spinaches
4 to 6 pickled pokeweed
4 to 5 Tbsps *denbu* shredded and
seasoned fish flesh

■作り方

1 182、183 ページを参照して、寿し飯を作ります。

2 108, 109 ページを参照して卵焼きを作ります。43 ページを参照してかんぴょうを戻します。かんぴょうは切らずに長いままにしておきます。43 ページを参照して干ししいたけを戻します。しいたけの石づき、軸を取り薄切りにします。ほうれん草は下ゆでし、冷水に取って水けをよく絞って、根の部分を切ります。山ごぼうの漬けものは汁けをよくきります。

3 巻きすに焼きのり 1 枚をのせ（ざらざらした裏面が上にくるように置く）、寿し飯を軽くまとめてのせ、焼きのりの上下 2cm を残して寿し飯を広げます。

4 3 の寿し飯の上に 2 の具材をバランスよくのせます。

5 手前の巻きすと焼きのりを一緒に持ち上げ、具材をかかえ込むように、向こう側に一気にかぶせます。

6 巻きすをぐっと押さえながら、丸く形を整え、両端を酢水で濡らしたふきんで、中へしっかりと 2 〜 3 回押します。

7 1 本を 6 〜 8 等分に切り分けます。包丁は 1 回切るたびに、酢水のついたふきんで濡らして切ります。

コツのコツ
★巻く具材の処理が終了したら、きっちりと水けをきっておきましょう。
★焼きのりではないのりは手早く両面を火であぶり、パリッとさせてから使用しましょう。

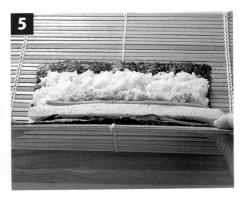

■ Directions

1 Make vinegared rice. (See P.182 and 183.)

2 Make an omelet (See P.108 and 109). Soften the dried gourd strip (See P.43). Leave the gourd strip as is without cutting. Soften the dried shiitake mushrooms (See P.43). Remove the stems of the mushrooms, and cut thinly. Boil the spinach in salted water, rinse in cold water, squeeze hard to remove moisture and cut off the roots. Remove the excess moisture of the pickled pokeweed.

3 Place a *nori* seaweed sheet on a *maki-su* bamboo mat. (Put the rough reverse side up.) Put the vinegared rice lightly on the nori sheet, and spread over the sheet leaving 3/4-inch at the top and bottom uncovered.

4 Place the core ingredients prepared in step 2 above on the rice evenly.

5 Lift the edges of both the bamboo mat and *nori* sheet nearest you, and bring over to meet the far edge of the sheet.

6 Gently but firmly press the bamboo mat around the roll to shape it. Push both ends of the roll towards the center firmly a few times using a cloth moistened with vinegar-added water.

7 Cut in sixths or eighths crosswise. Clean the knife with a vinegar water-moistened cloth between cuttings.

Tip on Tips
★ Make sure to remove the excess moisture from core ingredients after completing their preliminary preparations.
★ If you are not using a roasted seaweed sheet, toast each nori seaweed sheet by passing it over a high flame to make it dry and crispy just before rolling sushi.

Nigiri Sushi
にぎり寿し

ヘルシーでおいしくて世界中で人気の"にぎり寿し"を家庭で作る

It's healthy and popular worldwide and now you can make nigiri sushi at home

■材料（2〜3人分）

寿し飯 …… 米2カップ分	焼きのり ………… 1枚
えび ………… 5尾	おろしわさび ……… 適宜
まぐろ ……… 5切れ分	しょう油 ………… 適宜
たい ………… 5切れ分	しょうがの甘酢漬け … 適宜
いか ………… 1/3本	〈手酢〉
うに ………… 10片	水＋酢 ………… 適宜
いくら ……… 大さじ3	
卵焼き ……… 卵3個分	

■ INGREDIENTS (serves 2〜3)

Vinegared rice, cooked with
1 1/2 cups rice (360㎖)
5 shrimps
5 slices tuna
5 slices sea bream
1/3 squid
10 segments sea urchin
3 Tbsps salmon eggs
Omelet, cooked with 3 eggs

1 sheet toasted *nori* seaweed
Grated *wasabi* horseradish
Soy sauce
Sweet-vinegared ginger
〈**Tezu ("hand-vinegar")**〉
Water and vinegar

■ 作り方

1 182・183 を参照して、寿し飯を作ります。

2 えびは背わたを取り、まっすぐに伸ばして串を刺し、少量の水、酒、塩（すべて分量外）で炒り煮して殻をむき、腹から開きます。
※ 188 ページにイラスト解説があります。

3 まぐろのさくは厚さ 3 〜 5mm くらいの大きさに切ります。たい、いかはまぐろより少し薄めに切ります。
※ 188 ページにイラスト解説があります。

4 両手に手酢をつけ、右手で寿し飯を 20g くらい取り、軽くにぎりながらまとめます。左手にねたを取り、指の第二関節のあたりに広げます。右手は寿し飯を持ったまま人差し指でわさびを取り、左手のねたにつけます。
※ 188 ページにイラスト解説があります。

5 右手の寿し飯を、左手のねたの上にのせ、左手の親指で寿し飯の中央を軽く押し、右手の親指と中指で寿し飯の横を軽く押し、右手の人差し指で縦にくぼみをつけます。
※ 188 ページにイラスト解説があります。

6 ねたが上にくるようにひっくり返し、右手の人差し指と中指で押さえて寿し飯の形を整えます。
※ 188 ページにイラスト解説があります。

7 左手の上で、寿しを 180 度回転させ、右手の親指、人差し指で左右からはさみます。（えび、まぐろ、たい、いか、卵焼きはこの方法でにぎります）
※ 188 ページにイラスト解説があります。

8 うに、いくらは、のりを幅 3cm、長さ 12cm くらいの帯状に切り、にぎって形を整えた寿し飯のまわりに巻きます。寿し飯の上におろしわさびをのせ、ねたをのせます。
※ 188 ページにイラスト解説があります。

9 器に盛り、しょうがの甘酢漬け、しょう油を添えます。

❗ コツのコツ

★ 寿し飯は、あまり力を入れてにぎると、ご飯がつぶれてしまい、かたくなってしまうので、ふんわりとにぎるようにします。

★ にぎる時にあまり時間をかけると、寿し飯、ねたが体温で温まってしまうので、手早くにぎるようにします。

■ Directions

1 Make vinegared rice. (See P.182 and 183.)

2 Devein the shrimps, and skewer while straightening. Put the shrimps, as well as a small amount of water, sake and salt(except quantity), into a pot, and simmer while stirring until all the liquid is gone. Skin the shrimps, and open up the belly side.
※ Refer to P.188 for illustrated instructions.

3 Cut the fillet of tuna into 1/16 to 1/8 -inch pieces. Cut the sea bream and squid into slightly thinner pieces than the tuna.
※ Refer to P.188 for illustrated instructions.

4 Moisten your hands with hand-vinegar. Take about 20g rice in your right hand, and shape rice into a roughly rectangular form while rolling lightly. Lay a topping across the second joint of fingers of your left hand. Scoop up some wasabi with the index finger of the right hand while holding rice, and smear in the center of the topping in the left hand.
※ Refer to P.188 for illustrated instructions.

5 Put the rice in the right hand onto the topping in the left hand. Press the center of the rice lightly with the thumb of the left hand, press both sides of the rice lightly with the thumb and middle finger of the right hand and make a vertical indent on the top surface of the rice with the index finger of the right hand.
※ Refer to P.188 for illustrated instructions.

6 Turn the sushi over so that the topping faces up. Press and form the rice into a more defined shape with the index and middle fingers of the right hand.
※ Refer to P.188 for illustrated instructions.

7 Turn the sushi 180°on the palm of the left hand, and press both sides with the thumb and index finger of the right hand. (Follow the process from 4. to 7. for shrimp, tuna, sea bream, squid and omelet toppings.)
※ Refer to P.188 for illustrated instructions.

8 For sea urchin and salmon egg toppings, follow this process–Cut the nori sheet into about 1 1/5 × 4 3/4-inch long rectangles. Wind this *nori* rectangle around rolled and formed rice. Spread some grated *wasabi* on the rice, and add a topping.
※ Refer to P.188 for illustrated instructions.

9 Arrange the formed sushi rolls in a serving vessel, and garnish with the sweet-vinegared ginger. Offer also soy sauce for dipping.

❗ Tip on Tips

★ Be careful not to press the rice too hard, otherwise, the rice will be mashed, and become hard.

★ Don't spend too much time on rolling, otherwise the rice and topping will be warmed unnecessarily by your body heat. Roll as quickly as possible.

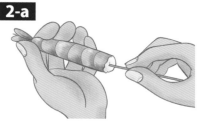

2-a

えびをまっすぐに伸ばして串を刺します。
Skewer the shrimp while straightening.

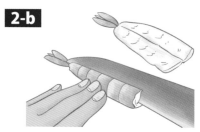

2-b

腹から開きます。
Open up the belly side.

3-a

まぐろのさくを厚さ3〜5mmくらいの大きさに切ります。
Cut the fillet of tuna into 1/16 to 1/8 -inch pieces.

3-b

たいはまぐろより少し薄めに切ります。
Cut the sea bream into slightly thinner pieces than the tuna.

4-a

右手で寿し飯を20gくらい取ります。
Take about 20g rice in your right hand.

4-b

軽く握りながらまとめます。
Shape rice into a roughly rectangular from while rolling lightly.

4-c

寿し飯がまとまったら、指の第2関節のあたりに乗せます。
Shape the rice and place across the second joints of your fingers.

4-d

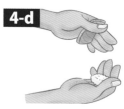

左手にねたを取り、指の第2関節あたりに広げます。
Lay a topping across the second joint of fingers of your left hand.

4-e

寿し飯を持ったまま、右手の人差し指でねたにわさびをつけます。
Smear some *wasabi* on the topping with the index finger of your right hand while holding the rice.

5-a

左手の親指で寿し飯の中央を軽く押します。
Press the center of the rice lightly with the thumb.

5-b

右手の人差し指で縦にくぼみをつけます。
Make a vertical indent on the top surface of the rice with the index finger of the right hand.

6-a

ねたが上にくるようにひっくり返します。
Turn the sushi over so that the topping faces up.

6-b

右手の人差し指と中指で押さえて寿し飯の形を整えます。
Press and form the rice into a more defined shape with the index and middle fingers of the right hand.

7

人差し指で左右からはさみます。
Press both sides with the thumb and index finger of the right hand.

8-a

のりを幅3cm、長さ12cmくらいの帯状に切ります。
Cut the *nori* sheet into about 11/5 × 4 3/4-inch long rectangles.

8-b

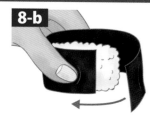

寿し飯のまわりにのりを巻きます。
Wind this nori rectangle around rolled and formed rice.

8-c

ねたをのせます。
Add a topping.

にぎり寿しのバリエーション

Variations of Sushi

186 ～ 188 ページで紹介したにぎり寿しや軍艦巻き以外にも、季節や旬によって数多くの寿しがあります。ここでは代表的なにぎり寿しや巻寿しを紹介します。

作り方は、186 ～ 188 ページを、巻き寿しは 184・185 ページを参照してください。

Depending on the season, you can find a variety of sushi ingredients other than nigiri sushi and gunkan sushi rolls illustrated on P.186 ～ 188. In this column, we introduce the typical ingredients used for them.
Please refer to P.186 ～ 188 for directions. For sushi rolls, see P.184 and 185.

にぎり寿し・Nigiri Sushi

まぐろ中トロ・Medium fatty tuna
脂がのっていて子どもにも人気の中トロ

It's called "*chutoro*" and it's very fatty and popular among children

あじ・Horse mackerel
青魚の代表で、脂がのりはじめる夏が旬

A representative of blue-skin fish, it's best enjoyed in summer as it starts getting fatty.

かんぱち・Great amberjack
脂がのりはじめる夏が旬

Great amberjack is best enjoyed in summer as it starts getting fatty.

甘えび・Northern shrimp
老若男女に人気の甘えび。えび類の寿しねたの代表

Popular among men and women of all generations. A common shrimps and prawns ingredient for sushi.

サーモン・Salmon
老若男女に人気。おもに回転寿司のねたになる

Popular among men and women of all generations. It's commonly served in sushi-go-round restaurants.

あなご・Conger ell
江戸前寿しを代表する一品

A typical *Edo*-style sushi ingredient.

ほたて・Scallop
かい類の寿しねたの代表

A common shellfish ingredient for sushi.

たこ・Octopus
日本人が大好きなたこ。生とゆでがある

Loved by the Japanese. Both boiled and raw can be used.

巻き寿し・Sushi Roll

かっぱ巻き・"*Kappa-maki*" Cucumber roll
"かっぱ" が好きなきゅうりを巻いた寿し

The name derives from an imaginative animal "kappa" that loves cucumber.

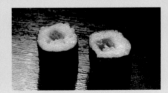
かんぴょう巻き・Gourd strip roll
滋味深いかんぴょうがおいしい。伝統的な巻き寿し

Wholesome tasty gourd strips are a traditional ingredient in sushi rolls.

鉄火巻き・Tuna roll
まぐろの赤身を巻いたもので、食べやすい

It's mild because the red meat of the tuna is used.

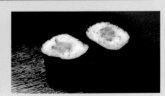
ねぎトロ巻き・Tuna and *naga-negi* onion roll
まぐろのトロと長ねぎを刻んだものを巻いた寿し

Minced fatty meat of tuna (toro) and *naga-negi* onions are rolled inside.

Hand-rolled Sushi
手巻き寿し

about 30min 約30分　1103kcal 1103キロカロリー

好きなものを巻いて食べれるから子どもも大好き、手巻き寿しでパーティーはいかが

How about a hand-rolled sushi party? Children and adults love to choose their favorite fillings to roll into their sushi

■材料（2〜3人分）

寿し飯 ······ 米 2 カップ分
焼きのり（手巻き寿し用）
·············· 10〜15 枚
※好みの大きさののりを使うとよい
まぐろ ·············· 5 切れ
ほたて ·············· 5 枚
いくら ·············· 大さじ 3
えび ·············· 5 尾
水・料理酒・塩 ··· 各少々
卵焼き ·········· 卵 3 個分
サラダ菜、エンダイブ、
かいわれ大根、大葉 ··· 各少々

〈いかめんたい〉
いか（刺し身用）··· 1/3 枚
めんたいこ ········· 1/2 腹

〈たくあん ＆ 炒りごま（黒）〉
たくあん ·········· 8cm
炒りごま（黒）··· 小さじ 1

〈コロコロあえ〉
たこ ·············· 1/2 足
セロリ ·············5cm
トマト ·············· 1/4 個
きゅうり ·········· 1/3 本

フレンチドレッシング ··· 大さじ 1
塩・こしょう ······ 各少々

〈アボガド ＆ ツナマヨ〉
アボガド ·········· 1/2 個
ツナ缶（小）··· 小1と1/2 缶
マヨネーズ ······ 大さじ 1
塩・こしょう ······ 各少々
レモン汁 ······· 小さじ 1

〈カレーチーズ〉
カッテージチーズ
·············· 大さじ 4
玉ねぎ ············· 1/8 個
あさつき ·········· 3〜4 本
カレー粉 ······ 小さじ 1/2
マヨネーズ··· 大さじ 1と1/2

■ INGREDIENTS (2 or 3)

Vinegared rice, cooked with 1
1/2 cups rice (360㎖)
10 to 15 toasted *nori* seaweed
(for hand-rolled sushi)
※ Use sny size according to your
preference.
5 slices tuna
5 scallop adductor muscles
3 Tbsps salmon eggs
5 shrimps
Pinch water, cooking sake, salt
Omelet, cooked with 3 eggs
Small quantity of *saradana*,
endive and green perilla leaves,
as well as young giant white
radish shoots

〈**For preparing squid with chili
pepper-flavored Alaska pollack roe**〉
1/3 fillet squid
1/2 piece *mentaiko* chili pepper-
flavored Alaska pollack roe

〈**For preparing pickled giant
white radish with black sesame**〉
3 -inch *takuan* pickled giant
white radish

1 tsp black parched sesame

〈**For preparing koro-koro-
ae dressed ingredients**〉
1/2 octopus tentacle
2 -inch celery
1/4 tomato
1/3 cucumber
1 Tbsp French dressing
Pinch salt and pepper

〈**For preparing avocado
with tuna mayonnaise**〉
1/2 avocado
1 1/2 small-size can of tuna
1 Tbsp mayonnaise
Pinch salt and pepper
1 tsp lemon juice

〈**For preparing curry cheese**〉
4 Tbsps cottage cheese
1/8 onion
3 to 4 leaves *asatsuki* chive
1/2 tsp curry powder
1 1/2 Tbsp mayonnaise

■ 作り方

1 182・183 ページを参照して、寿し飯を作ります。

2 まぐろを巻きやすい大きさに切ります。えびは背わたを取り、少量の水、料理酒、塩で炒り煮にして殻をむきます。108・109 ページを参照して、卵焼きを作り、巻きやすい大きさに切ります。

3 皮をむいたいかは細切りにし、ほぐしためんたいこと混ぜ合わせます。

■ Directions

1 Make vinegared rice. (See P.182 and 183.)

2 Cut the tuna slices into strips of easy-to-roll size. Devein the shrimps. Place the shrimps, as well as a small amount of water, cooking psake and salt in a pot, and simmer while stirring until all the liquid is gone. Skin the shrimps. Make an omelet (See P.108 and 109), and cut into strips of easy-to-roll size.

3 Cut the skinned squid into thin strips. Tear apart the mentaiko, and mix with the chopped squid.

2-a
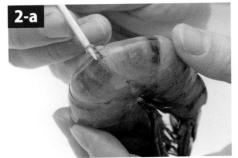

2-b

3

4 たくあんを3〜4cm長さのせん切りにし、炒りごま（黒）をまぶします。

5 たこ、水洗いしたセロリ、トマト、きゅうりは水けをふき取り、すべて5mm角に切り、ボウルなどに入れ混ぜ、塩、こしょうをし、フレンチドレッシングであえます。

6 アボガドは皮をむいて種を取り、粗みじん切りにし、ツナ、レモン汁、塩、こしょう、マヨネーズであえます。

7 玉ねぎは皮をむいてみじん切りにし、水にさらし、水けをきっておきます。あさつきは水洗いをし小口切りにします。ボウルに玉ねぎ、あさつき、カッテージチーズを入れ、カレー粉、マヨネーズであえます。

8 サラダ菜、エンダイブは水洗いし、食べやすい大きさに切ります。かいわれ大根は根を切り、水洗いします。大葉は水洗いし、かたい茎を切り取ります。

9 焼きのりに寿し飯、野菜、好みの具をのせ、巻いていただきます。

！ コツのコツ

★巻きに使用する野菜やせん切りにする野菜は下ごしらえをしたらきっちりと水けをきりましょう。

★巻く時に、寿し飯、具をたくさんのせすぎると巻けなくなるので注意しましょう。

4 Cut the *takuan* pickled giant white radish into julienne strips. Sprinkle on the black sesame.

5 Cut the octopus tentacle, washed celery, tomato and cucumber into 1/8-inch cubes, place in a bowl and mix. Add salt and pepper, and dress the ingredients with French dressing.

6 Peel the avocado and remove the seed. Chop coarsely and mix with the canned tuna, lemon juice, salt, pepper and mayonnaise.

7 Peel the onion and chop finely. Expose to cold water and remove excess water. Rinse the *asatsuki* chive leaves in cold water, and cut using the edge cut technique. Place the chopped onion, asatsuki chive leaves, cottage cheese, curry powder and mayonnaise in a bowl, and mix.

8 Rinse the *saradana* and endive leaves in cold water, and cut into bite-sized pieces. Remove the roots of the young giant white radish shoots, and rinse in cold water. Rinse also the green perilla leaves in cold water, and chop off the hard stalks.

9 Place the vinegared rice, as well as vegetables and other ingredients of your choice, on a toasted *nori* seaweed sheet, and roll.

！ Tip on Tips

★ Remove the moisture from vegetables thoroughly prior to using as is or chopping.

★ Be careful not to place too large a quantity of rice and ingredients on a nori seaweed sheet, otherwise rolling will be extremely difficult.

★ Simple boiled rice can also be used instead of vinegared rice.

Garnished Sushi
ちらし寿し

about 30 min 約30分

874 kcal 874キロカロリー

祝いの日や特別な日に作りたい、きれいでおいしい "ちらし寿し"

Garnished sushi is visually beautiful and as tasty as it looks. It's a festive dish for special days

■材料（2〜3人分）

寿し飯 ……… 2 カップ分

A
- 卵 …………… 2 個
- 砂糖 ……… 小さじ 1
- 塩 …………… 少々
- サラダ油 …… 適宜

B
- えび ………… 6 尾
- 水・塩 …… 各適宜
- だし汁 …… 大さじ 3
- 酢 …………… 大さじ 1
- 砂糖 ……… 小さじ 1
- 塩 …………… 少々

C
- 干ししいたけ … 4 枚
- だし汁 … 1/2 カップ
- 砂糖 ……… 大さじ 2
- みりん …… 大さじ 1
- しょう油 … 大さじ 1

D
- かんぴょう（乾）…10g
- 水 …………… 適宜
- 塩 …………… 適宜
- だし汁 …… 1 カップ
- 砂糖 ……… 大さじ 3
- しょう油 … 大さじ 2
- みりん …… 大さじ 2

E
- にんじん …… 1/2 本
- だし汁 … 1/2 カップ
- 砂糖 ……… 小さじ 1
- 塩 …………… 少々
- みりん …… 小さじ 1

F
- ごぼう ……… 1/3 本
- だし汁 … 1/3 カップ
- 砂糖 ……… 小さじ 1
- しょう油 … 小さじ 1
- みりん …… 小さじ 1

G
- れんこん …… 40g
- だし汁 …… 大さじ 3
- 酢 …………… 大さじ 2
- 砂糖 ……… 大さじ 1
- 塩 …………… 少々
- 酢水 ………… 適宜

H
- さやえんどう …8〜10枚
- 湯 …………… 適宜
- 塩 …………… 適宜

炒りごま（白）… 大さじ 1

■ INGREDIENTS (serves 2 or 3)

Vinegared rice, cooked with 1 1/2 cups rice (360 ㎖)

A
- 2 eggs
- 1 tsp sugar
- Pinch salt
- Vegetable oil

B
- 6 shrimps
- Water and salt
- 3 Tbsps stock
- 1 Tbsp vinegar
- 1 tsp sugar
- Pinch salt

C
- 4 dried shiitake mushrooms
- 2/5 cup stock (100 ㎖)
- 2 Tbsps sugar
- 1 Tbsp mirin sweet cooking sake
- 1 Tbsp soy sauce

D
- 10g dried gourd strip
- Water
- Salt
- 4/5 cup stock (200 ㎖)
- 3 Tbsps sugar
- 2 Tbsps soy sauce
- 2 Tbsp mirin sweet cooking sake

E
- 1/2 carrot
- 2/5 cup stock (100 ㎖)
- 1 tsp sugar
- Pinch salt
- 1 tsp mirin sweet cooking sake

F
- 1/3 burdock
- 2/7 cup stock (66㎖)
- 1 tsp sugar
- 1 tsp soy sauce
- 1 tsp mirin sweet cooking sake

G
- 40g lotus root
- 3 Tbsps stock
- 2 Tbsps vinegar
- 1 Tbsp sugar
- Pinch salt
- Vinegar-added water

H
- 8 to 10 snow peas
- Hot water
- Salt

1 Tbsp white parched sesame

■作り方

1 182・183 ページを参照して、寿し飯を作ります。

2 最初に具材を切ります。

A—卵は切るように溶きほぐし、砂糖と塩を混ぜ、こし器でこします。フライパンにサラダ油を薄く引き、卵液を流して薄焼き卵を作ります。焼き上がったら、冷ましてせん切りにし、錦糸卵を作ります。

B—だし汁、酢、砂糖、塩を合わせて調味液を作ります。えびは背わたを取り、小鍋に入れひたひたの水と塩を入れて炒り煮します。冷めたら殻をむいて、調味液に漬けておきます。

C—干ししいたけは、水で戻し、軸を切ります。小鍋にだし汁、砂糖、しいたけを入れ、弱火で5分煮ます。みりんとしょう油を加え、汁けがほとんどなくなるまで煮含めます。冷めたら5cm角に切ります。

D—かんぴょうはさっと水洗いし塩でよくもみ、塩けを水で洗います。鍋に多めの水とかんぴょうを入れてゆで、爪あとがつくくらい柔らかくなったら水洗いします。鍋にだし汁、砂糖、かんぴょうを入れて5分ほど弱火で煮ます。しょう油、みりんを加え、汁けがほとんどなくなるまで煮含めます。冷めた

ら1cmの長さに切ります。

E—にんじんは皮をむいて、半分は3cmの長さにせん切り、もう半分は5mmの厚さに切って花形に抜きます。鍋にだし汁、砂糖、塩、みりん、にんじんを入れ、煮汁で柔らかくなるまで弱火で煮含めます。

F—ごぼうは皮を包丁の背でこそげ、5～6mmの角切りにし、水にさらします。鍋にだし汁、砂糖、ごぼうを入れて5分くらい弱火で煮ます。しょう油、みりんを加え煮汁がほとんどなくなるまで煮ます。

1

2-A

2-B

2-C

■ Directions

1 Make vinegared rice. (See P.182 and 183)

2 Prepare ingredients as follows:
A—Beat the eggs with cutting strokes. Add the sugar and salt to the beaten eggs, and strain. Coat a frying pan thinly with vegetable oil, pour in the beaten eggs and make a paper-thin omelet. When cool, fold and cut into julienne strips.

B—Mix the stock, vinegar, sugar and salt to make seasoning liquid. Devein the shrimps. Put just enough salt and water in a pot to cover the shrimps. Add the shrimps to the pan, and simmer while stirring until all the liquid is gone. When cool, shell the shrimps, soak in the seasoning liquid and set aside.

C—Soak the dried shiitake mushrooms in cold water to soften, and remove the stems. Put the stock, sugar and shiitake mushrooms into a small pan, and place over a low heat for 5 min. Add the mirin sweet cooking sake and soy sauce, and simmer until the liquid is almost evaporated. When cool, cut the simmered shiitake mushrooms into 1/8-inch ×1/8-inch squares.

D—Rinse the dried gourd strip briefly in cold water, rub hard withsalted hands and wash away

the salt with cold water. Place the gourd strip and plenty of water in a pot, and boil. When the gourd strip becomes soft to the extent that you can leave a nail mark on the surface when pinching, rinse in cold water. Put the stock, sugar and gourd strip in a pot, and simmer over a low heat for about 5 min. Add the soy sauce and *mirin* sweet cooking sake, and simmer until the liquid is almost gone. When cool, cut the simmered gourd strip into 3/8-inch lengths.

E—Peel the carrot, and cut in half crosswise. Cut one half into about 1/16-inch wide julienne strips. Slice the remaining half into

G—れんこんは皮をむいて薄切りにし、半分はいちょう切りにし、酢水に漬けます。れんこんをさっと熱湯でゆで、熱いうちに合わせておいた調味液に漬けて味をなじませ、そのまま冷まします。

H—さやえんどうは筋を取り、塩を入れた湯でさっとゆで冷水に取ります。それを半分くらいの大きさに切ります。

3 人肌くらいになった寿し飯に、炒りごま、2で作ったしいたけ、ごぼう、かんぴょう、せん切りのにんじんを混ぜ合わせて器に盛り、錦糸卵を散らし、れんこん、えび、花形のにんじん、さやえんどうを彩りよく飾ります。

コツのコツ

★寿し飯を作る時に、合わせ酢を回しかけたご飯をしゃもじで切るようにほぐして、ご飯がつぶれないようにしましょう。つぶれるとべたついた寿し飯になってしまいます。

★ご飯がベタつかないように、うちわであおぎながら手早く切り混ぜましょう。

1/8-inch pieces, and stamp out into a flower shape. Place the stock, sugar, salt, *mirin* sweet cooking sake and both the shredded and sliced carrot in a pot, and simmer over a low heat until tender.

F—Scrape off the skin of the burdock using the back of a knife. Cut into 1/8 to 1/4-inch cubes, and rinse in cold water. Place the stock, sugar and burdock in a pot, and simmer over a low heat for about 5 min. Add the soy sauce and *mirin* sweet cooking sake, and continue to simmer until the liquid is almost gone.

G—Peel the lotus root, and slice thinly. Cut the slices into either half-moons or quarter-rounds. Immerse them in vinegar-added water. Boil briefly, and while hot, soak in the seasoning liquid made of the stock, vinegar, sugar and salt. Make sure that the half-moons or quarter-rounds are completely submerged in the liquid. Let stand until cool.

H—String the snow peas, boil briefly in boiling salted water and rinse in cold water. Cut into half-lengths.

3 When the vinegared rice is cooled to body temperature, mix it with the parched sesame, as well as the shiitake mushrooms, burdock, gourd strip and shredded carrot prepared in 2. above, and place everything into a serving vessel. Scatter the egg threads all over the rice, and decorate the surface colorfully with the lotus root, shrimps, carrot flowers and snow peas.

Tip on Tips

★ When mixing the vinegar dressing with rice using a flat wooden spoon to prepare vinegared rice, always use a sideways cutting motion to prevent the grains from being mashed. If mashed, the texture will become pasty.

★ Don't let the rice get too mushy. Mix it quickly using a sideways cutting motion while cooling the rice with a hand fan.

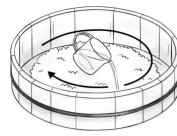

合わせ酢を外側から回しかけ、全体にまんべんなく回しかけます。
Sprinkle the vinegar dressing from the edge in a circular motion. Sprinkle evenly all over the rice.

うちわであおぎながら、しゃもじでご飯を切るように混ぜます。
Using a flat wooden spoon, toss the rice with horizontal, cutting strokes while cooling the rice with a hand fan.

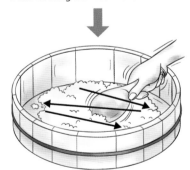

ご飯がベタつかないように手早く切り混ぜます。
Mix awiftly using a sideways cutting motion to prevent the rice from becoming mushy.

Sushi Pockets
いなり寿し

about **20**min 約20分 | **833**kcal 833キロカロリー

味のしみた油揚げと寿し飯のハーモニーがおいしい
A tasty combo of fully-flavored deep-fried tofu and vinegared rice

■材料（2～3人分）

寿し飯 …… 米2カップ分	〈干ししいたけ用だし汁の材料〉
油揚げ ……………… 6枚	だし汁 ……… 1/2カップ
炒りごま（白）… 大さじ3	砂糖 ………… 大さじ1
にんじん …… 1/4本分	みりん ………… 大さじ1
干ししいたけ … 4枚分	しょう油 ……… 大さじ1
〈にんじん用だし汁の材料〉	〈油揚げ用だし汁の材料〉
だし汁 …… 1/2カップ	だし汁 … 1と1/2カップ
砂糖 ……… 小さじ1	砂糖 ………… 大さじ3
塩……………… 少々	水あめ ……… 大さじ2
みりん …… 小さじ1	料理酒 …… 大さじ2
	しょう油 …… 大さじ3

■ INGREDIENTS (serves 2 or 3)

Vinegared rice, cooked with 1 1/2 cups rice (360㎖)	〈For simmering dried shiitake mushroomss〉
6 slices *abura-age* deep-fried tofu	2/5 cup stock (100㎖)
3 Tbsps white parched sesame	1 Tbsp sugar
1/4 carrot	1 Tbsp *mirin* sweet cooking sake
4 dried shiitake mushrooms	1 Tbsp soy sauce
〈For simmering carrot〉	〈**For simmering abura-age**〉
2/5 cup stock (100㎖)	1 1/4 cups stock (300㎖)
1 tsp sugar	3 Tbsps sugar
Pinch salt	2 Tbsps glucose
1 tsp *mirin* sweet cooking sake	2 Tbsps cooking sake
	3 Tbsps soy sauce

■作り方

1 182・183 ページを参照して、寿し飯を作ります。

2 にんじんの皮をむき、2〜3cm の長さのせん切りにします。干ししいたけは戻してから 5mm 角に切ります。にんじん、干ししいたけをだし汁で弱火で煮含め、取り上げておきます。
※干ししいたけの戻しかたは、43 ページを参照してください。

3 油揚げはまな板の上におき、菜箸を上から転がします。縦半分に切り指先で開きます。

4 3 の油揚げをゆでて油抜きをします。煮たてただし汁に入れ、料理酒、砂糖、水あめを加えて、約 5 分煮ます。

5 4 にしょう油を加えて落としぶたをし、汁けがなくなるくらいまで煮含めます。

6 寿し飯に炒りごま、2 のにんじん、干ししいたけを混ぜ合わせます。

7 油揚げの汁けを軽く絞ってから、6 の寿し飯をすみずみまで詰めます。形を整え、口を折りたたみます。

コツのコツ

★油揚げをたっぷりの湯で油抜きをしてから調理しましょう。

★具材の汁けをきらないと寿し飯が水っぽくなるので注意しましょう。

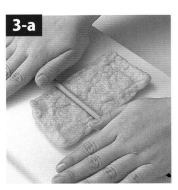

3-a

3-b

5

7-a

7-b

■ Directions

1 Make vinegared rice. (See P.182 and 183.)

2 Peel the carrot, and cut into 3/4 to 1 1/5-inch julienne strips. Soften the dried shiitake mushrooms, and cut into 1/8-inch cubes. Simmer the carrot and mushrooms in the simmering liquid over a low heat until seasoned thoroughly. Set aside.
※ Please refer to P.43 for how to reconstitute dried shiitake mushrooms.

3 Place the *abura-age* deep-fried tofu on a cutting board, and roll one cooking chopstick over it to make it easy to open. Cut the *abura-age* in half lengthwise, and open each pocket using the fingertips.

4 Boil the *abura-age* to remove excess oil. Place the *abura-age* in boiled stock, add the cooking sake, sugar and glucose, and simmer for about 5 min.

5 Add the soy sauce to the *abura-age* simmering liquid, cover with a drop-lid and simmer until the liquid is almost gone.

6 Add the white sesame, carrot and shiitake mushrooms to the vinegared rice, and mix.

7 Squeeze the *abura-age* lightly to remove moisture. Fill each *abura-age* pocket with the vinegared rice. Adjust the shape, and fold the opening.

Tip on Tips

★ Remove excess oil from *abura-age* by boiling it in plenty of water before cooking.

★ Make sure to eliminate as much moisture from each ingredient as possible. Otherwise, the vinegared rice will become damp.

にぎり寿しの発祥

Origin of Nigiri Sushi

　寿しの発祥は、米飯を使い魚介を発酵させた〝馴れ寿し〟だといわれています。その後、酢飯の上に魚介をのせた〝箱詰め寿し〟が登場します。

　現在、世界中で親しまれている〝にぎり寿し〟の発祥は、いつ頃なのでしょうか…。諸説ありますが、江戸時代の文化文政の頃、江戸に住む花屋與兵衛が考案したといわれています。

　当時のにぎり寿しは、大人のにぎりこぶし程の大きさがあり、まるでおにぎりのようだったといわれています。おしぼりもあるわけではなく、汚れた指をのれんで拭くのが通で、のれんの汚れ具合で江戸っ子たちは繁盛店であることを知ったみたいです。

　江戸時代のねたは、こはだ、車えび、さば、あじ、きす、あゆ、あかがいなどが代表になります。現在、人気のまぐろは下魚とされ、

江戸時代の寿しねたがよくわかる。小肌、鱚（きす）、車えび、あじ、あかがいなどが描かれている口絵

Illustration of spotted shad, prawns, horse mackerel, ark clam and other sushi ingredients, drawn during the *Edo* period, providing us with the sushi ingredient information of that time

『偲ぶ与兵衛の鮓』（小泉清三郎著　吉野昇雄［解説］主婦の友社刊〈1989年〉／国立国会図書館所蔵）

見向きもされませんでした。しかし、天保時代にまぐろが大量にとれたため、赤身をしょう油につけてにぎったところ人気になり、その後、にぎり寿しの定番になりました。

　現在、高級食材のトロは脂が強く、当時は捨てられていたといわれます。なんとも、もったいない話です。

The origin of sushi is believed to be "*nare*-sushi," made with rice and fermented seafood. Afterward, "*hakozume*-sushi," packed vinegared rice topped with seafood, appeared.

Currently nigiri sushi is enjoyed all over the world, but when did it get its start? There are several theories, but it's widely acknowledged that *Hanaya Yohei* from *Edo* (current Tokyo) came up with the dish during the *Edo* period.

It's said that nigiri sushi at that time used to be as big as an adult's fist. Back then, people wiped their fingers with shop curtains hung outside as wet wipes were not available. The people of *Edo* inspected those curtains to judge how popular the stores were.

Typical ingredients used during the *Edo* period were spotted shad, prawns, Spanish mackerel, horse mackerel, Japanese Sillago, *ayu* and ark clams. Tuna, popular now, wasn't used as an ingredient at first, but it became common after a large catch of tuna during the *Tempo* period. It's said that they soaked tuna meat in soy sauce and then made nigiri sushi. After that, it became a standard ingredient.

The fatty part of tuna, "*toro*," so commonly savored today—and very expensive—used to be discarded because it was thought to be too fatty. What a waste!

第十章
Chapter 10

Basic Japanese Tofu Dishes
和食の基本・豆腐料理

ヘルシーながら滋味あふれる味で、世界中で人気の豆腐料理。伝統的な冷ややっこ、豆腐田楽、
揚げ出し豆腐から、豆腐ステーキなどを紹介。豆腐のおいしさを堪能したい。
Tofu dishes are now very popular around the world for their healthy attributes and
flavorful taste. In this chapter, we introduce traditional chilled tofu, tofu *dengaku*, deep-
fried tofu with amber sauce and tofu steak. Enjoy these tasty tofu dishes.

Chilled Tofu
冷ややっこ

食欲の落ちる夏に最適な涼しげな " 冷ややっこ "
Refreshing chilled tofu is great on summer days when it's too hot to eat

■材料（4人分）

絹ごし豆腐（木綿豆腐でもよい）
···1丁
しょう油 ····················· 適宜
〈薬味〉
大葉（せん切り）············· 適宜
みょうが（小口切り）········ 適宜
万能ねぎ（小口切り）········ 適宜
しょうが（おろし）········· 適宜
削り節····················· 適宜
白ごま····················· 適宜

■ INGREDIENTS (serves 4)

1 cake "silken" tofu (or "cotton" tofu)
Soy sauce
〈**For condiments**〉
Green perilla leave, julienne-strip
Mioga Japanese ginger, edge-cut
Naga-negi onion, edge-cut
Bannnou-negi onion, edge-cut
Grated ginger
Dried bonito flakes
White sesame seeds

冷ややっこ Chilled Tofu (Image photo)

■作り方

1 ボウルに水をはり、あらかじめ冷蔵庫で冷やして冷水を作り、絹ごし豆腐を入れてラップをし、冷蔵庫に入れて食べる直前までよく冷やしておきます。

2 1の絹ごし豆腐を好みの大きさに切り、新しく冷水をはった器に入れます。

3 豆腐をすくい、しょう油と好みの薬味を添えていただきます。

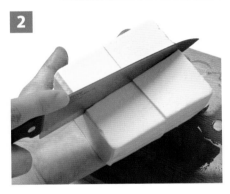

■ Directions

1 Fill a bowl with water and let it chilled in a refrigerator in advance. Put the tofu in the bowl and cover with plastic wrap. Let stand in the refrigerator to be chilled well until immediately before serving.

2 Cut the tofu into your favorite sizes and put into a serving bowl newly filled with chilled water.

3 Scoop it out of the bowl and place in individual cups. Pour on some soy sauce and garnish with your favorite condiments.

◆冷ややっこのタレのバリエーション・Variations of Sausce

しょう油マヨネーズ
Mayonnaise Soy Sauce

■材料（2人分）

しょう油	大さじ4
マヨネーズ	大さじ6
だし汁	大さじ4
白ごま	小さじ1

■作り方

ボウルにしょう油、マヨネーズ、白ごまを入れてよく混ぜ合わせ、だし汁を少しずつ加えてよく溶きのばします。

■ INGREDIENTS (serves 2)

4 Tbsps soy sauce
6 Tbsps mayonnaise
4 Tbsps stock
1 tsp white sesame

■ Directions

Put the soy sauce, mayonnaise and white sesame into a bowl, and stir well. Add the stock little by little to dissolve and thin down.

にんにくしょう油
Garlic Soy Sauce

■材料（2人分）

にんにく（すりおろし）	1片分
しょう油	大さじ2
オリーブオイル	大さじ4
酢	大さじ2
砂糖	小さじ1/4
あさつき（小口切り）	5本分
白ごま	小さじ2

■作り方

ボウルにすべての材料を入れ、よく混ぜ合わせてタレを作ります。

■ INGREDIENTS (serves 2)

1 clove garlic, grated
2 Tbsps soy sauce
4 Tbsps olive oil
2 Tbsps vinegar
1/4 tsp sugar
5 leaves *asatsuki* chive, edge-cut
2 tsps white sesame

■ Directions

Put all the ingredients into a bowl and stir well.

ごまみそ
Sesame Miso Sauce

■材料（2人分）

白みそ	大さじ2
練りごま（白）	大さじ1
砂糖	大さじ3
だし汁	大さじ4
ラー油	小さじ1

■作り方

すり鉢に白みそ、練りごま（白）を入れてすり混ぜ、砂糖、だし汁、ラー油を加えてよくすり合わせます。

■ INGREDIENTS (serves 2)

2 Tbsps white miso
1 Tbsp white sesame paste
3 Tbsps sugar
4 Tbsps stock
1 tsp *la-yu* spiced oil

■ Directions

Put the white miso and white sesame paste into a grinding bowl, and mix while grinding. Add the sugar, stock, and *la-yu* spiced oil into the bowl and grind well and mix.

マスタードソース
Mustard Sauce

■材料（2人分）

玉ねぎ（みじん切り）	大さじ4
パセリ（みじん切り）	大さじ1
マスタード	大さじ4
レモン汁	大さじ4
砂糖	大さじ1
塩	少々
こしょう	少々

■作り方

ボウルにすべての材料を入れ、よく混ぜ合わせてタレを作ります。

■ INGREDIENTS (serves 2)

4 Tbsps finely-chopped onion
1 Tbsp finely-chopped parsley
4 Tbsps mustard
4 Tbsps lemon juice
1 Tbsp sugar
Pinch salt
Pinch pepper

■ Directions

Put all the ingredients into a bowl and mix up well.

Tofu Steak with Fresh Tomato Sauce

豆腐ステーキ フレッシュトマトソース

about 20min
約20分

371 kcal
371キロカロリー

淡白な豆腐がおしゃれでおいしいステーキに変身
Transform plain tofu into a tasty and dressed-up steak

■材料 (2人分)

木綿豆腐	1丁
塩	少々
こしょう	少々
プチトマト	10 個
玉ねぎ	1/4 個
パセリ	1枝

A
バルサミコ酢	大さじ1
しょう油	大さじ 1/2
オリーブオイル	大さじ3

バジルの葉	適宜
オリーブオイル	大さじ1

■ INGREDIENTS (serves 2)

1 cake "cotton"tofu
Pinch salt
Pinch pepper
10 cherry tomatoes
1/4 onion
1 branch parsley

A
1 Tbsp balsamic vinegar
1/2 Tbsp soy sauce
3 Tbsps olive oil

Basil leaves
1 Tbsp olive oil

■作り方

1 木綿豆腐はキッチンペーパーで包み、重し（まな板など）をし、しっかりと水きりをします。
※豆腐の水けのきり方は、44 ページにも紹介しています。

2 プチトマトは水洗いして水けをきり、へたを取り縦半分に切り、次に横半分に切ります。パセリは水洗いして水けをきり、葉の部分を摘みみじん切りにします。玉ねぎは皮をむき、みじん切りにします。バジルの葉は水洗いして、水けをふき取っておきます。

3 ボウルに **A** と **2** のプチトマト、パセリ、玉ねぎを入れてよく混ぜ、ソースを作ります。

4 **1** の木綿豆腐を半分に切り、焼く直前にキッチンペーパーで表面の水分を軽くふき取り、塩、こしょうをふり下味をつけます。

5 フライパンにオリーブオイル大さじ1をひき、中火にかけて **4** の木綿豆腐を入れて両面に焼き色をつけます。
※豆腐を横から見て、中央部まで色が変化したら熱の通った証拠ですので、裏返しましょう。

6 器に **5** の木綿豆腐を盛り、上から **3** のソースをかけ、**2** のバジルの葉を飾ります。

コツのコツ
★ 使用する豆腐は、かための木綿豆腐を使用しましょう。
★ 木綿豆腐の表面全体をパリッと焼くとおいしいです。
★ 木綿豆腐を両面焼くために、裏返す時はフライ返しを使用すると便利です。

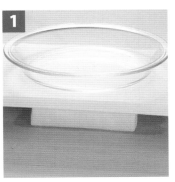

■ Directions

1 Wrap the tofu in kitchen paper and press to extract water firmly.
※ Also refer to P.44 for instructions on removing excess water from tofu.

2 Wash the cherry tomatoes in cold water, drain, and remove the stalks and cut lengthwise into halves then crosswise into quarters. Rinse the parsley in cold water, drain, and pluck off the leaves. Peel the onion. Chop the parsley and onion finely. Rinse the basil leaves in cold water and wipe dry.

3 Put **A**, the cherry tomatoes, parsley, and onion into a bowl and mix well to complete the sauce.

4 Cut the tofu into halves. Wipe the surface gently with kitchen paper to remove moisture immediately before frying. Sprinkle the salt and black pepper to season beforehand.

5 Heat the olive oil in a frying pan and place over a medium heat. Fry the tofu in the pan until both surfaces are browned.
※ You can tell whether the tofu has cooked when you see its color changed to the center looking from the side. If cooked, flip it over.

6 Arrange the tofu on a plate and pour the sauce prepared in 3. above. Garnish with the basil leaves.

Tip on Tips
★ Use a firm "cotton" tofu.
★ Frying the tofu until it's crispy is the key to enhancing its flavor.
★ Use a spatula to flip the tofu so both sides fry.

Tofu *Dengaku*
豆腐田楽

田楽みits濃厚さが淡白な豆腐とベストマッチの日本の伝統食

田楽みその濃厚さが淡白な豆腐とベストマッチの日本の伝統食

A traditional Japanese meal pairing thick *dengaku* miso and plain tofu

■材料（2人分）

木綿豆腐 …………… 1丁

A
┌ 赤みそ ………… 50g
│ 砂糖 ……… 大さじ2
│ みりん …… 大さじ1
│ だし汁 …… 大さじ5
└ ごま油 ………… 適宜

サラダ油 ………… 適宜

木の芽 …………… 適宜

■ INGREDIENTS (serves 2)

1 cake "cotton" tofu

A
┌ 50g red miso
│ 2 Tbsps sugar
│ 1 Tbsps *mirin* sweet cooking sake
│ 5 Tbsps stock
└ Sesame oil

Vegetable oil

Kinome (young leaves of sansho Japanese pepper)

みそ田楽（こんにゃく）　Miso *Dengaku* (Devil's tongue)
(Image photo)

■作り方

1 木綿豆腐は半分の厚さに切り、キッチンペーパーで包み、上から重し（まな板など）をし、水けをよくきります。
※豆腐の水けのきり方は、44 ページにも紹介しています。

2 小鍋に A を入れ、弱火にかけてよく混ぜて田楽みそを作ります。
※弱火にし、絶対に焦がさないようにしましょう。
※田楽みそは好みによって材料の分量を調節しましょう。

3 1の豆腐を幅 3 〜 4cm くらいの棒状に切り、竹串に刺します。

4 焼き網にハケで油を塗り、中火で 3 の豆腐の両面に焼き色をつけます。

5 4を器に盛り、2 の田楽みそを塗り、木の芽を添えます。

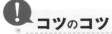

コツのコツ

★木綿豆腐の水けをきっちりときらないと、焼く時に崩れたり、仕上がりが水っぽくなってしまいます。

★田楽みそを作る際は、必ず弱火にし、焦がさないようにしましょう。焦がしたら最初から作り直しましょう。

第十章●和食の基本の豆腐料理 ● Basic Japanese Tofu Dishes

1

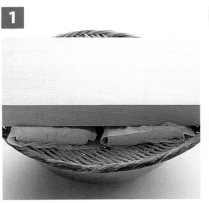

3-a

3-b

4

■ Directions

1 Cut the tofu in half. Wrap in kitchen paper, and press lightly to squeeze out water.
※ Also refer to P.44 for instructions on removing excess water from tofu.

2 Put the **A** mixture into a small pot, and place over a low heat while stirring to make the *dengaku* miso sauce.
※ Remember to turn the heat to low to avoid the sauce from burning.
※ Adjust the quantity of ingredients to accommodate your taste.

3 Cut the tofu into 3/4 to 1 1/5-inch bars, and skewer each piece with a bamboo skewer.

4 Apply the sesame oil over a cooking grill using a brush, and fry the tofu over a midium heat until both the top and bottom sides of each piece are browned.

5 Arrange the tofu on plates. Pour on the *dengaku* miso sauce, and garnish with the kinome.

Tip on Tips

★ Remove excess moisture thoroughly from tofu before cooking, otherwise, it will crumble when frying, and the resultant taste will be bland.

★ When preparing *dengaku* miso, always use low heat and do not let the miso burn. If it burns, give it another try.

Deep-fried Tofu with Amber Sauce
揚げ出し豆腐

about
20min
約20分

235kcal
235キロカロリー

ほっとするおいしさで酒のつまみにも喜ばれる
Comfort food that goes great with sake

■材料（2人分）

絹ごし豆腐 ………… 1丁	薄口しょう油 … 小さじ2
大根おろし …… 大さじ3	みりん ………… 小さじ1
赤唐辛子 …… 1/3本	
あさつき …… 2〜3本	※その他の添えものとして、さっ
糸がつお ………… 適宜	とゆでたさやえんどうや、ゆでて小
片栗粉 …………… 適宜	口切りにしたおくら、三つ葉、せ
揚げ油 …………… 適宜	ん切りにした大葉などを添えても
だし汁 ……… 1/3カップ	おいしいです。

■ INGREDIENTS (serves 2)

1 cake "silken" tofu
3 Tbsps grated giant white radish
1/3 red pepper
2 or 3 leaves *asatsuki* chive
Fine dried bonito shreds
Katakuriko starch
Oil for deep-frying
2/7 cup stock (66㎖)

2 tsps light soy sauce
1 tsp *mirin* sweet cooking sake

※ It is also tasty to use swiftly boiled snow peas, edge-cut boiled *okra*, trefoil and julienne-strip green perilla leaves as other garnishes.

■作り方

1 絹ごし豆腐はふきんやペーパータオルに包んでバットにのせ、冷蔵庫に30分くらいおいて余分な水分をきります。

2 赤唐辛子は種を取ってぬるま湯で戻し、みじん切りにして大根おろしと混ぜ、もみじおろしを作ります。あさつきは小口切りにします。

3 1の豆腐を半分に切り、片栗粉を薄くつけ、170℃に熱した油で揚げます。

薄いきつね色になって浮いてきたらバットに取り出して油をきります。

4 小鍋にだし汁、薄口しょう油、みりんを入れて煮たて、かけ汁を作ります。

5 器に3の豆腐を盛って4のかけ汁を張り、2のもみじおろし、あさつき、糸がつおをのせていただきます。

■ Directions

1 Wrap the silken tofu with a cloth or paper towel, and place on a tray. Let stand for about 30 min in a fridge to eliminate excess moisture.

2 Remove the seeds of the red pepper, and soak in lukewarm water to soften. Chop finely, and mix with the grated giant white radish to make a *momiji-oroshi* condiment. Cut the *asatsuki* chive leaves using the edge cut technique.

3 Cut the tofu in half, coat thinly with *katakuriko* starch and deep-fry in oil preheated to 340°F. When the tofu turns light brown, and floats up to the surface, take out of the pan and drain on a tray.

4 Place the stock, light soy sauce and *mirin* in a small pot, and bring to the boil to make sauce.

5 Arrange the tofu on plates, and pour on the sauce. Garnish with *momiji-oroshi* condiment, chopped

asatsuki chive leaves and fine dried bonito shreds.

Simmering Tofu
湯豆腐

しみじみとおいしくて心が安らぐシンプルな冬の定番鍋料理

A popular dish for winter, it's a simple and warming hot pot

湯豆腐 Simmering tofu (image photo)

■材料（4人分）

絹ごし豆腐 …………	2丁
長ねぎ …………	1/2本
削りがつお ……	1パック
昆布 …………	20cm
水 …………	7〜8カップ
塩 …………	少々
しょう油 …………	適宜

■ INGREDIENTS (serves 2)

2 cakes "silken" tofu
1/2 *naga-negi* onion
1 packet dried bonito flakes
8 -inch *konbu* kelp
5 4/5 or 6 3/5 cups water (1400〜1600㎖)
Pinch salt
Soy sauce

■作り方

1 昆布は乾いたふきんでさっとふき、鍋に入れて水をはり、30分くらいおきます。

2 絹ごし豆腐は一度水にさらしてから、1丁を6〜8等分くらいに切ります。

3 1の鍋を火にかけ、煮たつ前に、塩をひとつまみと2の豆腐を静かに入れます。
※あまり沸騰させないように注意しましょう。

4 3の絹ごし豆腐が温まったら、豆腐をすくい、しょう油にくぐらせ、小口切りにした長ねぎ、削りがつお、薬味を添えていただきます。
※絹ごし豆腐をすくう専用の穴あきじゃくしか、穴あき玉じゃくしを使用しましょう。

！ コツのコツ

★絹ごし豆腐はとても柔らかいので、丁寧に扱いましょう。

★豆腐は一度水にさらすことで、臭みを取ることができます。

★鍋に塩をひとつまみ入れると、豆腐が煮えすぎてもかたくなりにくくなります。

★沸騰させると豆腐が壊れてしまいますので注意しましょう。

◆湯豆腐に適した食材◆
Suggestions for your tofu hot pot

シンプルでおいしい湯豆腐ですが、豆腐のほかに下の食材をプラスしてもおいしいです。
This easy dish is tasty with tofu alone or you can add other ingredients, like those listed below.
◆はまぐり・Clams
◆あさり・Short-necked clams
◆たら・Cod
◆豚肉（しゃぶしゃぶ用）・Thinly sliced pork for shabu-shabu
◆水菜・Potherb mustard leaves
◆春菊・Shungiku or garland chrysanthemum
◆長ねぎ・Naga-negi onion
◆しいたけ・Shiitake mushroom

■ Directions

1 Briefly wipe the *konbu* kelp with a dry cloth. Place the kelp in a pot, and fill the pot with water. Let stand for about 30 min.

2 Soak the silken tofu in cold water, and cut each cake into sixths or eighths.

3 Place the pot with the kelp over heat. Add a pinch of salt and the tofu gently before the water in the pan comes to the boil.
※ Take care not to boil too long.

4 When the tofu from step 3 is warmed, scoop it out of the pot and place in individual bowls. Pour on some soy sauce, and garnish with the *naga-negi* onion sliced using the edge cut technique, dried bonito flakes and other condiments.
※ When you scoop the tofu, use a slotted spoon or a straining ladle.

！ Tip on Tips

★ The silken tofu is very soft so make sure to handle it with care.

★ By soaking tofu in cold water, its odor can be effectively eliminated.

★ Put a pinch of salt into the pot before heating tofu. Salt will prevent tofu from hardening even when it is over-cooked.

★ Take care not to let the water boil too long or the tofu will crumble.

Tofu in *Ogasawara*-Style

小笠原豆腐

柔らかい絹ごし豆腐をあんかけと花がつおでいただく
Enjoy soft silken tofu with starchy sauce and bonito flakes

■材料 (2人分)

絹ごし豆腐 ……… 1丁		水……… 大さじ3	
A	水……… 1/4カップ	**C**	葛粉 (片栗粉でも可)
	葛粉 (片栗粉でも可)		……… 大さじ1
	……… 大さじ2	花がつお ……… 適宜	
だし汁 … 1と1/2カップ		辛子 ……… 適宜	
B	料理酒 … 大さじ1		
	みりん …… 大さじ1		
	薄口しょう油 …小さじ1/2		
	塩 ……… 小さじ1/4		

■ INGREDIENTS (serves 2)

1 cake "silken" tofu

A
- 1/5 cup water (50mℓ)
- 2 Tbsps powdered arrowroot (or starch)

1 1/4 cup broth (300mℓ)

B
- 1 Tbsp cooking sake
- 1 Tbsp *mirin* sweet cooking sake
- 1/2 tsp light soy sauce
- 1/4 tsp salt

C
- 3 Tbsps water
- 1 Tbsp powered arrowroot (or starch powder)

Bonito flakes

Mustard paste

■作り方

1 器に **A** を入れて葛粉を溶き、鍋に水1ℓ (分量外) と溶いた葛粉を加えてよく混ぜながら弱火にかけて葛湯を作ります。

2 絹ごし豆腐は半分に切り1の葛湯に入れ、弱火で温めます。

3 器に **C** を入れて葛湯を溶いておきます。

4 別の鍋にだし汁、**B**、3 を入れてかき混ぜながら弱火にかけ葛あんを作ります。

5 器に2の絹ごし豆腐を盛りつけ、4の葛あんをかけ、豆腐のまわりに花がつおをかけ、豆腐の上に辛子を添えます。

■ Directions

1 Place **A** into a bowl and dissolve the powdered arrowroot. Put 1 liter of water into a pot with the dissolved arrowroot. Place over low heat while stirring well to make "*kuzuyu*" arrowroot water.

2 Cut silken tofu in half and put into the pot from step 1. Warm over low heat.

3 Place **C** into a bowl and dissolve the powdered arrowroot.

4 Put broth, **B** and the dissolve powdered arrowroot from step 3 into another pot. Place over low heat while stirring to prepare the arrowroot sauce.

5 Transfer the silken tofu from step 2 into a serving bowl. Pour the arrowroot sauce from step 4 and garnish with bonito flakes so they surround the tofu. Put a little mustard paste on top.

第十一章
Chapter 11

Basic Japanese Salads and Marinated Dishes

和食の基本・サラダ・あえもの

サラダはみんな大好きな定番のポテトサラダを紹介。季節の野菜、山菜、魚介類などを使用して作るあえもの。コツを覚えれば誰でもおいしいあえものができるはず。

Here, we introduce a very popular potato salad as a dressed dish. There are various marinated dishes using vegetables, wild plants and seafood in season. Anyone can prepare delicious marinated foods once you get the hang of these tips.

Potato Salad
ポテトサラダ

about 30 min
約30分

471 kcal
471 キロカロリー

子どもはもちろん大人も大好きなサラダの定番
A standard, loved by children and also adults

■材料（2人分）

じゃがいも	…………	4 個
にんじん	…………	1/2 本
玉ねぎ	…………	1/2 個
きゅうり	…………	1 本
スイートコーン	………	50g
塩	…………	適宜
マヨネーズ	……	大さじ 4
牛乳	…………	大さじ 1
練りからし	……	小さじ 1

塩・こしょう	………	少々
チャービル	…………	適宜

※一般的にサラダに使うじゃがいもは男爵が多いが、手に入るものを使用すればよいでしょう。メークイーンはねっとりとした食感で、男爵はほくほくとした食感になります。また、みずみずしくて柔らかい新じゃがを使ってもおいしいです。

■ INGREDIENTS (serves 2)

4 potatoes
1/2 carrot
1/2 onion
1 cucumber
50g sweet corn
Salt
4 Tbsps mayonnaise
1 Tbsp milk
1 tsp mustard paste

Pinch salt and pepper
Chervil

※ Generally Danshaku potato is used for potato salad, though any kind of potato can be used. Use of May Queen provides viscous texture and Danshaku steamy and soggy texture. It is tasty to use new potato that has a succulent and soft texture.

■作り方

1 じゃがいもは皮をむいて、6〜8等分に切って水につけてアクを取ります。にんじんは皮をむき、厚さ2mmのいちょう切りにします。

2 きゅうりは厚さ2mmの輪切りにし、塩でもんで絞って水けをきります。玉ねぎは薄くスライスします。

3 鍋に1のじゃがいもとにんじんを入れ、ひたひたの水に塩を加えて強火にかけ、沸騰したら弱火にし、じゃがいもに竹串がスーと通るまでゆでます。にんじんは柔らかくなったら取り出します。

4 3のじゃがいもがゆで上がったら鍋の湯を捨て、再び火にかけて水分を飛ばします。

5 ボウルにマヨネーズ、牛乳、練りからしを入れスプーンなどでよく混ぜ合わせ、4のじゃがいもを熱いうちに加えて、混ぜ合わせます。

6 5に3のにんじん、2のきゅうり、玉ねぎ、スイートコーンを入れてあえます。塩、こしょうをして味を調え、冷蔵庫で冷やします。器に盛り、チャービルを添えていただきます。

> **!** **コツのコツ**
>
> ★ゆでたじゃがいもの水分を飛ばすことで仕上がりがよくなります。この時に焦がさないように注意しましょう。
>
> ★じゃがいもは熱いうちに潰しましょう。
>
> ★マヨネーズ、牛乳、練りからしの分量は、好みで調整しましょう。

■ Directions

1 Peel the potatoes, cut into sixths or eighths and soak in cold water to eliminate bitterness. Peel the carrot, and cut into about 1/16-inch quarter-rounds.

2 Cut the cucumber into 1/16-inch rounds, rub in salt and squeeze to drain. Slice the onion thinly.

3 Place the chopped potatoes and carrot in a pot. Fill the pot with just enough water to cover the vegetables, add the salt and boil over a high heat. When it comes to the boil, reduce the heat to low and continue to simmer until the potatoes become tender enough for a bamboo skewer to pierce without difficulty. Take the carrot out of the pot whenever they are tender.

4 When the potatoes are tender enough, discard the hot water from the pot and place over heat again to evaporate the moisture of the potatoes.

5 Place the mayonnaise, milk and mustard in a bowl, and mix well with a spoon, etc. Add the potatoes to the bowl while still hot, and mash.

6 Add the carrot, cucumber, onion and sweet corn, and mix. Adjust the flavor with salt and pepper, and cool everything in the fridge. Arrange in individual bowls, and garnish with chervil.

> **!** **Tip on Tips**
>
> ★ Evaporating the moisture of boiled potatoes will make the results even better.
>
> ★ Be sure to mash potatoes while they are still hot.
>
> ★ Adjust the amount of mayonnaise, milk and mustard to your taste.

Marinated Cucumber, *Wakame* Seaweed, and *Shirasu* Dried Young Sardine with Sweet Vinegar Sauce

きゅうり・わかめ・しらすの甘酢あえ

about **10** min
約10分

55 kcal
55キロカロリー

やさしい味で体にもよい一品
A mild but very healthy side dish

■材料（2人分）

きゅうり …………… 1本
わかめ（塩蔵） …… 10g
しらす干し …… 大さじ1
塩 …………………… 少々
〈甘酢の材料〉
酢 ………………… 大さじ2
砂糖 ……………… 大さじ2
塩 ………………… 小さじ1/8
だし汁 …………… 大さじ2

※その他の具材として、小さめに
切ったちくわ、ほやなどを加えて
もよいし、しらすの代わりにジャ
コを使ってもおいしい。

■ INGREDIENTS (serves 2)

1 cucumber
10g *wakame* seaweed (salt cured)
1 Tbsp *shirasu* dried young sardine
Pinch salt
〈Fore preparing sweet vinegar sauce〉
2 Tbsps vinegar
2 Tbsps sugar
1/8 tsp salt
2 Tbsps stock

※ Thinly sliced *chikuwa* fish paste roll and ascidian can also be added to the ingredients. *Jako*, boiled and dried baby sardines, can be used instead of *shirasu*.

■作り方

1 ボウルに酢、砂糖、塩を入れてかき混ぜ、完全に溶かします。だし汁を加えて甘酢を作ります。冷蔵庫で冷やしておきます。

2 きゅうりは塩をまぶし、まな板の上でころがして板ずりし、水洗いして小口切りにします。塩を少々加えた水につけてしんなりさせ、手で絞って水けをきります。

3 わかめは水につけて戻し、筋を取って食べやすい大きさに切り、熱湯にくぐらせて冷水に入れます。ペーパータオルなどで水けをきります。

4 しらす干しはザルに入れ、熱湯を回しかけ、水けをきります。

5 2、3、4の具材は食べる直前まで冷蔵庫で冷やし、具材からしみ出た水けをきってから1の甘酢であえます。

■ Directions

1 Put the vinegar, sugar, and salt in a bowl and stir until dissolved completely. Add the stock to complete the vinegar sauce and let stand until cool in a refrigerator.

2 Salt the cucumber and roll onto a cutting board. Rinse in cold water and cut by using the edge cut technique. Soak in salted water until softened. Squeeze out to drain with hands.

3 Soak the *wakeme* seaweed in cold water to soften, string, and cut into bite-sized pieces. Blanch the seaweed in boiling water and soak in cold water. Wipe dry with a paper towel.

4 Place the *shirasu* dried young sardines on a sieve, pour boiling water over, and drain.

5 Let the ingredients of 2, 3, and 4 above rest in a refrigerator until immediately prior to serving. Drain the water of the ingredients and mix well with the sweet vinegar sauce prepared in 1 above.

❗ コツのコツ・Tip on Tips

★きゅうり、わかめ、しらすの下処理をしたら出来上がりが水っぽくならないように水けをよくきります。また、冷蔵庫で冷やした具材はあえる前に水けをよく取りましょう。

★ After preparing cucumber, wakeme seaweed, and *shirasu* dried young sardine, drain well to prevent the ingredients to become too watery. Furthermore, remove the water from the chilled ingredients in a refrigerator before mixing with the vinegar sauce.

Cucumber and Celery mixed with salted *Konbu* kelp
きゅうりとセロリの塩昆布あえ

about **5** min 約5分 / **25** kcal 25キロカロリー

もう一品欲しい時にすぐに出来るのが嬉しい

Here's a quick side when you want another dish on your table

■材料 (1 人分)

きゅうり	1本
セロリ	1/3 本
みょうが	1本
塩	少々
ごま油	小さじ 1/2
塩昆布	10g

■ INGREDIENTS (serves 1)

1 cucumber
1/3 stalk celery
1 *mioga*
Small quantity of salt
1/2 tsp sesame oil
10g salted *konbu* kelp

■作り方

1 きゅうりは所々皮をむいて乱切りに、セロリは筋を取ってから斜め薄切り、みょうがは縦半分に切ってから斜め薄切りにして、水にさらしてからザルにあげて水けをきります。

2 ボウルに1のきゅうり、セロリ、みょうがを入れ、塩、ごま油、塩昆布であえれば出来上がりです。

■ Directions

1 Partially peel the cucumber, and cut into wedges while rotating it. String the celery, and slice diagonally. Cut the mioga in half lengthwise first, and then slice diagonally. Soak the mioga in cold water, and drain on a basket.

2 Put the cut cucumber, celery, and *mioga* in a bowl, and mix with the salt, sesame oil, and salted *konbu* kelp.

❗ コツのコツ・Tip on Tips

★水にさらしたみょうがの水けをよくきりましょう。水けをよくきらないと、仕上がりが水っぽくなり、味が薄くなるので注意しましょう。

★ Drain the *mioga* well. Otherwise, the dish will be watery when finished, and its taste will be too weak.

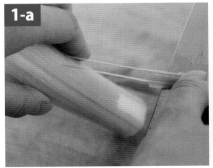
1-a

1-b

Bamboo Shoot with *Kinome* Dressing
たけのこの木の芽あえ

春のいぶきと味覚を口いっぱいに感じる
Bamboo shoots are like a taste of the start of spring

■材料（2人分）

ゆでたけのこ …… 100g	
いか（胴の部分）…1/2 杯	
A ┌ だし汁 … 1/2 カップ	
│ みりん …… 小さじ 1	
│ 薄口しょう油 小さじ 1/2	
└ 塩 ……… 小さじ 1/4	

B ┌ 西京みそ ……… 30g	
│ みりん …… 大さじ 1	
└ 砂糖 … 大さじ 1/2	
ほうれん草（葉先）…… 3 枚	
木の芽……… 10 枚	

■ INGREDIENTS (serves 2)

100g boiled bamboo shoots
1/2 squid (body part)

A ┌ 2/5 cup stock (100 ㎖)
│ 1 tsp *mirin* sweet cooking sake
│ 1/2 tsp light soy sauce
└ 1/4 tsp salt

B ┌ 30g *Saikyo miso*
│ 1 Tbsp *mirin* sweet cooking sake
└ 1/2 Tbsp sugar

3 spinach leaves
10 *kinome*, or young leaves of *sansho* Japanese pepper

■ 作り方

1 たけのこは短冊切りにし、鍋に **A** の調味料と一緒に入れて煮立てたらそのまま冷ましておきます。

2 いかは皮をむいて鹿の子（縦横か斜めに交差する切り目）に包丁目を入れ、たけのこと同じくらいの大きさの短冊切りにし、さっと湯通しをしてザルに上げ、しっかりと水けをきっておきます。

3 木の芽みそを作ります。
(a) 耐熱容器に **B** を入れてラップをし、電子レンジ（600W）で約30秒加熱し、手早く混ぜ合わせて、練りみそを作ります。
※少量の場合は電子レンジを使うと便利です。

(b) ほうれん草は水洗いしたあと、耐熱皿にのせてラップをし電子レンジ（600W）で約30秒加熱したら水にさらしてアクを抜き、汁けを絞って細かく刻んでからすり鉢ですります。

(c) (b)のすり鉢に葉だけをつんだ木の芽を入れて香りが出るようにすりつぶしたら、(a)の練りみそを入れて合わせます。

4 食べる直前に汁けをきった、**1** のたけのこ、**2** のいか、**3** の **(c)** の木の芽みそであえて器に盛ります。木の芽を上に飾るときれいです。

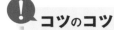
コツのコツ
★使用する食材（たけのこ、いか、ほうれん草）の水けをよくふき取り、使用しましょう。
★木の芽みそを作る時は、最後に木の芽を入れるのがコツです。より木の芽の香りがします。

3-a 3-b 3-c

■ Directions

1 Cut the bamboo shoots into rectangles. Put the bamboo shoots in a pot together with **A**, bring to the boil, and allow it to stand to cool.

2 Skin the squid, and make shallow cuts in the *kanoko* pattern (parallel vertical and horizontal lines or diagonal lines crossing each other). Cut the squid into the same size pieces as the bamboo shoots. Blanch the squid, and thoroughly drain it on a sieve.

3 Make *kinome* miso.
(a) Put **B** in a heat-resistant vessel, and cover it with plastic wrap. Microwave (600w) for about 30 sec, and swiftly stir to make a thick miso sauce.

※ If the quantity is small, use a microwave to cook simply!

(b) Rinse the spinach with cold water, put it in a heat-resistant container covered with plastic wrap, and microwave (600w) for about 30 sec. Soak the spinach to remove the bitterness. Squeeze the spinach, finely chop, and grind in a mortar.

(c) Add only the *kinome* leaves to the mortar and grind until the flavor emerges. Add the thick miso sauce prepared in (a), and mix.

4 Just before serving, mix the drained bamboo shoots and squid with the *kinome* miso sauce, and place it on a serving dish. Garnish with *kinome* leaves on top to make the dish beautiful.

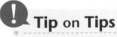
Tip on Tips
★ Wipe off excess moisture from all ingredients (bamboo shoots, squid and spinach) while preparing.
★ The key to prepare good *kinome* miso is to add the *kinome* last. This enhances the *kinome* scent.

Chicken Breast Fillet with Sesame Vinegar
鶏ささ身のごま酢がけ

about **15**min
約15分

156kcal
156キロカロリー

ごま酢が鶏ささ身と野菜に相性がよく食欲をそそる
Sesame vinegar is excellent on chicken and vegetables and whets your appetite.

■材料（2人分）

鶏ささ身 …………… 3本	酢……… 大さじ 1/2
きゅうり ………… 1/2 本	薄口しょう油… 大さじ 1
にんじん …………4cm	A 砂糖 …… 小さじ 2
大根…………………4cm	だし汁 …… 大さじ 1
かいわれ大根… 1/4 パック	炒りごま（白）… 大さじ 1
塩・料理酒 ……… 各少々	

■ INGREDIENTS (serves 2)

3 fillets chicken breast
1/2 cucumber
1 1/2-inch carrot
1 1/2-inch giant white radish
1/4 package young giant white radish shoots

Small quantity of salt and cooking sake

A
- 1/2 Tbsp vinegar
- 1 Tbsp light soy sauce
- 2 tsps sugar
- 1 Tbsp stock

1 Tbsp white parched sesame

■作り方

1 炒りごまを小鍋で炒ります。すり鉢にごまを入れてすり、粒の半分くらい残っている状態になったら、**A** を順に入れてよくすり混ぜます。

2 鶏ささ身は筋と皮を取り、料理酒と塩を少々入れた熱湯でゆでて冷まし、身をほぐします。

3 きゅうりは塩をふってまな板の上で転がし、水洗いし4cm の長さのせん切りにします。にんじん、大根は皮をむいて4cm の長さのせん切りにし、かいわれ大根は根を取り、3 〜 4cm の長さに切ります。これらの野菜はさっと水に放し、水けをきっておきます。

4 器に、2 のささ身と 3 の野菜を合わせて皿に盛り、1 のごま酢をかけます。

■ Directions

1 Toast the sesame seeds in a small pot. Transfer to a grinding bowl, and grind until half-ground. Add the ingredients of **A**, and grind and mix well.

2 Remove the sinew and skin from the chicken fillets, place in boiling water with a small amount of cooking sake and salt added and let stand until cool. When cool, break into pieces with your hands.

3 Salt the cucumber, and roll onto a cutting board. Rinse in cold water and cut into 1 1/2-inch long julienne strips. Peel the carrot and giant white radish, and cut into 1 1/2-inch long julienne strips. Chop off the roots of the young giant white radish shoots, and cut into 1 1/5 to 1 1/2-inch lengths. Rinse these vegetables in cold water briefly, and drain.

4 Arrange the chicken pieces and vegetables in bowls, and pour on the sesame vinegar.

❗ コツのコツ・Tip on Tips

★炒りごま（白）を焦がさないように炒って、ごまの香りをよく出しましょう。

★ Be careful not to scorch the white sesame to bring out the best aroma.

Uzaku
うざく

食欲の落ちる夏に最適な栄養ある一品
A perfect summer side dish when the heat ruins your appetite

■材料（2人分）

うなぎの蒲焼き … 1/2 尾	
きゅうり ………… 1/2 本	A ┌ 酢 ………… 50cc
料理酒 …………… 適量	├ 薄口しょう油… 大さじ1
塩 ………… 小さじ 1/2	└ みりん … 大さじ 1/2

■ INGREDIENTS (serves 2)

1/2 grilled eel with sauce	A ┌ 50cc vinegar
1/2 cucumber	├ 1 Tbsp light soy sauce
Cooking sake	├ 1/2 Tbsp *mirin* sweet cook-
1/2 tsp salt	└ ing sake

■作り方

1 うなぎの蒲焼きに料理酒を少々塗り、オーブントースターで軽く焼き、約1cm幅に切ります。

2 きゅうりは水洗いし、水けをきり縦半分に切り、斜め薄切りにします。ボウルに塩水（水100cc〈分量外〉に、塩を合わせる）を作り、きゅうりを約5分ひたし、しんなりしたら水けを絞っておきます。

3 Aを合わせて三杯酢を作ります。**1**のうなぎ、**2**のきゅうりに、それぞれ三杯酢を適量加えてあえ、器に盛ります。

■ Directions

1 Apply a small quantity of cooking sake to the grilled eel, and lightly heat in a toaster oven. Cut the eel into 3/8-inch-wide pieces.

2 Wash the cucumber, and drain. Cut it in half lengthwise first, and then slice thin diagonally. Make salty water by dissolving the salt in 2/5 cup water (extra quantity) in a bowl. Soak the cucumber in the bowl for about 5 min. When the cucumber softens, squeeze out the water.

3 Blend the ingredients of **A** to make *sanbaizu* dressing. Mix the eel prepared in 1 and drained cucumber with a proper quantity of the dressing, and arrange in a serving dish.

❗ コツのコツ・**Tip** on **Tips**
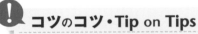

★きゅうりの水けをしっかり絞らないと、仕上がりが水っぽくなるので注意しましょう。

★うなぎに酒を塗り、オーブントースターで焼くと身が柔らかくなります。

★ Note that if the water is not squeezed out well, the finished dish will be watery.

★ Apply a little cooking sake to the grilled eel and heat in a toaster oven to make the eel nice and soft.

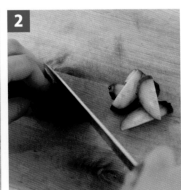

Kidney Beans with Sesame Dressing
いんげんのごまあえ

about **12** min
約 **12** 分

172 kcal
172 キロカロリー

ごま風味がいんげんにからんでおいしい
Tasty kidney beans dressed with sesame sauce

■材料（2 人分）

さやいんげん	100g
塩	少々
炒りごま（白）	大さじ 3
A ┌ 砂糖	大さじ 1
├ サラダ油	大さじ 1
└ しょう油	大さじ 1

■ INGREDIENTS (serves 2)

100g pod kidney beans
Pinch salt
3 Tbsps white parched sesame
A ┌ 1 Tbsp sugar
├ 1 Tbsp vegetable oil
└ Tbsp soy sauce

■作り方

1 さやいんげんは筋を取り、熱湯に塩を入れ、2 〜 3 分ゆでます。冷水に入れ水けをよくきり、3cm の長さに切ります。

2 小鍋で炒りごまを炒り、熱いうちにすり鉢ですります。

3 2 のごまがねっとりとしてきたら A を入れ、なめらかになるようにすり、あえ衣を作ります。

4 1 のさやいんげんを 3 のすり鉢に入れて、あえ衣とまんべんなくあえます。

■ Directions

1 String the pod kidney beans, place in boiling salted water and boil for a few minutes. Soak in cold water, drain and cut into 1 1/5-inch lengths

2 Toast the sesame seeds, and grind in a grinding bowl while they are still hot.

3 When the sesame seeds are half-pastelike, add the ingredients of **A** and continue to grind to make a smooth-textured dressing.

4 Place the kidney beans into the grinding bowl, and mix well with the dressing.

❗ コツのコツ・Tip on Tips

★ゆでたさやいんげんはよく水けをふき取ります。水けが多いと出来上がりが水っぽくなります。

★ Wipe the kidney beans well to remove moisture thoroughly after boiling. If they are not wiped sufficiently dry, the results will be washy.

Basic Japanese Rice and Noodle Dishes

和食の基本・ご飯もの・麺類

日本の食卓を賑わす数々のご飯ものと麺類。コツさえ覚えればおいしいご飯ものと麺類を家庭で楽しめるはず。
Rice and noodle dishes are standard fare on Japanese tables. By following these tips, you can enjoy tasty rice and noodle dishes at home.

Seasoned Tuna on Rice
まぐろのづけ丼

about **10** min
約10分

559 kcal
559キロカロリー

白いご飯とづけにしたまぐろとの相性がよく、食欲をそそる
Seasoned tuna and white rice will tempt all your tastebuds

■材料 (2 人分)

まぐろのさく ……	150g
長ねぎ………………	8cm
大葉 ………………	2枚
炒りごま（白）…	小さじ2
わさび……………	適宜
ご飯…………	丼2杯分
しょう油 …	大さじ1と1/2
料理酒 ………	大さじ1
みりん………	大さじ1/2

※その他のつけ合わせとして、刻みのりやもみのり、きゅうりのせん切りや薄切り、みょうがの薄切り、かいわれ大根などを好みでつけ合わせるとよいでしょう。また、ご飯を寿し飯（182、183 ページ参照）に代えてもよいでしょう。

■ INGREDIENTS (serves 2)

150g tuna
3 -inch *naga-negi* onion
2 green perilla leaves
2 Tsps white parched sesame
Wasabi
2 *donburi* bowl portions of rice
1 1/2 Tbsps soy sauce
1 Tbsp cooking sake
1/2 *mirin* sweet cooking sake

※ Shredded *nori* seaweed, julienne-strip or thinly-sliced cucumber, thinly-sliced *mioga* Japanese ginger, or young giant white radish shoots can be used as a garnish. Also, vinegared rice (see P.182 and 183) can be used instead of white rice.

■ 作り方

1 まぐろのさくは薄めのそぎ切りにします。
※下の写真を参照してください。

2 器にしょう油、料理酒、みりんを合わせ、1のまぐろを入れてなじませ、ラップをして約5分冷蔵庫におきます。

3 長ねぎは約4cmの長さに切り、縦に包丁を入れて開き、芯を取り除き、白い部分を重ね合わせ包丁でせん切りにします。せん切りにした長ねぎは水にさらして、水けをきります。

4 水洗いした大葉は、水けをふき取りせん切りにし、水にさらして水けをきり、

3の長ねぎと合わせます。

5 丼にご飯を盛り、汁をきった2のまぐろをのせて炒りごまをふり、4とわさびを添えていただきます。
※まぐろの汁けは、箸で器にふり落とす程度でよいでしょう。

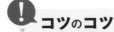
コツのコツ
★まぐろのづけダレに好みでわさびを入れてもおいしいです。
★使用するまぐろは、脂の多いトロより赤身がおいしいです。
★づけダレは好みで分量を調整しましょう。

■ Directions

1 Save the tuna into thin pieces.
※ See the picture above.

2 Mix the soy sauce, cookng sake and *mirin* in a bowl, and add the tuna. Make sure each piece of the tuna is completely soaked in the sauce. Cover the bowl with wrap, and let stand for 5 min in a fridge.

3 Cut the *naga-negi* onion into 1 1/2-inch lengths. Make a lengthwise incision with your knife to open, remove the onion's core and discard. Place the white layers onto others and shred into fine strips. Expose to cold water and drain.

4 Cut the green perilla leaves into julienne strips, rinse in cold water and drain. Mix the *naga-negi* onion with the chopped green perilla leaves.

5 Put the rice into individual donburi bowls. Place the drained tuna on top of the rice, and sprinkle over the white parched sesame. Garnish with the ingredients prepared in step 4 and wasabi.
※ Sprinkle just a bit of the sauce drained from the tuna into the bowls—no more than you can shake off the end of your chopsticks.

Tip on Tips
★ Evaporating the moisture of boiled potatoes will make the results even better.
★ It's better to use the lean part rather than the fatty part of the tuna.
★ Adjust the amount of sauce according to your taste.

Pork Cutlet on Rice
かつ丼

ボリュームたっぷりで満足できる " かつ丼 "
A juicy pork cutlet over rice is always a hearty and satisfying dish

■材料（2 人分）

ロースかつ ………… 2 枚
玉ねぎ………… 1/2 個
卵………………… 3 個
さやいんげん ……… 4 本
ご飯………… 丼 2 杯分

A
┌ だし汁 … 1/2 カップ
│ 料理酒 … 大さじ 1
│ 砂糖 …… 大さじ 1
│ みりん …… 大さじ 2
└ しょう油 … 大さじ 2

※かつ丼には一般的に脂肪があり味にコクのあるロースかつを使いますが、脂肪分が気になる人や、さっぱりとした味が好きな人はヒレかつを使うとよいでしょう。また、チーズや大葉などをはさんで一緒に揚げてもおいしいです。

■ INGREDIENTS (serves 2)

2 pork cutlets
1/2 onion
3 eggs
4 string beans
2 *donburi* bowl portions of rice

A
┌ 2/5 cup stock (100 ㎖)
│ 1 Tbsp cooking sake
│ 1 Tbsp sugar
│ 2 Tbsps *mirin* sweet cook-ing sake
└ 2 Tbsps soy sauce

※ Generally pork loin, fatty and rich in flavor, is used for this dish but if you are avoiding fat or like lighter taste, use pork tender loin cutlet instead. Deep-frying the cutlet with cheese or green perilla leaves is also tasty.

■作り方

1 ロースかつは食べやすい大きさに切ります。玉ねぎは皮をむき、くし切りにします。さやいんげんは筋を取り、塩を入れた熱湯でさっとゆでて冷水に取り、斜め薄切りにします。卵は軽く溶きほぐします。

2 Aを合わせてよくかき混ぜて、煮汁を作ります。

3 丼に温かいご飯を盛っておきます。

4 親子用鍋または小さなフライパンに、2 の煮汁の半分を入れて煮たて、1 の玉ねぎ（半分）を入れてさっと煮ます。1

人分のロースかつをのせ、卵（半量）を外側から回しかけふたをします。

5 4 の鍋をゆすりながら 30 秒ほど煮てふたを開け、さやいんげん（半量）を散らして火を止め、3 の丼に移し入れます。

※煮る時間を調整して、卵のかたさを好みに合わせるとよいでしょう。

コツのコツ

★卵は溶きすぎないのがポイントです。また、卵は溶きすぎるとかたくなってしまいます。

★卵を 2 度にわけてかけると、卵のトロトロ感が出せます。

★あまりロースかつを煮込まず、衣のサクサク感を残しましょう。

第十二章●和食の基本・ご飯もの・麺類 ● Basic Japanese Rice and Noodle Dishes

1

4-a

4-b

■ Directions

1 Cut the pork cutlets crosswise into pieces that are a little larger than bite-sized. Peel the onion, and cut lengthwise into wedges. String the beans, boil in salted water briefly, expose to cold water and slice diagonally into thin pieces. Beat the eggs lightly.

2 Mix all the ingredients of **A**, and stir well.

3 Put hot rice into individual donburi bowls.

4 Put only a half amount of the liquid prepared in 2. above into an *oyako-nabe* pan (a pan specially made for cooking *donburi* bowl rice dishes) or a small frying pan,

and bring to the boil. Add half the number of onion wedges from step 1, and simmer briefly. Add a portion of pork cutlet pieces. Pour a half amount of the lightly beaten eggs gently along the circular edge of the simmering sauce, and cover.

5 Simmer for about 30 sec while shaking the pan from step 4 gently. Uncover the pan, scatter half of the string beans and turn off the heat. Put everything onto the rice in one of the *donburi* bowls. Repeat this process for the other portion.

※Adjust the time of simmering the eggs to accommodate your taste.

Tip on Tips

★ Don't beat the eggs too hard. Otherwise, they will become stiff.

★ By pouring the eggs in twice, they will remain soft and lightly cooked.

★ Do not simmer the pork cutlet too long. Try to keep the batter nice and crispy.

Chicken'n'Egg on Rice
親子丼

about 12 min / 約12分

764 kcal / 764キロカロリー

卵がふわとろで、鶏肉がおいしく体にやさしい丼の定番

This hearty rice bowl of soft eggs and scrumptious chicken is a classic

■材料（2人分）

鶏もも肉		100g
玉ねぎ		1/2 個
卵		3 個
三つ葉		4〜5 本
ご飯		丼 2 杯分
A	だし汁	1/3 カップ
	料理酒	大さじ 2
	砂糖	大さじ 2
	みりん	大さじ 2
	しょう油	大さじ 2 と 1/2

※鶏もも肉は皮や肉につやがあり、皮の毛穴がぷくっと盛り上がっているものが新鮮です。また、古くなってくると色つやがなくなり、肉も柔らかくなってくるので、肉の赤味が強く、かたく弾力のあるものを選ぶとよいでしょう。

■ INGREDIENTS (serves 2)

100g chicken thighs

1/2 onion

3 eggs

4 or 5 stalks trefoil

2 *donburi* bowl portions of rice

A
- **2/7 cup stock (66 ㎖)**
- **2 Tbsps cooking sake**
- **2 Tbsps sugar**
- **2 Tbsps *mirin* sweet cooking sake**
- **2 1/2 Tbsps soy sauce**

※ Fresh chicken thigh has glossy skin and flesh, and its skin's pores are swelled. It looses a good complexion and firmness when getting old. Choose those of which the flesh is firm and resilient and has a good red color on the flesh.

■作り方

1 鶏もも肉は脂肪と余分な皮を包丁で切り除き、一口大のそぎ切りにします。

2 玉ねぎは皮をむき、薄切りにします。三つ葉は水洗いし、2〜3cmの長さに切っておきます。卵3個は軽く溶きほぐします。

3 **A**を合わせてよくかき混ぜ、半分（1人分）に分けておきます。

4 丼に温かいご飯を盛っておきます。

5 親子鍋に**3**の汁の半分を入れて煮たて、**1**の鶏もも肉、**2**の玉ねぎを入れて煮ます。

6 鶏もも肉、玉ねぎに熱が通ったら、**3**の卵液半分（1人分）を外側から回しかけ、ふたをします。鍋をゆすりながら30秒ほど煮ます。卵のかたさは好みでよいでしょう。

7 **6**に三つ葉を散らし、火を止めて**4**の丼に移し入れます。

コツのコツ

★卵は軽く溶きほぐすことで、仕上がりがふわふわになります。

★卵のかたさは好みで火の通しを調整しましょう。かたいのが好きであれば長めに煮て、柔らかいのが好きであれば短かめに煮ればよいでしょう。

★卵液を回しかける場合は、外側から中央に回しかけます。

■ Directions

1 Remove excess fat and skin from the chicken thighs, and shave into bite-sized pieces.

2 Peel the onion, and slice thinly. Cut the trefoil stalks into 3/4 to 1 1/5-inch lengths. Beat the eggs lightly.

3 Mix **A** and stir well. Separate the sauce into two portions. Set aside.

4 Put the hot rice into individual donburi bowls.

5 Add half of the sauce prepared in step 3 into an *oyako-nabe* pan (a pan specifically made for cooking rice bowl dishes) and bring to a boil. Add the chicken thighs from step 1 and the onion from step 2 and simmer.

6 After the chicken thighs and onions are cooked, pour half of the beaten eggs (for 1 portion) from the circular edge of the pan and cover with a lid. Simmer for about 30 seconds while shaking the pan. Cook the eggs to your desired firmness.

7 Scatter the trefoil stalks onto the ingredients from step 7. Turn off the heat and transfer to bonburi bowls.

Tip on Tips

★ By gently beating the eggs, you can get a soft and light finish.

★ If you prefer firmer eggs, simmer the sauce longer than indicated above, and for softer eggs, simmer the sauce only for a short time.

★ When adding the beaten eggs, pour in a circular motion from the outside edge to the center of the pan.

Mixed Rice
五目炊き込みご飯

香り高い炊き込みご飯を特別な日にいただく

Aromatic mixed rice is suitable for special occasions

■材料（2〜3人分）

米	2 カップ
鶏もも肉	80g
にんじん	6cm
ごぼう	1/3 本
干ししいたけ	2 枚
こんにゃく	1/3 枚
三つ葉	3〜4 本
料理酒（鶏肉の下味用）	小さじ 1
だし汁	1 カップ
しいたけの戻し汁	1/2 カップ
砂糖	小さじ 1 と 1/2
料理酒	大さじ 2
薄口しょう油	大さじ 1 と 1/2
塩	小さじ 1/2

■ INGREDIENTS (serves 2 or 3)

1 1/2 cups rice (360㎖)

80g chicken thighs

2 1/3 -inch carrot

1/3 burdock

2 dried shiitake mushrooms

1/3 devil's tongue

3 or 4 stalks trefoil

1 tsp cooking sake (for seasoning chicken prior to cooking)

4/5 cup stock (200 ㎖)

2/5 cup shiitake mushroom soak-ing water (100 ㎖)

1 1/2 tsps sugar

2 Tbsps cooking sake

1 1/2 Tbsps light soy sauce

1/2 tsp salt

■作り方

1 米は炊く30分前にとぎ、ザルに上げて水けをきっておきます。

2 鶏もも肉は余分な脂肪と皮を取り、2cm大のそぎ切りにし、料理酒をふりかけて約10分おきます。にんじんは3cmのせん切りに、ごぼうは包丁の背で皮をこそげてから、ささがきにし水にさらしてアクを取ります。干ししいたけは水（1カップ）につけて戻し、軸を切ってせん切りにします。戻した汁を2分の1カップ分取っておきます。こんにゃくは3cmの長さの拍子切りにし、熱湯でさっとゆがきます。

3 鍋にだし汁、しいたけの戻し汁、2の具材を入れて軽く煮たってきたら、砂糖、料理酒を入れて1〜2分煮ます。次に薄口しょう油と塩を加えてさっと煮ます。

4 ザルの下にボウルをおき、3をザルにあけ、具材と煮汁を分けて冷ましておきます。

5 炊飯器に1の米と4の煮汁を入れ、足りない分は水を入れます。4の具を入れて軽く混ぜ、炊き上げます。

6 炊き上がったら10分ほど蒸らし、具が均等になるように混ぜ、三つ葉を散らしていただきます。

❗ コツのコツ

★炊飯器によっては、煮汁が熱いと炊飯器が反応しない場合があるので冷ましてから炊き上げましょう。

★鶏もも肉の余分な脂身を取り、酒をふりかけ臭みを取ります。

■ Directions

1 Wash the rice 30 min prior to cooking, and drain on a sieve.

2 Remove excess fat and skin from the chicken thighs, shave into 3/4-inch pieces, sprinkle on the sake and let stand for about 10 min. Cut the carrot into 1/16-inch julienne strips. Scrape off the skin of the burdock with the back of a knife, cut using the *sasagaki* shaving technique and rinse in cold water to remove bitterness. Soak the shiitake mushrooms in 4/5 cup of water to soften, remove the stem and cut into julienne stripes. Reserve the 2/5 cup of water in which the mushrooms were soaked. Cut the devil's tongue into 1/16-inch bar rectangles, and parboil in boiling water quickly.

3 Pour in the stock, mushroom soaking water and all the ingredients prepared in 1. above into a pot, and heat everything. When it begins to boil lightly, add the sugar and cooking sake, and continue to simmer for 1 or 2 min. Add the light soy sauce and salt, and continue to simmer briefly.

4 Prepare a sieve with a bowl underneath. Transfer all the ingredients in the pot onto the sieve. Let the solids on the sieve and the liquid in the bowl stand separately until cool.

5 Place the rice in the simmering liquid. If there is not enough simmering liquid, add some water. Add the solid ingredients on the sieve, and mix everything lightly. Turn on the cooker.

6 When cooking is finished, keep the cooker covered and let stand for about 10 min until the grains have settled. Open the lid, and mix the rice so that the ingredients will spread evenly. Scatter the trefoil stalks before serving.

❗ Tip on Tips

★ Cook the mixed rice after these ingredients become cool because some rice cookers do not work if the liquid is hot.

★ Remove excess fat from the chicken thighs, and sprinkle cooking sake over it prior to cooking to eliminate the odor.

Chicken Curry
チキンカレー

about 80 min 約80分

641 kcal 641キロカロリー

スパイスのきいた本格的カレーを家庭で作る
Prepare an authentic and spicy curry at home

■材料（4人分）

鶏手羽元……………… 8 本
玉ねぎ……………… 3 個
塩・こしょう …… 各少々
バター……………… 30g
塩……… 小さじ 1 と 1/2
カレー粉 …… 大さじ 3
ガラムマサラ … 小さじ 2
水……… 2 と 1/2 カップ
サラダ油……… 大さじ 1
ご飯…………… 4 皿分

■ INGREDIENTS (serves 4)

8 chicken drumsticks
3 onions
Small quantity of salt and pepper
30g butter
1 1/2 tbsps salt
3 Tbsps curry powder
2 tbsps galam masala
2 1/8 cups water (500㎖)
1Tbsp vegetable oil
4 portions rice

◆ カレーに適した材料◆
Ingredients suited to add in curry

◆豚肉・Pork
◆牛肉・beef
◆えび・shrimp
◆ホタテ・scallop
◆じゃがいも・potato
◆にんじん・carrot
◆たけのこ・bamboo shoot
◆なす・eggplant

■作り方

1 玉ねぎは皮をむいて、たて半分に切り、繊維に沿ってさらに薄切りにします。フライパンにバターを入れて溶かし、玉ねぎを入れて炒めたら塩小さじ2分の1を加えてさらに炒めます。

2 1を木ベラでバターを全体にからめ、玉ねぎがしんなりと透き通ってきたら、焦げないようによく混ぜ合わせ、玉ねぎの水分を飛ばします。

3 2の玉ねぎがきつね色になってきたら弱火にしてさらに根気よく混ぜ合わせて、玉ねぎに照りが出てくるまで炒め続け、全体があめ色になったら火を止めて粗熱を取ります。

4 鶏手羽元全体に塩、こしょうをふりかけておきます。

5 鍋にサラダ油大さじ1を入れて中火で熱し、4の鶏手羽元を入れます。全体がきつね色になるまで焼き、カレー粉を加えて香りがたつまでさらに弱火で炒めます。

6 5に3の玉ねぎ、塩小さじ1と水2と1/2カップを加えて中火にかけ、ふたをして約30分鶏手羽元が柔らかくなるまで煮込みます。最後にガラムマサラを入れ約3～5分煮込みます。

7 皿にご飯を盛り、6のチキンカレーをかけていただきます。

！コツのコツ

★玉ねぎはあめ色になるまで炒めることでカレーに甘味とコクがでます。時間を短縮したい場合はみじん切りにするか、電子レンジで軽く加熱してから炒めてもよいでしょう。

★鶏手羽元を表面がきつね色になるまで焼き、旨味を閉じ込めます。

★ガラムマサラは、香りが飛んでしまうので、最後の仕上げに入れましょう。

■ Directions

1 Peel the onions and cut lengthwise into two pieces. Cut into thin slices along their fiber. Melt the butter in a frying pan. Add the onions and fry. Add a half tsp salt and continue to fry.

2 Use a wooden spatula to stir the onions from step 1 in the butter until they are completely coated. When the onions become soft and transparent, stir well to prevent them from burning. Let the moisture of the onions evaporate.

3 When the onions from step 2 become light brown, reduce the heat to low. Keep stirring patiently until the onions glisten. When the onions become golden brown, turn off the heat and set aside to cool.

4 Sprinkle the salt and pepper on the chicken drumsticks.

5 Pour 1 Tsp vegetable oil into a pot and place over medium heat. Add the chicken drumsticks from step 4 and fry until light brown. Add the curry powder and continue to cook over low heat until aromatic.

6 Add the onions from step 3, 1tsp salt and 2 1/8 cups of water into the pot. Place a lid over the pot and turn the heat to medium. Simmer for about 30 minutes until the chicken drumsticks soften. Finally add the garam masala and simmer for about 3 to 5 minutes.

7 Arrange the rice on a plate, ladel the chicken curry over it and serve.

！Tip on Tips

★ The key to sweet and rich curry is to fry the onions until golden brown. When you want to shorten the time, chop the onions finely or quickly cook in a microwave prior to frying.

★ By frying the chicken drumsticks until light brown, the meat will hold its flavor within.

★ Add the garam masala last or the aroma will be spoiled.

Fried Rice with Leaf Mustard
高菜炒飯

about **20**min
約20分

539kcal
539キロカロリー

高菜漬けの香りがご飯とからんでおいしい和風炒飯

A delicious Japanese-style fried rice with the aroma of pickled leaf mustard

■材料（2人分）

ご飯	1合分
高菜漬け（水けをきったもの）	60g
牛薄切り肉	80g
長ねぎ	1/2本
塩	適宜
こしょう	少々
しょう油	大さじ1
白ごま	大さじ1
サラダ油	大さじ2

〈牛肉用下味〉

料理酒	小さじ1
しょう油	小さじ1

※フライパンで半熟の状態に炒めた卵を加えると味がまろやかになります。また、仕上げに辛子明太子、じゃこ、山椒の実の佃煮などを好みに合わせて少量散らし、風味を楽しむのもよいでしょう。ただし、塩けが強いので、材料の塩、こしょうを少なめにするのがコツです。

■ INGREDIENTS (serves 2)

170g boiled rice
60g pickled leaf mustard, drained
80g beef, thinly sliced,
1/2 *naga-negi* onion
Salt
Small quantity of pepper
1 Tbsp soy sauce
1 Tbsp white sesame
2 Tbsps vegetable oil
〈Beef seasoning〉
1 tsp cooking sake
1 tsp soy sauce

※ Addition of softly pan-fried beaten eggs makes the taste mellower. It is also enjoyable to add a small quantity of *karashi-mentaiko* flavored Alaska Pollack roe, jako boiled and dried baby sardines, seasoned sansho Japanese pepper seeds. But remember to reduce the amount of salt and pepper since these ingredients are saline.

■ 作り方

1 牛薄切り肉は 2cm 幅に切り、ボウルに下味の材料と牛肉を入れよくもみこんでおきます。

2 高菜、長ねぎをみじん切りにします。

3 ボウルにご飯を入れてほぐしておきます。冷やご飯の場合は、レンジで温め直してほぐしておきます。

4 油ならしをした中華鍋に、サラダ油大さじ 2 を入れて強火でよく熱し、**2** の長ねぎと **1** の牛肉を入れ炒め合わせ、牛肉に火が通ったら **2** の高菜を入れてさらに炒めます。

5 **4** の高菜がしんなりしてきたら、ご飯を入れて全体を混ぜ合わせ、鍋を前後に動かし、お玉やヘラなどでほぐしながらご飯がばらばらとなるまで炒めます。

6 **5** に塩、こしょうをふり入れてさらに炒め、しょう油を鍋肌から回し入れ、炒め合わせます。

7 仕上げに白ごまをふりかけ、さっと混ぜて器に盛ります。

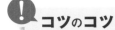

コツのコツ

★ 高菜漬けが塩辛すぎるものは水洗いして塩分を抜き、よく水けを絞るとよいでしょう。

★ 鍋を火から離さないで炒めるのがコツです。

■ Directions

1 Cut the beef into 3/4-inch pieces. Put the beef seasoning ingredients into a bowl, add the beef and mix all the ingredients well with the hands.

2 Chop the leaf mustard and naga-negi onion finely.

3 Put the boiled rice into a bowl, and loosen any lumps. When using cold boiled rice, re-heat in a microwave before loosening.

4 Before you start cooking, heat a wok coated with some oil for a moment, and remove the oil. Put 2 Tbsps of vegetable oil into the wok, and place over a high heat. Add the chopped *naga-negi* onion and the seasoned beef, and fry. When the beef is heated through, add the leaf mustard, and continue to fry.

5 When the leaf mustard becomes tender, add the rice and mix it all well. Fry until each grain of rice is fried and dry while shaking the wok back and forth and loosening any lumps with a ladle or spatula.

6 Sprinkle on the salt and pepper, and continue to fry. Don't put the soy sauce directly onto the rice, but on the wok's inner surface around the rice, and fry together.

7 To finish off cooking, sprinkle on the white sesame, and mix briefly before transferring to serving plates.

Tip on Tips

★ When pickled leaf mustard is too salty, rinse it in cold water to remove the salt, and squeeze out the moisture.

★ The key is to fry without taking the wok off the heat.

Tea-and-Rice
お茶漬け

about **8** min
約**8**分

349 kcal
349キロカロリー

飲んだ後や軽い食事にサラッと食べられるお茶漬け
An easy dish to make and eat after drinking and yummy as a snack

■材料（2人分）
ご飯	2杯分
さけの切り身	1切れ
大葉	4枚
炒りごま（白）	適宜
お茶	適宜

■ INGREDIENTS (serves 2)
2 bowl portions boiled rice
1 fillet chum salmon
4 green perilla leaves
White parched sesame
Japanese green tea

お茶漬け
Tea-and-rice (Image photo)

■作り方

1　さけは両面を焼いて身をほぐしておきます。

2　大葉は水洗いし、水けをふき取りせん切りにします。

3　茶碗にご飯を盛り、1のさけをのせ、2の大葉をのせ、炒りごまを上から散らします。

4　3に熱いお茶を注いでいただきます。

❗ コツのコツ

★お茶は熱いものを使用しましょう。

★温めただし汁を使用してもおいしいです。

★ご飯をさっと水で洗ってぬめりを取るとさらっとしたお茶漬けになります。

★さけは塩けのあるものが、おいしいです。

◆ バリエーション

※さけの代わりに

● 梅干し
● めんたいこ
● 高菜漬け
● 塩昆布
● おろしわさび
● 葉わさび漬け

※お茶の代わりにだし汁を使用

だし汁1と2分の1カップ、塩小さじ4分の1、しょう油小さじ1を合わせて温めます。

第十二章・和食の基本・ご飯もの・麺類 ● Basic Japanese Rice and Noodle Dishes

■ Directions

1　Grill both sides of the chum salmon fillet, and tear the flesh.

2　Rince the green perilla leaves in cold water and remove excess water. Then cut into julienne strips.

3　Put the rice into bowls. Place the torn flesh of the chum salmon on top of the rice, and sprinkle over the green perilla leaves and white sesame.

4　Pour hot tea over the rice.

❗ Tip on Tips

★ Tea you pour over the rice shold be hot.

★ It's also tasty to use heated soup stock instead of tea.

★ Rinsing the rice in cold water briefly to eliminate the scum prior to putting it into a bowl, will make the rice smoother and easier to swallow.

★ Salty salmon will taste better than unsalted ones.

◆ Variations

※ Instead of salmon

● Pickled plum
● Seasoned cod roe
● Pickled leaf mustard
● Salted kelp
● Grated *wasabi*
● Pickled *wasabi* leaf

※ Use soup stock instead of tea

Mix 1 1/4 cups of soup stock, 1/4 tsp salt and 1 tsp soy sauce in a pot and heat it.

Soba Noodles in a Basket
ざるそば

about **20**min
約20分

620kcal
620キロカロリー

そばの風味とのどごしのよさを堪能する " ざるそば "
Cold buckwheat noodles are a tasty treat that are fun to eat

■材料（2人分）
そば（乾燥）…… 300g
刻みのり ……………… 適宜
わさび ………………… 適宜
長ねぎ…………………… 適宜
〈つゆ用材料〉
みりん ……… 1/4 カップ
だし汁 ………… 1 カップ
しょう油 …… 1/4 カップ

■ INGREDIENTS (serves 2)
300g dried *soba* buckwheat noodles
Shredded *nori* seaweed
Wasabi
Naga-negi onion
〈For preparing dipping sauce〉
1/5 cup *mirin* sweet cooking sake(50 ㎖)
4/5 cup stock (200 ㎖)
1/5 cup soy sauce (50 ㎖)

ざるそば　Soba noodles in a basket(Image photo)

■作り方

1 鍋にみりんを入れ、煮たたせてからだし汁、しょう油を加えてひと煮たちさせ、冷ましておきます。

2 長ねぎは小口切りに、わさびは生を使う時は、水洗いしておろし金ですりおろします。

3 鍋に湯を沸かしそばを入れてゆで、流水でもみ洗いをします。

4 そばをザルにあけて水けをきって器に盛り、刻みのりをかけます。そばつゆと薬味のわさび、ねぎを添えます。

! コツのコツ

★つけそばのつゆは、だし汁４：しょう油１：みりん１の割合にします。

■ Directions

1 Place the *mirin* in a pot, and bring to the boil. Add the stock and soy sauce, boil briefly and let stand until cool.

2 Slice the *naga-negi* onion using the edge cut technique. When using fresh *wasabi*, rinse it in cold water and grate.

3 Bring water to the boil in a pot. Place the *soba* noodles in the pot to boil, and rub and rinse in running fresh water.

4 Drain the *soba* noodles on a sieve, and place on serving baskets. Sprinkle on the shredded *nori* pieces. Ladle the dipping sauce into bowls, and place the *wasabi* and *naga-negi* onion condiments on small dishes.

! Tip on Tips

★ To prepare dipping sauce, stock, soy sauce and *mirin* should be used at a ratio of 4 : 1 : 1, respectively.

天ぷらそば
Soba Noodles with Tempura

■材料（２人分）

そば（乾）	200g
えびの天ぷら	4 尾
長ねぎ	1/4 本
三つ葉	3 ～ 4 本
差し水用水	適宜
〈つゆ用材料〉	
水	4 カップ
煮干し	20 尾
削りかつお	30g
料理酒	大さじ 3
しょう油	大さじ 3
みりん	大さじ 3
塩	小さじ 1/2

■作り方

❶ 煮干しは頭と腹わたを除き縦半分にさきます。鍋に水と煮干しを入れ中火にかけ、ひと煮たちしたら火を弱め、アクをすくい、料理酒、しょう油、みりん、塩、削りかつおを入れて、再び沸騰させ20 ～ 30 秒煮たたせたら火を止め、削りかつおが鍋の底に沈んだらふきんでこします。

❷ 大きめの鍋に湯を沸かし、そばを入れて箸でかき混ぜながらゆでます。ふきこぼれそうになったら、もう一度２分の１カップのさし水を入れます。ザルに上げて湯をきり、流水でもみ洗いをし、ぬめりを取り、水けをきります。

❸ 鍋に湯を沸かし、2のそばを入れてさっと温めて水けをきり、丼に入れ、えびの天ぷらをのせ、1のつゆを張り小口切りにした長ねぎと、水洗いし 3cm の長さに切った三つ葉をのせます。

■ INGREDIENTS (serves 2)

200g dried *soba* buckwheat noodles
4 tempura deep-fried shrimps
1/4 *naga-negi* onion
3 or 4 stalks trefoil
Cold water (to be added while boiling noodles)
〈**For preparing broth**〉
3 1/3 cups water (800 ㎖)
20 *niboshi* small dried sardines
30g dried bonito flakes
3 Tbsps cooking sake
3 Tbsps soy sauce
3 Tbsps *mirin* sweet cooking sake
1/2 tsp salt

■ Directions

❶ Remove the heads and entrails from the dried sardines, and tear each in half lengthwise. Place the water and dried sardines in a pot, and bring to the boil over a medium heat. After boiling briefly, reduce the heat and skin off the foam. Add the cooking sake, soy sauce, *mirin*, salt and dried bonito flakes, and bring to the boil again to simmer for 20 to 30 sec. Remove from the heat. When all the bonito flakes have set on the bottom of the pot, strain through a cloth.

❷ Bring water to the boil in a large pot. Place the *soba* noodles in the pot, and boil while stirring with chopsticks. When the water rolls up to the edges of the pot, pour in 2/5 U.S. cup of cold water. Drain the noodles on a sieve, rub and rinse in running fresh water to eliminate slipperiness and drain again.

❸ Bring water to the boil in a pot. Plunge the noodles into the boiling water to re-warm. And drain. Put the noodles into *donburi* bowls, and place the deep-fried shrimps on top. Pour on the broth prepared in 1. above, and garnish with the *naga-negi* onion, sliced using the edge cut technique and the trefoil stalks, cut into 51/2-inch lengths.

Chilled *Somen* Noodles
冷やしそうめん

about
10 min
約10分

326 kcal
326キロカロリー

涼しげな冷やしそうめんは、暑い夏に最適
Chilled *somen* noodles are the best on a hot summer day

■材料（2人分）

そうめん（乾）…150g（3束）	削りがつお ………… 15g
みょうが …………… 1個	砂糖 ………… 大さじ1
あさつき ………… 3〜4本	薄口しょう油 … 大さじ2と1/2
大葉 ………… 4〜5枚	みりん ………… 大さじ1
しょうが ………… 1片	
差し水用水 … 1/2 カップ	※そうめんは水けをきって器に盛
〈つゆの材料〉	り、戻してだし汁で煮た干ししい
水………… 1 カップ	たけ、炒り煮したえび、錦糸卵、
	せん切りにしたきゅうりやハムなど
	をのせてもおいしい。

■ INGREDIENTS (serves 2)

150g (3 bunches) dried *somen* fine noodles
1 *mioga*
3 or 4 leaves *asatsuki* chive
4 or 5 leaves green perilla
1 knob ginger
2/5 cup cold water (to be added when boiling noodles) (100㎖)
〈**For preparing dipping sauce**〉
4/5 cup water (200㎖)

15g dried bonito flakes
1 Tbsp sugar
1 1/2 Tbsps light soy sauce
1 Tbsp *mirin* sweet cooking sake

※ Drain *somen* noodles and arrange in a bowl, and simmered dried-shiitake in stock, fried and simmered shrimp, and julienne-strip eggs, cucumber and ham can be used as tasty toppings.

■作り方

1 鍋につゆの材料を入れて強火で煮たて、中火にします。アクを取りながら1分程煮て火を止め、削りがつおが鍋の底に沈んだらふきんでこして冷やしておきます。

2 みょうがは縦半分に切ってから薄切りに、あさつきは小口切りにします。大葉は水洗いしてからせん切りにし、水にさらしてからペーパータオルなどで水けをきります。しょうがは皮をむいてすりおろします。

3 鍋に湯を沸かし、そうめんを入れ、箸でかき混ぜ鍋底にくっつかないようにします。沸きこぼれそうになったら

差し水カップ2分の1を入れます。麺に芯がなくなったら流水でもみ洗いします。

4 器に水と氷を入れ、そうめんを盛り、**1**のつゆと**2**の薬味を添えていただきます。

■ Directions

1 Place all the dipping sauce ingredients in a pot, and bring to the boil over a high heat. When it comes to the boil, reduce the heat to medium. Simmer for about 1 min while skimming off foam, and remove from the heat. When all the bonito flakes have settled on the bottom of the pot, strain through a cloth and let stand until cool.

2 Cut the *mioga* in half lengthwise, and slice thinly. Slice the *asatsuki* chive leaves using the edge cut technique. Wash the green perilla leaves and cut them into julienne strips. Pat dry with paper towels after exposing to water. Peel the ginger and grate it.

3 Put water in a pot and bring to a boil. Add the *somen* noodles and stir to keep the noodles from sticking. When the water boils over the pot, add 2/5 cup of water. When the noodles are completely cooked to the core, rinse and rub the noodles in running water.

4 Place water and ice in a serving bowl, and arrange the noodles. Serve with the dipping sauce from step 1 and condiments from step 2.

❗ Tip on Tips

★ Take a strand out, expose to cold water and bite to see how well the noodles are cooked.

★ Cook the noodles swiftly over a high heat and rinse well in cold running water to remove slipperiness. This will make the noodles smoother and tastier.

★ Because fine noodles are coated with oil, you need to remove it by rinsing them in running water after boiling.

Udon Noodles with Deep-fried Tofu
きつねうどん

about 12 min 約12分

449 kcal 449キロカロリー

薄味の上品なつゆと油揚げがおいしいうどん
A bowl of tasty *udon* noodles in a light, savory broth is even yummier with deep-fried tofu

■材料（2人分）

生うどん ……………… 2 玉
油揚げ ……………… 1 枚
長ねぎ ……………… 1/4 本
かいわれ大根 …… 1/4 パック
〈油揚げ用〉
だし汁 ………… 1/2 カップ
料理酒 ……… 大さじ 1
砂糖 ………… 大さじ 1
みりん ……… 大さじ 1/2
しょう油 …… 大さじ 1/2
〈つゆ用材料〉
水 ……………… 4 カップ
昆布 ……………… 10cm
削りかつお ……… 30g
料理酒 ……… 大さじ 3
薄口しょう油 … 大さじ 1と1/2
塩 ……………… 小さじ 1
みりん ……… 大さじ 2

■ INGREDIENTS (serves 2)

2 portions fresh *udon* wheat noodles
1 *abura-age* deep-fried tofu
1/4 *naga-negi* onion
1/4 package young giant white radish shoots
〈**For preparing deep-fried tofu**〉
2/5 cup stock (100 ㎖)
1 Tbsp cooking sake
1 Tbsp sugar
1/2 Tbsp *mirin* sweet cooking sake
1/2 Tbsp soy sauce
〈**For preparing broth**〉
3 1/3 cups water (800 ㎖)
4 -inch *konbu* kelp
30g dried bonito flakes
3 Tbsps cooking sake
1 1/2 Tbsps light soy sauce
1 tsp salt
2 Tbsps *mirin* sweet cooking sake

■作り方

1 油揚げは熱湯をかけて油抜きし、半分に切ってから三角形に切ります。だし汁を熱し、料理酒、砂糖、油揚げを入れて2〜3分煮ます。みりんとしょう油を加え、落としぶたをして汁けがなくなるまで弱火で煮含めます。長ねぎは小口切りにします。かいわれ大根は根を切ります。

2 鍋に水と昆布を入れて、中火にかけ、沸騰直前に昆布を取り出します。煮たったら、削りがつおを入れてひと煮し、火を止めます。削りがつおが鍋の底に沈んだら、ふきんでこします。だし汁を鍋に入れて煮たて、料理酒、薄口しょう油、塩、みりんを入れてひと煮たちさせます。

3 鍋に湯を沸かし、うどんをほぐしながら入れてゆで、流水でよく水洗いをします。

4 3のうどんを熱湯でさっと温めて水けをきり、温めておいた丼に入れ、1の油揚げをのせ、あつあつのつゆを張ります。1の長ねぎ、かいわれ大根を添えていただきます。

! コツのコツ

★ 油揚げを油抜きすることで、仕上がりが油っぽくなりません。

★ うどんをもみ洗いすることで、だし汁がにごらず、つるっとしたうどんに仕上がります。

★ 丼にお湯を入れて温めておきましょう。

■ Directions

1 Pour boiling water over the *abura-age* to eliminate excess oil, cut in half and cut further into triangles. Place the cooking sake, sugar and deep-fried tofu triangles in the hot stock, and simmer for a few minutes. Add the *mirin* and soy sauce, cover with a drop-lid and simmer over a low heat until all the liquid is gone. Slice the *naga-negi* onion using the edge cut technique. Chop off the roots of the young giant white radish shoots.

2 Place the water and *konbu* kelp in a pot, and bring to the boil over a medium heat (the kelp must be removed from the pot immediately before coming to the boil). When it comes to the boil, add the dried bonito flakes, boil briefly and turn off the heat. When all the flakes have set on the bottom of the pot, strain through a cloth. Place this strained stock in a pot, and bring to the boil. Add the cooking sake, light soy sauce, salt and *mirin*, and boil briefly.

3 Place the *udon* noodles–while loosening each portion–in boiling water, and boil. Rinse the noodles well in running fresh water.

4 Plunge the noodles into hot water to re-warm them, drain and put into warmed *donburi* bowls. Place the *abura-age* on top of the noodles. Pour on the hot broth, and garnish with the *naga-negi* onion and young giant white radish shoots.

! Tip on Tips

★ Eliminate the excess oil from the *abura-age* to keep the finish from getting too oily.

★ Make sure the boiled noodles are rinsed well. This will result in clear broth and smooth noodles.

★ Pour a little hot water into the serving bowls to warm them beforehand.

Udon Noodles in the Pot
鍋焼きうどん

about **20**min 約20分 | **589**kcal 589キロカロリー

寒い日にふうーふうーいいながら食べたい鍋焼きうどん
Enjoy an *udon* noodle hot pot while blowing your breath to the noodles on a cold winter day

■材料（2人分）

ゆでうどん ………… 2玉	〈つゆ用材料〉
えびの天ぷら ……… 2尾	水 …………… 4カップ
かまぼこ ……… 4切れ分	削りかつお ………… 40g
しいたけ ………… 2枚	料理酒 ……… 大さじ3
きぬさや ……… 4〜6枚	砂糖 ……… 小さじ1
お麩 ………… 小6枚	しょう油 ……… 大さじ3
長ねぎ ……… 1/3本	みりん ……… 大さじ3
卵 …………… 2個	塩 ……… 小さじ1/2

■ INGREDIENTS (serves 2)

2 portions fresh *udon* wheat noodles	〈**For preparing broth**〉
2 tempura deep-fried shrimps	3 1/3 cups water （800㎖）
4 slices *kamaboko* fish paste	40g dried bonito flakes
2 shiitake mushrooms	3 Tbsps cooking sake
4 to 6 *kinusaya* Chinese pea pods	1 tsp sugar
6 small dried wheat glutens	3 Tbsps soy sauce
1/3 *naga-negi* onion	3 Tbsps *mirin* sweet cooking sake
2 eggs	1/2 tsp salt

■作り方

1 しいたけは石づきと軸を取り飾り包丁を入れます。きぬさやは筋を取って塩ゆでし、冷水に取り水けをきります。麩は水につけて戻しておきます。長ねぎは小口切りにします。

2 鍋につゆ用の材料を入れて強火にかけ、煮たったら中火にし、アクをすくいながら1分程煮て火を止めます。削りがつおが鍋の底に沈んだらふきんでこします。

3 うどんを軽くゆで、流水でよく水洗いをし、水けをきっておきます。

4 土鍋に2のつゆ、3のうどん、1のしいたけ、お麩を入れてふたをして火にかけ煮たったら、かまぼこ、1のきぬさや、えびの天ぷらをのせ、卵を割り入れ、ふたをして約30秒煮ます。火を止めて、薬味に1の長ねぎをのせていただきます。

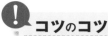

コツのコツ

★ゆでたうどんを水洗いすることで、だしがにごりません。

★卵は血が入っていたり、殻が入ってしまう可能性があるので、別の器に一度割り、確認してから鍋に入れましょう。

★天ぷらはすぐしんなりするので最後に入れるとよいでしょう。

1-a

1-b

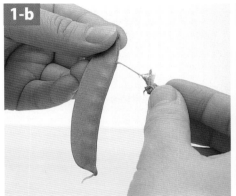

3

■ Directions

1 Chop off the stems of the shiitake mushrooms, and make a cross-shape incision on each cap. String the *kinusaya* pea pods, boil in salted water, rinse in cold water and drain. Soak the wheat glutens in cold water to soften. Slice the *naga-negi* onion using the edge cut technique.

2 Place all the ingredients necessary for preparing the broth in a pot, and bring to the boil over a high heat. When it comes to the boil, reduce the heat to medium and simmer for about 1 min while skimming off foam before turning off the heat. When all the bonito flakes have settled on the bottom of the pot, strain through a cloth.

3 Lightly boil the noodles, rinse well in running water and drain. Set aside.

4 Place the strained broth, *udon* noodles, shiitake mushrooms and wheat glutens in a clay serving pot, cover the pot and bring to the boil. When the broth begins to boil, place the *kamaboko* fish paste, *kinusaya* pea pods and deep-fried shrimps on top of the noodles, and finally add the eggs. Cover the pot again, and simmer for 30 sec. Remove from the heat, and garnish with the *naga-negi* onion.

Tip on Tips

★ Rinsing the cooked noodles in water will keep your broth clear.

★ Remember to crack the eggs in a separate bowl before adding to the pot so you don't end up with eggshells or eggy blood spots in your dish.

★ Place tempura shrimps last in the serving pot. Otherwise, they will become soggy in the broth.

243

Japanese-style Chow Mein
焼きそば

ソース味が食欲をそそるみんなが大好きな " 焼きそば "
Everyone loves to indulge in yummy "*Yakisoba*" sauce and the noodles

■材料（4人分）

蒸し麺	2 玉
豚肉（薄切り）	60g
桜えび（乾）	5g
キャベツ	3 枚
もやし	100g
にんじん	30g
きくらげ	大1 枚
サラダ油	大さじ 2
塩・こしょう	各少々

A
- オイスターソース … 大さじ1
- ウスターソース … 小さじ 2
- しょう油 … 小さじ 2
- 料理酒 … 大さじ 2
- 塩・こしょう … 各少々

青のり・紅しょうが … 各適宜

■ INGREDIENTS (serves 4)

2 portions cooked
yakisoba wheat noodles
60g pork, thinly sliced
5g dried *sakura* shrimps
3 cabbage leaves
100g bean sprouts
30g carrot
1 large cloud ear mushroom
2 Tbsps vegetable oil

Pinch salt and pepper

A
- 1 Tbsp oyster sauce
- 2 tsps Japanese-style Worcestershire sauce
- 2 tsps soy sauce
- 2 Tbsps cooking sake
- Pinch salt and pepper

Green laver
Beni-shoga red vinegared ginger

■作り方

1 豚肉は2〜3cm幅に切り、塩、こしょうで下味をつけます。キャベツは1cm幅の短冊切りに、にんじんは皮をむき、細切りに、もやしは水洗いします。きくらげは水で戻し、細切りにします。**A**の調味料をボウルに混ぜておきます。

2 フライパンにサラダ油大さじ2をひき、1の豚肉、キャベツ、にんじん、もやし、きくらげを順に入れて炒め、蒸しめんを加えて炒めます。

3 2に桜えび、**A**の調味料を加えて炒めます。

4 器に盛り、青のりをふり、紅しょうがを添えます。

> **! コツのコツ**
> ★蒸し麺に焼き目をしっかりとつけてから炒めると、おいしくできます。

■ Directions

1 Cut the pork into 3/4 to 1 1/5-inch pieces, and season with salt and pepper. Cut the cabbage leaves into 3/8-inch wide rectangles. Peel the carrot, and cut into thin strips. Rinse the bean sprouts in cold water. Soak the cloud ear mushrooms in cold water to soften, and cut into thin strips. Mix all the seasonings of **A** in a bowl, and set aside.

2 Spread 2 Tbsps vegetable oil over the frying pan, and add the pork, cabbage leaves, carrot, bean sprouts and cloud ear mushrooms in this order, and fry. Then, add cooked noodles and fry.

3 Add the *sakura* shrimps and seasonings of A to 2, and fry.

4 Arrange on individual plates. Sprinkle on the green laver, and garnish with the *beni-shoga* red vinegared ginger.

> **! Tip on Tips**
> ★ To enhance the taste of the dish, fry the noodles until both sides are browned first.

焼きうどん
Fried *Udon* Noodles

■材料（2人分）	
ゆでうどん	2玉
豚こま切れ肉	80g
キャベツ	2枚
長ねぎ	1/2本
にんじん	4cm分
しいたけ	2枚
かまぼこ	4cm分
かつお節	適宜
松葉のり	適宜
あさつき	3〜4本
サラダ油	大さじ1
塩・こしょう	各少々
しょう油	大さじ1
ソース	大さじ2

■ INGREDIENTS (serves 2)

- 2 portions cooked *udon* wheat noodles
- 80g pork, chopped
- 2 leaves cabbage
- 1/2 *naga-negi* onion
- 1 1/2-inch carrot
- 2 shiitake mushrooms
- 1 1/2-inch *kamaboko* fish paste
- Dried bonito flakes
- Nori seaweed fine shreds
- 3 or 4 leaves *asatsuki* chive
- 1 Tbsp vegetable oil
- Pinch salt and pepper
- 1 Tbsp soy sauce
- 2 Tbsps Japanese-style Worcestershire sauce

■作り方

❶ 豚こま切れ肉は一口大に、長ねぎは斜め薄切りに、キャベツはざく切りにします。にんじんは1cm幅の短冊切り、しいたけは石づきと軸を取り、薄切りにします。かまぼこは5〜6cmの厚さに切り、半分にします。

❷ ゆでうどんはザルに入れ、さっと熱湯をかけてほぐし、水けをよくきります。

❸ フライパンに油を入れ熱し、1の豚こま切れ肉を炒め、1のにんじん、キャベツ、しいたけ、長ねぎ、かまぼこを炒めます。野菜がしんなりしたら2のうどんを入れて炒め、塩、こしょうをし、しょう油とソースで味をつけます。

❹ 3を皿に盛り、かつお節、小口切りのあさつき、松葉のりをのせていただきます。

■ Directions

❶ Cut the pork into bite-sized pieces. Slice the *naga-negi* onion diagonally and thinly. Chop the cabbage leaves coarsely. Cut the carrot into 3/8-inch rectangles. Chop off the stems of the shiitake mushrooms, and slice thinly. Slice the *kamaboko* fish paste into about 1/8-inch pieces, and cut the slices in half.

❷ Place the cooked *udon* noodles on a sieve, pour boiling water over them quickly to loosen each portion and drain well.

❸ Heat the vegetable oil in a frying pan, and fry the chopped pork. Add the *naga-negi* onion, carrot, cabbage, shiitake mushrooms and *kamaboko* fish paste, and fry. When the vegetables are tender, add the *udon* noodles and fry. Season with the salt, pepper, soy sauce and Japanese-style Worcestershire sauce.

❸ Arrange in individual bowls, and garnish with the dried bonito flakes, *asatsuki* chive leaves chopped using the edge cut technique and nori seaweed shreds.

第十二章・和食の基本・ご飯もの・麺類 ● Basic Japanese Rice and Noodle Dishes

Cold Chinese Noodles
冷やし中華

about **10** min
約10分

923 kcal
923 キロカロリー

夏になるとむしょうに食べたくなる冷やし中華
Chilled Chinese noodles will cool you down during hot summer

■材料 (2人分)

中華麺 (生麺) ······ 2 玉	水 ············· 小さじ 1
長ねぎ ············· 1/2 本	サラダ油 ············· 適宜
きゅうり ············· 1 本	〈ごまダレ〉
トマト ············· 1 個	ごま ············· 大さじ 1
ハム ············· 4 枚	芝麻醤 ············· 大さじ 3
小えび ············· 4 尾	スープ (顆粒スープの素小さじ
好みの海藻 (乾燥) 適宜	1/2+ 湯大さじ 2) ··· 大さじ 2
リーフレタス ·········· 適宜	酢 ············· 大さじ 3
ごま油 ············· 小さじ 1	砂糖 ············· 大さじ 4
〈薄焼き卵用材料〉	しょう油 ············· 大さじ 4
卵 ············· 2 個	ごま油 ············· 小さじ 2
塩 ············· 少々	マスタード (練りからし)
片栗粉 ·········· 小さじ 1	············· 小さじ 1/2

■ INGREDIENTS (serves 2)

2 portions Chinese noodles (uncooked)	1 tbsp *katakuriko* starch
1/2 *naga-negi* onion	1 tbsp water
1 cucumber	Vegetable oil
1 tomato	〈**For preparing sesame sauce**〉
4 slices ham	1 Tbsp sesame
4 small shrimp	3 Tbsps Chinese sesame paste
Dried seaweed of your preference	2 Tbsps soup (1/2 tbsp stock powder + 2 Tbsps hot water)
Leaf lettuce	3 Tbsps vinegar
1 tbsp sesame oil	4 Tbsps sugar
〈**For preparing egg crepe**〉	4 Tbsps soy sauce
2 eggs	2 tbsps sesame oil
Small amount of salt	1/2 tbsp mustard paste

■作り方

1 小さめのボウルに卵を割り入れ、塩を少々入れて泡立てないように軽くほぐし、片栗粉に水を加えてよく混ぜ合わせた水溶き片栗粉を加えてかき混ぜます。

2 平たいフライパンを強火で十分熱したら弱火にして、サラダ油をしみ込ませたペーパータオルなどでフライパン全体に薄く油をひきます。1の卵液を流し入れ、卵液がかたまらないうちに、フライパンを回しながら薄く伸ばして焼きます。

3 2の卵の表面まで軽く火が通ってきたら、竹串を端に入れて周囲から丁寧に

はがしていき、フライパンの中央まで竹串を動かして裏返しやすくしてから、両手で卵の周囲を持って、破れないように一気に裏返します。

4 裏側は余熱で火を通すかんじで軽く焼き、3の要領で裏返し、盆ザルの裏側にあけて冷ましておきます。続けて、残った卵液を同じように焼き冷ましておきます。冷めたら長さ6cmくらいの細切りにします。

5 水洗いしたきゅうりは薄く斜め切りにしてから、せん切りにして冷水に約10分さらしてシャキッとさせ、水けをきっておきます。

6 海藻は水につけて戻し、戻ったらザルにあけて水けをきっておきます。リーフレタスは水洗いして水けをきって適当な大きさに切っておきます。

7 ハムも細切りにします。長ねぎは約4cmに切り、縦に包丁を入れて芯を取り除き、白い部分を重ねて縦に細く切って白髪ねぎにして、水にさらし水けをきっておきます。トマトはへたを取り除き、薄切りにします。

■ Directions

1 Break the eggs in a small bowl. Add the salt and beat lightly without whipping. Add the water to the *katakuriko* starch, mix together and pour into the bowl and stir.

2 Place a flat frying pan over high heat. After heating sufficiently, turn to low heat. Soak a paper towel in vegetable oil and apply the oil thinly on the entire surface of the pan. Pour the egg from step 1 into the pan and spread it thinly by rotating the pan before the egg hardens.

3 When the eggs from step 2 have cooked lightly to the surface, work a bamboo skewer around the edge and peel the crepe from the pan

gently. Move the bamboo skewer toward the center of the pan so that you can easily flip it over. Holding the edges of egg crepe with both hands, flip over at once.

4 Fry the reverse side lightly with the remaining heat then flip again in the same manner with step 3. Transfer to a reverse side of a flat sieve basket and set aside to cool. Immediately fry another egg crepe with the remaining egg and let it cool. When both crepes are cool, cut them thinly into 2 1/4-inch lengths.

5 Wash the cucumber, cut into thin slices diagonally and then into

julienne strips. Expose to chilled water for about 10 minutes to keep crisp. Drain excess water.

6 Reconstitute the dried seaweed with water then transfer to a sieve and drain. Rinse the lettuce leaves, drain excess water and cut into bit sizes.

7 Cut the ham into julienne strips. Cut the *naga-negi* onion into about 1 1/2-inch lengths and then cut into the center lengthwise to remove the core. Stack the white parts and cut lengthwise into julienne strips. Expose to water and drain. Remove the stem of the tomato and cut into thin slices.

8 小えびは背わたを竹串などで取り、小さめの鍋に入れ酒、塩少々（分量外）を入れて中火にかけます。えびがピンク色にかわり、中まで火が通るまで炒りながら煮ます。あら熱が取れたら殻をむきます。

9 カップにごまダレの材料を混ぜ合わせ、冷やしておきます。

10 鍋にたっぷりの湯を沸かしておき、中華麺をほぐしながら入れ、中華麺が少し柔らかくなったら菜箸でゆっくりとほぐしながらゆでていきます。

11 中華麺を1本つまんでかたさを調べてみて、芯がなくなるまでゆでます。ゆで上がったらザルにあけ、流水で手早く洗いぬめりを取って水けをきっておきます。

12 水けをきった中華麺をボウルに入れ、ごま油小さじ1を加え麺全体にからめて、麺がくっつかないようにします。

13 皿に12の中華麺を盛り、6のリーフレタス、4の薄切り卵、7のハム、5のきゅうり、7の白髪ねぎ、トマト、8のえび、6の海藻を盛りつけ、9のごまダレをかけていただきます。

！コツのコツ

★ 薄焼き卵に片栗粉を加えることにより、卵にコシを与え、薄く焼いた時に破れにくくなります。

★ 薄焼き卵は、表面が焼けてないうちに裏返すと破れてしまうので注意しましょう。卵を均等に伸ばして焼くのがポイントです。

★ ゆでた中華麺は流水でよく手でもむように洗い、麺のぬめりを取りコシを強くします。

★ 水洗いした中華麺の水けをよくきりましょう。水けをきらないと仕上がりが水っぽくなってしまうので注意しましょう。

7-a

7-b

11

8 Remove the entrails from the shrimp with a bamboo skewer. Put the shrimp in a small pot with sake and extra small amount of salt. Place over medium heat. Braise the shrimp until pink and cooked completely. When cool, remove the shells.

9 Mix all the ingredients for the sesame sauce together in a cup and chill in the refrigerator.

10 Fill a pot with plenty of water and bring to a boil. Put the Chinese noodles in the pot while unraveling. As the noodles soften, unravel them slowly with cooking chopsticks.

11 Test a noodle by pinching with your fingers. When cooked completely, transfer to a sieve and rinse quickly in running water to remove the slack. Drain excess water.

12 Put the drained noodles in a bowl. Add 1 tbsp sesame oil and spread all over the noodles to prevent from sticking together.

13 Arrange the noodles from step 12 on a plate. Garnish with the leaf lettuce from step 6, julienne strips of egg from step 4, ham from step 7, cucumber from step 5, *naganegi* onion and tomato from step 7, shrimp from step 8 and seaweed from step 6. Pour the sesame sauce from step 9 and eat.

！Tip on Tips

★ The *katakuriko* starch gives the eggs firmness and prevents them from tearing when fried thinly.

★ If you flip the egg crepe before the surface is cooked, it'll tear easily. The key is to spread the egg evenly.

★ Rub the boiled noodles well with your hands in running water to remove the slime and give the noodles body.

★ Drain the rinsed noodles well or you'll have a watery finish.

第十三章
Chapter 13

Basic Japanese One-Pot Dishes
和食の基本・鍋料理

寒い日が続くとむしょうに食べたくなる鍋料理。ひとつの鍋で家族全員が食べられ、幸せな気分になれるのが鍋料理の魅力。豪華なすき焼きから、定番のおでん、寄せ鍋などを紹介。

One-pot dishes are good to eat on cold days. A single pot can serve an entire family and make everyone warm and happy. In this chapter, we introduce hearty sukiyaki, classic oden, the all-in-one-pot and more.

Sukiyaki (Kanto-style)
すき焼き（関東風）

甘辛い牛肉が生卵とからんで食がすすむごちそう
This delicacy of salty-sweet beef in beaten raw eggs satisfies all appetites

■材料（4人分）

牛ロース肉（すき焼き用）	……	400g
焼き豆腐	…………………	1丁
長ねぎ	…………………	2本
春菊	…………………	1束
しめじ	…………………	1パック
えのきだけ	…………………	1袋
しらたき	…………………	1玉

A	しょう油	……	1/2カップ
	みりん	………	1/2カップ
	料理酒	……	1/4カップ
	水	…………	1/4カップ
	砂糖	…………	大さじ3

牛脂	…………………	少々
卵	…………………	4個

■ INGREDIENTS (serves 4)

400g beef loin, thinly sliced for sukiyaki
1 cake grilled tofu
2 *naga-negi* onions
1 bunch *shungiku* chrysanthemum leaves
1 packet *shimeji* mushrooms
1 pack of enokidake mushroom
1 knot *shirataki* filaments

- 2/5 cup soy sauce (100㎖)
- 2/5 cup *mirin* sweetcooking sake (100㎖)
- **A** 1/5 cup cooking sake (50㎖)
- 1/5 cup water (50㎖)
- 3 Tbsps sugar

Small quantity of beef suet
4 eggs

■作り方

1　Ａの材料を鍋に入れて、ひと煮たちさせ割り下を作ります。

2　焼き豆腐は8等分に切ります。長ねぎは斜め切りに、春菊は水洗いし、葉をつみ取ります。しめじは石づきを取り、小房に分けます。えのきだけは根元を切り落とします。しらたきは水からゆで、沸騰させて水にあけ、水けをきって食べやすい長さに切り分けます。

3　鍋を熱して牛脂を入れたら火を弱め、牛肉を広げて入れて焼き、色が変わりはじめたら1の割り下を注ぎ、強火にして肉をさっと煮ます。そこに他の具材を加え、煮えた順に溶き卵をつけていただきます。

！コツのコツ

★牛脂はすき焼きに旨味やコクを出すので、必ず使用しましょう。

★しらたきは肉をかたくする成分が含まれているため、肉の横におかないようにしましょう。

★牛肉は火を通しすぎるとかたくなりますので、火が通ったら早めに食べましょう。

◆関西風すき焼き◆
Sukiyaki (Kansai-style)

関西風すきやきは、鍋を熱したら牛脂を溶かし、牛肉を広げ入れてそこに直接砂糖をふりかけ、割り下（砂糖を入れない）をいれるのが関西風です。関東風は割り下に砂糖を入れます。

To prepare the sukiyaki in the kansai-style, add the beef suet after heating the pan. Let it melt and spread the sliced beef in the pan. Sprinkle sugar directly on the beef then pour the sauce (without the sugar). In the kanto-style, the sugar is added to the sauce beforehand.

1

2-a

2-b

3

■ Directions

1　Place all the ingredients in a pot, and boil briefly to make the simmering sauce.

2　Cut the tofu into eights. Cut the *naga-negi* onion diagonally. Rinse the *shungiku* chrysanthemum in cold water, and pluck off the leaves. Chop off the hard tips of the stems of the *shimeji* mushrooms, and divide into portions. Remove the stem tips of the enokidake mushrooms. Place the *shirataki* filaments in a pot filled with cold water, and bring to the boil. Plunge the *shirataki* into cold water, drain and cut into lengths that are easy to eat.

3　Heat a sukiyaki pan, place the beef suet in the pan and reduce the heat. Spread the beef slices over the bottom of the pan, and sprinkle. Pour on the simmering sauce prepared in 1. above. Turn up the heat to high, and simmer the beef briefly. Add the other solid ingredients. Set each place with an individual dipping bowl into which an egg has been broken. Each diner can choose something simmered from the pot, and dip it into the beaten egg to eat.

！Tip on Tips

★ Beef suet gives sukiyaki a full-bodied flavor, so be sure to use some.

★ Since *shirataki* filaments contain a component that makes meat tough, don't place them beside the meat.

★ Beef tends to get tough when cooked too long. Eat as soon as it's cooked.

Shabu-Shabu
しゃぶしゃぶ

ポン酢とごまダレで牛肉をいくらでも食べられる "しゃぶしゃぶ"

Shabu-Shabu and its tasty sauces of ponzu and sesame keep you coming back for more

■材料 (4人分)

しゃぶしゃぶ用牛肉
………… 500 〜 600g
木綿豆腐 ………… 1 丁
白菜 ……………… 1/4 株
春菊 ……………… 1/2 束
長ねぎ ………… 約 2 本
昆布 ……………… 10cm
水 ………… 8 〜 10 カップ

〈つけタレ〉
ポン酢しょう油 …… 適宜
ごまダレ (市販のもの) … 適宜
〈薬 味〉
もみじおろし ……… 適宜
青ねぎ …………… 適宜

■ INGREDIENTS (serves 4)

500 to 600g beef for shabu-shabu
1 cake "cotton" tofu
1/4 whole Chinese cabbage
1/2 bunch *shungiku* chrysanthemum leaves
About 2 *naga-negi* onions
4 -inch *konbu* kelp
6 5/8 to 8 1/2 cups water
(1600 〜 2000㎖)

〈**For preparing dipping sauce**〉
Commercially prepared *ponzu*
sauce (citrus juice and soy sauce)
Commercially prepared sesame sauce
〈**For condiments**〉
Momiji-oroshi grated giant white
radish with red pepper
Ao-negi onion

■作り方

1 昆布は乾いたふきんでさっとふき、水を入れた鍋に入れて30分くらいおきます。

2 白菜は水洗いし、ざく切りにします。春菊はかたい茎の部分を切り、水洗いして葉を摘み取ります。長ねぎは斜め切りにします。木綿豆腐は一口大に切ります。

3 1の鍋を火にかけ、沸騰する直前に昆布を取り出します。

4 3の鍋に2の白菜、春菊、長ねぎ、木綿豆腐を入れて火を通します。

5 野菜、木綿豆腐に火が通ったら、肉を箸で持ち、一枚ずつ湯に泳がせます。

6 肉の色が変わったら、もみじおろし、小口切りにした青ねぎを添えたつけダレにつけていただきます。

! コツのコツ

★鍋に牛肉を入れると、アクが浮いてくるので、こまめに取りましょう。

★牛肉は火を通しすぎるとかたくなるので、軽く火が通る程度にするとよいでしょう。

★野菜は火の通りにくいものから順に入れていきましょう。

豚肉のしゃぶしゃぶ
Pork Shabu-Shabu

■材料（4人分）

しゃぶしゃぶ用豚肉 …	約600g
白菜	1/4個
水菜	1束
長ねぎ	約2本
えのきだけ	1袋
ポン酢しょう油	適宜

■ INGREDIENTS (serves 4)

600g thinly-sliced pork
1/4 Chinese cabbage
1 bundle of potherb mustard
2 naga-negi onions
1 pack of enokidake mushroom
Ponzu soy sauce

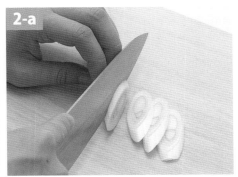

■ Directions

1 Briefly wipe the *konbu* kelp with a dry cloth. Soak the kelp in a pot filled with cold water for about 30 min.

2 Rinse the Chinese cabbage in cold water, and cut coarsely. Chop off the hard stalks of the *shungiku* chrysanthemum, rinse in cold water and pluck off the leaves. Cut the *naga-negi* onions diagonally. Cut the tofu into bite-sized pieces.

3 Place the pot with the kelp over heat, and take the kelp out of the pot immediately before it comes to the boil.

4 Add the Chinese cabbage, shungiku, *naga-nagi* onions and tofu to the pot, and simmer until heated through.

5 When the vegetables and tofu are cooked, lift a slice of beef with chopsticks and plunge it into the simmering broth. Cook the beef slice by slice.

6 When the red meat becomes pink, each diner dips it in either *ponzu* or sesame sauce, which is mixed with *momiji-oroshi* and *ao-negi* onions sliced using the edge cut technique.

! Tip on Tips

★ After putting beef in the broth, foam appears on its surface. So, skim the broth occasionally while dining.

★ Beef is delicious when only slightly heated. So, be careful not to over-cook it.

★ Add vegetables in the order of their hardness.

All in One-Pot
よせ鍋

about 15 min / 約15分

280 kcal / 280キロカロリー

だし汁と食材から出た味が最高に旨い鍋料理

A heavenly hot pot with mixed flavor of soup stock and various ingredients

■材料（4人分）

はまぐり	8 個
えび	4 尾
金目だいの切り身	2 切れ
鶏もも肉	1 枚
白菜	1/4 株
水菜	1/2 株
長ねぎ	1 本
しいたけ	4 枚
しめじ	1 パック

A ┌ だし汁 …… 7 カップ
  │ 料理酒 … 1/2 カップ
  │ 塩 …… 小さじ 3/4
  └ 薄口しょう油 … 大さじ1

あさつき	適宜
すだち	適宜
紅葉おろし	適宜
ポン酢しょう油	適宜

■ INGREDIENTS (serves 4)

8 live hard-shell clams
4 shrimps
2 fillets sea bream
1 chicken thigh
1/4 whole Chinese cabbage
1/2 bunch *mizuna* potherb mustard
1 *naga-negi* onion
4 shiitake mushrooms
1 packet *shimeji* mush-
rooms

A ┌ 5 3/5 cups stock (1400 ㎖)
  │ 2/5 cup cooking sake (100㎖)
  │ 3/4 tsp salt
  └ 1 Tbsp light soy sauce

Asatsuki chive leaves
Sudachi lime
Momiji-oroshi grated gi-
ant white radish with red
pepper
Ponzu soy sauce

■作り方

1 はまぐりはよく水洗いをし、汚れを落とします。殻と殻を打ち合わせ、鈍い音がするものは除きましょう。えびは背わたを取り、水けをふき取っておきます。金目だいは食べやすい大きさに切り、ザルにのせて、さっと熱湯を回しかけたら、氷水に入れ、水けをふき取っておきます。鶏もも肉は余分な脂身、皮を除き一口大のそぎ切りにします。

2 白菜はよく水洗いし、ざく切りにします。水菜はよく水洗いし、4cmの長さに切ります。長ねぎは斜め切りにします。しいたけは石づきと軸を切り取り、飾り包丁を入れます。しめじは石づき

を取り、小房に分けます。

3 鍋にＡを入れて煮立て、1の魚貝類、鶏もも肉など、だしの出るものや火の通りにくいものから入れて、ひと煮たちさせ、アクを取ります。

4 3が煮えたら、2の具材を入れて煮ます。煮えたら小鉢に取り、小口切りのあさつき、紅葉おろし、すだちなどを添えて、ポン酢しょう油と鍋の汁でいただきます。

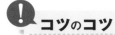

コツのコツ

★はまぐりの殻と殻を合わせて、鈍い音のするものは死んでいる場合が多いので使用しないようにしましょう。

★金目だいに熱湯を回しかけることによって魚の臭みを取り除くことができます。

★魚介類、肉類などだしの出るものや、火の通りにくい具材（きのこ類、白菜の芯の部分など）を先に入れましょう。

1-a

1-b

2

3

■ Directions

1 Prepare the ingredients preliminarily. Scrub the clamshells clean. Do not use the ones you hear dull sounds when striking with each other. Devein the shrimps and wipe dry. Cut the sea bream into bite-sized pieces and place on a sieve. Pour boiling water over briefly and soak in chilled water with ice. Drain and wipe dry. Remove excess fat and skin of the chicken thigh and cut into bite-sized thin slices.

2 Wash the Chinese cabbage well in cold water and cut coarsely. Wash the *mizuna* potherb mustard well in cold water and cut into 1 1/2-inch lengths. Cut the *naga-negi* onion diagonally. Remove the stems of the shiitake mushrooms, and make a cross-shape incision on each cap. Chop off the tips of the *shimeji*

mushroom stems and divide into portions.

3 Put **A** in a pot and bring to the boil. Put the ingredients that would add flavors to the stock, such as the seafood and chicken thighs, and the ones that take time to be cooked first. When it comes to the boil, skim off the foam.

4 When the ingredients from step 3 are cooked, add the ingredients from step 2 and simmer. After all the ingredients are cooked, serve in individual small bowls and provide each diner with the condiments such as the edge-cut *asatsuki* chives, *momiji-oroshi* grated *daikon* radish with red pepper and sliced *sudachi*

lime. Eat with *ponzu* soy sauce and simmering soup in the pot.

Tip on Tips

★ Strike the shells of the clams with each other. Do not use the ones that sound dully since it is likely that those may be dead.

★ Remove odors of fish by pouring boiling water over sea bream.

★ Add the seafood and meat to the pot first so they add their flavors to the soup, and also other ingredients like mushrooms and the heart of the Chinese cabbage as these take more time to cook.

Chicken One-pot
鶏の水炊き

about **40**min 約40分

416kcal 416キロカロリー

ぽん酢と鶏もも肉の相性が抜群においしいヘルシー鍋料理

A healthy hot pot that pairs *ponzu* soy sauce and juicy chicken thighs

■材料（4人分）

鶏もも肉（骨つきぶつ切り）	…	600g
豆腐	…	1丁
白菜	…	1/4株
春菊	…	1/2束
しいたけ	…	4個
えのきだけ	…	1袋
長ねぎ	…	2本
くずきり	…	適宜
水	…	8～10カップ
だし昆布	…	15cm
料理酒	…	1/2カップ
大根おろし	…	適宜
あさつき	…	適宜
ぽん酢しょう油	…	適宜

※鶏もも肉の他に手羽肉を使ってもよい
でしょう。また、その他の具材として水
菜、しめじなどを加えてもおいしい。

■ INGREDIENTS (serves 4)

600g chicken thighs with bones,
chopped into pieces

1 cake tofu

1/4 whole Chinese cabbage

1/2 bunch *shungiku* chrysanthemum leaves

4 shiitake mushrooms

1 pack of enokidake mushroom

2 *naga-negi* onions

Kudzu filaments

6 5/8 to 8 1/2 cups water (1600～2000㎖)

6 inch *konbu* kelp

2/5 cup cooking sake (100㎖)

Grated giant white radish

Asatsuki chive leaves

Commercially prepared *ponzu*
sauce (citrus juice and soy sauce)

※ Chicken wings can be used instead
of chicken thigh. *Mizuna* potherb
mustard and *shimeji* mushrooms can
also be added to the ingredients.

■作り方

1 鶏もも肉はさっと湯引きにします。

2 鍋に水とだし昆布を入れて30分くらいおき、料理酒、1の鶏もも肉を入れて強火にかけ、煮たったら弱火にし、アクを取りながら、汁が2分の1になるくらいまで煮込みます。

3 豆腐は6〜8等分に切り、白菜は水洗いしざく切りに、春菊は水洗いして葉を摘み取ります。しいたけは石づき

と軸を取り、飾り包丁を入れます。えのきだけは根元を切り落とし、長ねぎは5〜6mm幅の斜め切りにします。くずきりは熱湯で透き通るまでゆでて水けをきっておきます。

4 2の鶏もも肉が柔らかくなったら、3の具材を入れて煮ます。大根おろし、小口切りのあさつき、ぽん酢しょう油を添えます。

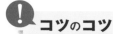

❗ コツのコツ

★鶏もも肉は熱湯に入れアクや臭みを取ってから使用しましょう。また、湯通しした鶏もも肉を鍋に入れてから火にかけて煮込むことで、鶏もも肉からだしがよく出て、柔らかく仕上がります。

★春菊（青菜類）は、食感が悪くなるので、最後に加えて熱を通しすぎないようにしましょう。

■ Directions

1 Blanch the chicken thighs.

2 Set the water and *konbu* kelp, and let stand for about 30 min. Add the cooking sake and blanched chicken thighs, and bring to the boil over a high heat. When it comes to the boil, reduce the heat to low and simmer until the liquid is reduced to 2/3 while skimming off foam.

3 Cut the tofu into sixths or eighths. Rinse the Chinese cabbage in cold water, and chop coarsely. Rinse the *shungiku* chrysanthemum in cold water, and pluck off the leaves. Remove the stems from the

shiitake mushrooms, and make a cross-shape incision on each cap. Chop off the tips of the enokidake mushroom stems. Cut the *naga-negi* onions into 3/16 inch-thick diagonal slices.Boil the kudzu filaments until transparent, and drain.

4 When the chicken thighs are tender, add the ingredients prepared in 3. above and simmer. Provide each diner with the condiments (grated giant white radish and *asatsuki* chive leaves chopped using the edge cut technique) and *ponzu* sauce.

❗ Tip on Tips

★ Plunge chicken into boiling water before use to eliminate bitterness and odor. This blanching operation will also help add the flavor of the chicken to the broth more efficiently, and make the meat tender when simmered.

★ Add *shungiku* (and greens) lastly since they loose the crunchy texture easily when overcooked.

Oden Stew
おでん

寒い冬にむしょうに食べたくなる体が温まる " おでん "
During cold winter, Oden will warm you up

■材料 (4人分)

大根… 400g (中1/3本)	昆布 (15cm 長さのもの)
こんにゃく ……… 1/2 丁	………………… 4 枚
すじ ……………… 120g	〈煮汁の調味料〉
ちくわ …………… 1本	┌ だし汁 …… 8 カップ
さつま揚げ (ごぼう巻き) … 4本	A │ しょう油 … 大さじ 3 と1/2
がんもどき ……… 4 個	│ 塩 ……… 小さじ 1
ゆで卵 …………… 4 個	└ みりん …… 大さじ 3
はんぺん ………… 1 枚	練り辛子 ………… 適宜

■ INGREDIENTS (serves 4)

1/3 middle-size (400g) giant white radish
1/2 cake devil's tongue
120g beef containing ample sinews
1 *chikuwa* fish paste rolls
4 cakes *satsuma-age* deep-fried fish paste (Burdock roll)
4 cakes *ganmodoki* deep-fried tofu
4 boiled eggs

1 cake *hanpen* white boiled fish paste
4 pieces *konbu* kelp (each 6 inches long)
〈For simmering〉
A
6 2/3 cups stock (1600㎖)
3 1/2 Tbsps soy sauce
1 tsp salt
3 Tbsps *mirin* sweet cooking sake
Mustard paste

■作り方

1 昆布は水につけて柔らかくし、結び昆布にします。

2 大根は3cmの厚さの輪切りにして皮をむき、面取りをして隠し包丁を入れます。米のとぎ汁（分量外）でかためにゆで、水でよく洗います。

3 こんにゃくはさっとゆで、両面に浅く斜めに切り込みを入れ、三角形に切ります。

4 さつま揚げ、がんもどき、ちくわは熱湯にくぐらせて油抜きし、ちくわは斜め輪切りにします。

5 ゆで卵は殻をむき、すじは1.5cm幅に切り、串に刺します。

6 鍋に煮汁の調味料Aを入れて味つけし、2の大根、3のこんにゃくを入れて煮ます。

7 6が煮たったらさらに20分程煮て、1の昆布、5のゆで卵を加え、さらに10分煮ます。煮汁が少なくなってきたら補います。

8 4のちくわ、さつま揚げ、がんもどき、5のすじ、はんぺんを加えて7～8分煮ます。

9 8を器に盛り、練り辛子をつけていただきます。

❗ コツのコツ

★具を入れる順番は火の通りの悪いもの、味のなじみにくいものから先に入れます。

★煮たてると汁がにごるので、火加減は弱火を保ち、煮汁が減ったら補うとよいでしょう。

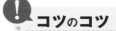

■ Directions

1 Soak the *konbu* kelp in cold water to soften, and make a knot with each piece.

2 Cut the giant white radish into 1 1/5-inch rounds, peel, bevel the edges and make a cross-shape incision on one flat side of each slice. Boil the slices in the water used for washing rice until half tender, and rinse well in cold water.

3 Boil the devil's tongue briefly, and make a diagonal shallow incision on both sides. Cut each piece into triangles.

4 Plunge the *satsuma-age*, *ganmodoki* and *chikuwa* into boiling water to eliminate excess oil. Cut the *chikuwa* diagonally into rounds.

5 Shell the boiled eggs. Cut the beef into 1/2-inch pieces and stick it bamboo skewers.

6 Mix all the ingredients of A in a pot. Add the giant white radish from step 2 and devil's tongue from step 3, and bring to a boil.

7 When it comes to the boil, continue to simmer for 20 min. Add the *konbu* kelp and boiled eggs from step 5, and simmer for 10 min. When the simmering liquid is reduced, add some more seasonings to the pot.

8 Add the *chikuwa* from step 4, *satsuma-age*, *ganmodoki*, beef from step 5 and *hanpen*, and simmer for 7 to 8 minutes.

9 Arrange in a bowl. Each diner can spread some mustard paste onto each ingredient, and eat.

❗ Tip on Tips

★ Put hard-to-cook and hard-to-season ingredients into the pot first.

★ Use a low heat throughout cooking because boiling strongly will cause the simmering liquid to lose clarity. When the liquid is reduced, add the seasonings.

全国の代表的な鍋料理
Hot-Pot Dishes of Japan

ふぐ鍋　Boiled Fugu stew

　晩秋から初春にかけてよく食べられるのが、鍋料理です。ひとつの鍋に肉類、魚介類、野菜類などが入り、手軽で栄養満点なため、家庭ではもちろんのこと、居酒屋などでもよく食べられています。

　本書では家庭でよく食べられる寄せ鍋、すき焼き、しゃぶしゃぶ、鶏の水炊きなどの代表的な鍋料理を紹介していますが、ここでは各都道府県の食材などを使用した特徴ある代表的な鍋料理を紹介します。

Hot-pot dishes are frequently enjoyed from the late fall to the early spring. Various kinds of ingredients such as meats, seafood and vegetables can be added to a single pot. They are often eaten at home and also at Japanese-style pubs since they are very simple to prepare and at the same time very nourishing.

In this book, we introduce typical hot-pot dishes prepared at home—the all-in-one-pot, sukiyaki, shabu-shabu and chicken one-pot. But in this column, we introduce one-pot dishes from each prefecture using local ingredients.

かきの土手鍋（広島）
Oyster and vegetable stew with miso (Hiroshima)

石狩鍋、ジンギスカン（北海道）
Ishikari stew, Mongolian mutton barbecue (Hokkaido)

だご汁、ふぐ鍋（大分）
Dagojiru, Boiled Figu stew (Oita)

きりたんぽ鍋（秋田）
Kiritanpo-Nabe (Akita)

水炊き、くえ鍋（福岡）
Chicken One-pot, Longtooth grouper and vegetable stew (Fukuoka)

いも煮（山形）
Imoni〈stewed taro〉(yamagata)

たらのじゃっぱ汁（青森）
Tara-no-Jappajiru〈A fishy miso soup〉(Aomori)

ふくちり（山口県）
Fuku-Chiri〈Boiled Figu stew〉(Yamaguchi)

たら鍋（富山）
Tara-Nabe〈pasific cod hot pot〉(Toyama)

牛しゃぶしゃぶ、すき焼き、鴨すき（滋賀）
Beef Shabu-shabu, Sukiyaki, Kamo-suki (shiga)

南部はっと鍋（岩手）
Nambu Hatto-Nabe (Iwate)

かに鍋（福井）
Crab stew (Fukui)

かき鍋（宮城）
Oyster and vegetable stew (Miyagi)

鴨鍋、ハモ鍋、湯豆腐（京都）
Duck stew, *Hamo-Nabe*〈daggertooth pike conger hot pot〉, Simmering Tofu (kyoto)

あんこう鍋（茨城）
Ankou-Nabe〈monk-fish hot pot〉(Ibaraki)

すき焼き、しゃぶ鍋、ボタン鍋（兵庫）
Sukiyaki, Shabu-Nabe, Wild boar stew (Hyogo)

いわしのつみれ鍋（千葉）
Sardine mince and vegetable stew (Chiba)

かきの土手鍋（広島）
Oyster and vegetable stew with miso (Hiroshima)

どじょう鍋、柳川鍋、おでん、ねぎま鍋、すき焼き（東京）
Loach hot pot, *Yanagawa-Nabe*〈a pot of loachs boiled in soy sauce with eggs and burdock〉, Oden stew, *Negi* and tuna stew, sukiyaki〈Kanto-style〉(Tokyo)

ぶたしゃぶ（鹿児島）
Pork Shabu-shabu (Kagoshima)

いのしし鍋、静岡おでん（静岡）
Wild boar stew, Shizuoka-style *Oden* stew (Shizuoka)

飛鳥鍋（奈良）
Asuka-Nabe (Nara)

みそおでん（愛知）
Miso-*Oden* stew (Aichi)

くえ鍋（和歌山）
Longtooth grouper and vegetable stew (Wakayama)

牛しゃぶしゃぶ、すき焼き（三重）
Beef Shabu-shabu, Sukiyaki (Mie)

てっちり、うどんすき、くじらのハリハリ鍋、関東煮〈おでん〉（大阪）
Boiled Figu stew, Udon-Suki, *Harihari-Nabe*〈whale meat and poyherb mustard stew〉, *Kantoni*〈Oden stew〉(Osaka)

※上記の鍋料理は代表的なものとなり、各地にさまざまな鍋料理がある
※ The above are only representative examples. Every region enjoys a variety of one-pot dishes.

第十四章
Chapter 14

Basic New Year O-sechi Cuisine
基本の正月料理

正月料理は、お母さんがゆっくりできるようにと考えられた料理。数の子は "子孫繁栄" を願うように、ひとつひとつに縁起をかついでいる。

The New Year's feast dishes will stay tasty for days so the mothers can rest during the New Year Holidays. Also every dish comes with an extra bit of goodness: it is believed that herring roe will bring prosperity to descendants.

How to pack foods in *ichi-no-juu* (first box) of the tiered box

お重の詰め方（壱の重）

彩りよく、よりおいしそうに料理をお重に詰めていくための、コツや基本を壱の重で紹介

The basics and useful tips for packing foods in the tiered box, beautiful to see and appealing to the appetite, are introduced below for the case of ichi-no-juu (first box)

■作り方

1 黒豆を小さな器（ゆず釜、竹筒など）に入れ、お重の中央に置きます。次に紅白のかまぼこを、紅が右上にくるように、互い違いに詰めます。

2 錦玉子、伊達巻を少しずつずらして詰めます。

3 料理と料理の間に仕切りとして、笹の葉や葉らんを置きます。

4 昆布巻は結び目を上にして重ねて盛り、高さを揃えます。

5 栗きんとんは、栗とあんのバランスをよく詰めます。

6 田作り（ごまめ）の頭を左にして重ねて盛り、高さを揃えます。

※お頭のある魚、えびなどは頭を左にして詰めます。

■ Directions

1 Put kuro-mame into a small vessel such as yuzu-gama (hollowed-out citron) or take-zutsu (hollow bamboo container), and place it at the center. Pack the red-and-white kamaboko alternately, with the red portion located on the upper-right side of the box.

2 Pack nishiki-tamago (yellow and white colored egg cake) and date-maki by staggering them a bit.

3 Place bamboo grass leaves or aspidistra leaves between foods to separate them.

4 Stack kobu-maki one above the other, with the knot facing up. Align the height of the stacks.

5 Pack kuri-kinton, checking the balance between chestnuts and mashed sweet potatoes.

6 Stack tazukuri (gomame) one above the other, with the head on the left side. Align the height of the stacks.

※ Fish cooked whole and shrimps are placed with the head on the left side.

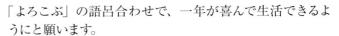

■ 田作り（ごまめ）　*Tazukuri(Gomame)*
Dried young anchovies

かつては田畑の肥料にされていた片口いわしを使うため、豊作を願います。

Wish for good harvest: Japanese anchovies were once used as fertilizer for rice paddies and fields.

■ 数の子　*Kazu-no-ko*
Herring roe

卵の数が多いことから、子孫繁栄を願います。

Wish for being blessed with children: *Kazu-no-ko* literally means "many roes."

■ 黒豆　*Kuro-mame*
Sweetened black beans

まめに働き（勉強）、まめ（健康）に暮らせることを願います。

Wish for working and studying hard and living in good health: In addition to beans, mame means "diligent" hin Japanese.

■ 伊達巻　*Date-maki*
Rolled omelet

伊達者（しゃれ者）たちが着ていたドテラに似ていたことから伊達巻と呼ばれます。巻きものに形が似ていることから、知識が増えるといわれます。

This food is so called because of its resemblance to the *dotera kimono* (worn by a *date-mono* or dandy). It is believed that knowledge increases when you eat *date-maki*, which looks like a rolled book.

伊達巻
Date-maki
(Rolled omelet)

■ 昆布巻　*Kobu-maki*
Kelp rolls

「よろこぶ」の語呂合わせで、一年が喜んで生活できるようにと願います。

Wish for living pleasantly throughout the year: From the harmonious sound between *kobu* (kelp) and *yorokobu* (rejoice).

■ お多福豆　*Otafuku-mame*
Big broad beans

福が多いことを願っています。

Wish for great happiness: *Tafuku* literally means "much good luck."

■ 紅白なます　*Kohaku-namasu*
A dish of raw fish and vegetables seasoned in vinegar and decorated in red-and-white stripes

お祝ごとに使う水引をイメージしています。

This food resembles the lucky red-and-white strings used for celebratory envelopes.

■ ぶりの焼きもの　*Buri-no-yakimono*
Grilled Japanese amberjack

ぶりが出世魚であることから、出世を願います。

Wish for a successful career: Japanese amberjack is called by different names as it grows large, which is indicative of a person rising to a high position in their career.

■ たいの焼きもの　*Tai-no-yakimono*
Grilled sea bream

「めでたい」の語呂合わせです。

Harmonious sound between tai (sea bream) and *mede-tai* (happy).

■ えびの焼きもの　*Ebi-no-yakimono*
Grilled shrimp

ひげが長く、腰が曲がっていることから老人を連想させ、長寿を祈願します。

Wish for longevity: The long barbels and the bent figure remind us of an old man enjoying longevity.

Sweetened Black Soybeans
黒豆

about **80**min 約80分

276kcal 276キロカロリー

手まひまかけてじっくり煮込んだ黒豆がしみじみと旨い
It takes time and effort to simmer tasty black soybeans

■材料（2〜3人分）

黒豆	1/2 カップ
砂糖	100g
水	適量
しょう油	大さじ 1/2

■ INGREDIENTS (serves 2〜3)

2/5 cup black soybeans (100 ㎖)
100g sugar
Water
1/2 Tbsp soy sauce

黒豆
Sweetened black soybeans

(Image photo)

■作り方

1 黒豆を水で洗い、豆の3倍量の水、1と2分の1カップに一晩漬けます。

2 1の戻した水ごと鍋に入れて中火にかけ、アクを取りながら煮たて、常に豆にゆで汁がかぶるように差し水をしながら40〜50分、強めの弱火で落としぶたをして煮ます。

3 2の豆が柔らかくなったら火を止めます。別鍋に砂糖と水1カップを合わせ入れ、ひと煮し、蜜を作ります。

4 3の豆の汁けをきって蜜に一晩漬けて冷まします。

5 4を汁ごと鍋に移し、弱火にかけ、しょう油を加えて約15分煮て火を止め、味を含ませます。

❗ コツのコツ

★黒豆が柔らかく煮えたら、蜜に一晩漬けて甘さを含ませます。

★作り方の2では、常に豆にゆで汁がかぶるように差し水をするため、火もとから離れないようにしましょう。

★煮豆（煮物）は、火を止めてから味が食材にしみ込みます。

◆ 黒豆の縁起 ◆
A bit about black soybeans

◆黒豆を食べて、まめに働き、学び、まめ（健康）に暮らせることを願います。これは、黒豆とまめの語呂合わせになります。

◆ Japanese tradition tells us that eating black soybeans helps to fulfill our wish that we are able to work hard, learn and live a healthy life. This belief originates in a Japanese homophone: the word "mame," meaning beans also refers to healthy in old Japanese.

■ Directions

1 Rinse the black soybeans in cold water, and soak in 1 1/4 cups water (three times the quantity of black soybeans) over night.

2 Place the black soybeans and the water used to reconstitute in step 1 into a pot, and bring to the boil over a medium heat while skimming off foam. Cover with a drop-lid, and simmer over a slightly stronger low heat for 40 to 50 min.

3 Turn off the heat after the beans from step 2 soften. Prepare the syrup. Combine sugar and 4/5 cup of water in a pot and bring to a boil.

4 Drain excess water from the beans from step 3. Soak into the syrup over night and let cool.

5 Transfer everything to a pot, and place over a low heat. Add the soy sauce, and simmer for about 15 min before turning off the heat.

❗ Tip on Tips

★ When black soybeans become tender after boiling, let them rest in the syrup over night to thoroughly absorb the sweetness.

★ During step 2, remember to stay with the pot to add water so the simmering liquid always covers the beans.

★ Simmered beans (and other simmered dishes) start absorbing the flavor after the heat is turned off.

265

Sweet Chestnut Puree
栗きんとん

甘くておいしい " 栗きんとん " は、豊かな一年を願う料理

Make this sweet and tasty chestnut puree and share your hope for a prosperous year

■材料（4人分）

さつまいも ‥‥‥‥ 500g
くちなしの実 ‥ 2〜3個
砂糖 ‥ 1と1/2 カップ
栗の甘露煮‥‥‥‥ 12個
栗の蜜‥‥‥‥ 1/2 カップ
みりん ‥‥‥‥‥ 大さじ 3

☐ INGREDIENTS (serves 4)

500g sweet potato
2 or 3 dried gardenia pods
1 1/4 cups sugar (300㎖)
12 candied chestnuts
2/5 cup chestnut syrup (100㎖)
3 Tbsps *mirin* sweet cooking sake

◆栗きんとんの縁起◆
A bit about chestnut puree

◆栗きんとんの色合いを、黄金色に輝く財宝にたとえ、豊かさを願っています。

◆ The golden color of sweet chestnut puree is a metaphor for golden treasure and a hope for prosperity.

■作り方

1 さつまいもは 1cm 幅の輪切りにし皮を厚くむき、水にさらして（何回か取りかえる）アクを抜きます。

2 くちなしの実をくだいて、ガーゼにくるみます。

3 鍋に 1 のさつまいもとひたひたの水を入れ、2 のくちなしの実を入れて火にかけます。沸騰したら弱火にし、竹串がすっと入るくらいになるまでゆでます

4 3 の湯を捨て、熱いうちにさつまいもを裏ごしします。
※冷めると裏ごししにくくなり、きれいに裏ごしが出来ません。

5 鍋に 4 の裏ごしたさつまいも、栗の蜜、砂糖を加えて、強火にかけ練り込みます。照りが出たら栗の甘露煮とみりんを入れて弱火にし、ゆっくりと練り、水分をとばします。
※絶対に焦がさないように注意しましょう。焦がしてしまったら最初から作り直しましょう。

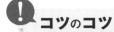

コツのコツ

★さつまいもを水にさらし、アクを抜くことで、くどくない甘味がでます。

★さつまいもは熱いうちに、裏ごしにしましょう。冷めるとかたくなり、裏ごししにくくなります。

★弱火で常に鍋を練り、焦がさないように注意しましょう。

■ Directions

1 Cut the sweet potato into 3/8-inch thick rounds, peel and soak in cold water (change water several times) to eliminate bitterness.

2 Crush the dried gardenia pods and wrap in gauze.

3 Place the sweet potato from step 1 and the gardenia pod from step 2 in a pot. Add enough water to cover and place over heat. When it comes to the boil, reduce the heat to low and simmer until the potatoes become tender enough for a bamboo skewer to pierce smoothly.

4 Discard the water from step 3. Strain the potato while hot.
※ Once the potato is cooled, it'll be hard to strain smoothly.

5 Add the strained potato from step 4, chestnut syrup and sugar, and mix well while heating over a high heat. When the mixture becomes glossy, add the chestnuts and mirin, reduce the heat to low and mix gently to cook off the excess moisture.
※ Pay special attention to make sure it doesn't burn. If it burns, give it another try.

Tip on Tips

★ By exposing the potato to water, you can remove bitterness and enhance its sweetness.

★ Strain the potato while it's still hot. It hardens as it cools so it becomes difficult to strain.

★ Remember to stir constantly at low heat without letting it burn.

Red And White Salad
紅白なます

about **15**min
約15分

72kcal
72キロカロリー

めでたい "水引き" にみたてた紅白なます

The colors of this salad are inspired by the red-and-white strings used to wrap gifts

■材料（2～3人分）

大根	……………	200g
にんじん	…………	20g
ゆず皮	…………	少々
塩	…………	少々

〈甘酢の材料〉

酢	…………	1/4 カップ
だし汁	………	1/3 カップ
砂糖	………	大さじ 3
塩	………	小さじ 1/4

■ INGREDIENTS (serves 2 or 3)

200g giant white radish
20g carrot
Small quantity of *yuzu* rind
Pinch salt

〈**For preparing dressing**〉

1/5 cup vinegar (50㎖)
2/7 cup stock (66㎖)
3 Tbsps sugar
1/4 tsp salt

■作り方

1 大根とにんじんを約 4cm に切り、皮を
  むいて 4cm の長さのせん切り（28 ペー
  ジ参照）にします。

2 1 をボウルに入れて、塩少々をふり入れ
  てもみます。しんなりとさせ、甘酢を
  しみ込みやすくさせます。

3 甘酢の材料を小鍋に入れて、砂糖が
  溶けるまで温め、冷ましておきます。

4 2 の塩もみしたにんじんと大根の水け
  をペーパータオルに包んで取るか、両
  手で絞って取り、ボウルなどに入れま
  す。3 の甘酢にゆずの皮のせん切りを

入れ、軽くあえてからにんじんと大根
を漬けます。1 時間くらいおいて味を
しみ込ませてからいただきます。

! コツのコツ

★ 大根とにんじんに塩を入れ軽くもみ、
水けが出てきたら強めにもんで柔らかくし
ます。

★ 塩もみすることで、甘酢がしみ込みや
すくなります。

★ 1 時間ほど漬けておくと、味がしみ込
みおいしくなります。

◆紅白なますの縁起◆
Origin of Red-and-White Salad

◆日本でお祝いごとに使用する"水引
き"をイメージして作られたのが、よく
正月にいただく「紅白なます」です。

◆ This red-and-white salad has its origin in
"*mizuhiki*," the red and white gift wrapping
strings used on formal
celebratory occasions.
It's one of the traditional
Japanese New Year's
dishes.

めでたい時に使用する紅白の水引き
Red and white *mizuhiki* used
on celebratory occasions

■ Directions

1 Cut the giant white radish and
  carrot into 1 1/2 inch lengths. Peel
  them and cut into 1 1/2 inch-long
  julienne strips. (See P. 28)

2 Put the ingredients from step 1 in
  a bowl and sprinkle with a pinch
  of salt. Rub the giant white radish
  and carrots with the salt so they
  soften. This will help them soak
  up the sweet vinegar sauce.

3 Place the dressing ingredients in a
  small pot, and heat until the sugar
  melts. Let stand until cool.

4 Remove excess moisture from the
  salt-rubbed carrot and giant white
  radish from step 2 by wrapping
  them in paper towels or squeezing
  them with both hands. Place in a

bowl. Add the *yuzu* rind julienne
strips into the sweet vinegar sauce
from step 3 and mix lightly. Then
soak the carrot and giant white
radish. Set aside for about an hour
while the vegetables absorb the
seasoning and then serve.

! Tip on Tips

★ Rub the salted giant white radish
and carrot lightly at first, and when
liquid begins to appear, press the
vegetables harder to soften them.

★ A salt rub helps the ingredients
absorb the sweet vinegar sauce.

★ The ingredients will fully absorb
the seasonings over an hour and
become more delicious.

お節料理（お重）に欠かせない紅白なます
Red-and-white salad is a necessity among the
New Year's dishes

269

Kazunoko Herring Roe
数の子

子孫繁栄を願って正月にいただく " 数の子 "

Herring roe is a symbol of the wish to be gifted with children and it's another traditional Japanese New Year's dish

■材料 (2〜3人分)

塩数の子‥‥‥‥ 100g
〈漬け汁用材料〉
だし汁 ‥‥‥‥ 1/2 カップ
薄口しょう油 ‥大さじ1と1/2
調理酒 ‥‥‥‥ 大さじ1

■ INGREDIENTS (serves 2 or 3)

100g salted *kazunoko* herring roe
〈**For preparing soaking liquid**〉
2/5 cup stock (100 ㎖)
1 1/2 Tbsps light soy sauce
1 Tbsp cooking sake

数の子
Kazunoko herring roe

(Image photo)

■作り方

1 塩数の子はたっぷりの水に一晩漬けて、塩出しします。途中2〜3回水をかえて塩けを抜きます。数の子についている白い膜は、手や竹串で丁寧に取ります。

2 漬け汁用材料を合わせて小鍋に入れ、ひと煮たちさせ、冷ましておきます。

3 1の数の子の水けをペーパータオルなどでふき取り、2の漬け汁に漬けて味を含ませます。一日くらいおいてからいただきます。

◆数の子の縁起◆
A bit about herring roe

◆数の子を正月に食べると子孫繁栄につながるといわれています。これは、にしんが多くの卵を産むことにあやかってのことです。

◆ It's believed that you'll be blessed with children if you enjoy herring roe on New Year's Day. This follows the example of herring that they have many eggs.

第十四章・基本の正月料理 ● Basic New Year O-sechi Cuisine

1-a

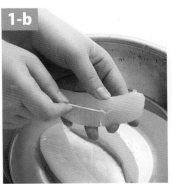

1-b

2

3

■ Directions

1 Leave the salted herring roe in plenty of cold water over night to eliminate salt. Change the water a few times during this desalting process. Thoroughly remove the white coating of the roe with your hand or a bamboo skewer.

2 Mix all the soaking liquid ingredients in a small pot, and boil briefly. Let stand until cool.

3 Wipe off the excess moisture from the herring roe with paper towels, and soak in the liquid prepared in 2. above so that the roe absorbs the seasonings. Let the roe rest in the liquid for 1 day or so before eating.

漬け汁がしみて、コリコリとした食感がおいしい。酒のつまみにもなり、正月料理に欠かせない「数の子」

Its flavor and crunchy texture are delightful. Herring roe goes well with sake and is an indispensable New Year's dish.

Tazukuri (*Gomame*, or Small Dried Sardines)
田作り（ごまめ）

一年の豊作を願う縁起が込められている

This dish is prepared and served with a prayer for a good harvest

■材料（4人分）

ごまめ ・・・・・・・・・・・・・・・・・ 50g
砂糖 ・・・・・・・・・・・・・・ 大さじ 2
しょう油 ・・・・・・・・・・ 大さじ 1
水 ・・・・・・・・・・・・・・・・ 小さじ 2
料理酒 ・・・・・・・・・ 大さじ 1/2
サラダ油・・・・・・・・・・・・・・・・ 適量

■ INGREDIENTS (serves 4)

50g *gomame*, or small dried
sardines
2 Tbsps sugar
1 Tbsp soy sauce
2 tsps water
1/2 Tbsp cooking sake
Vegetable oil

■作り方

1 ごまめは平皿に重ならないように並べ、電子レンジに 1 分かけます。取り出してかき混ぜて再び電子レンジで 30 秒ずつ 4 ～ 5 回かけます。（冷めた時にごまめがカリカリになっていれば OK です）。

2 鍋に砂糖、しょう油、水を入れ中火にかけ、煮立って泡が大きくなったら 1 のごまめを入れ、手早くかき混ぜてからめ、火を止めて料理酒をふって混ぜます。

3 薄くサラダ油を塗ったバットに 2 を手早くあけ、広げて冷まします。

■ Directions

1 Scatter the *gomame* on a flat plate so that the fish do not overwrap each other, and microwave for 1 min. Stir, and microwave 4 to 5 times, for 30 sec each. (If the *gomame* is crispy, when cool, it's done.)

2 Put the sugar, soy sauce, and water in a pan, and heat over a medium flame. When it comes to the boil and large bubbles begin to form, put the *gomame* in, and quickly stir to allow the fish to be coated with the sauce. Turn off the heat, sprinkle with the cooking sake, and stir.

3 Quickly spread the *gomame* on a cooking tray thinly smeared with vegetable oil, and allow the fish to cool.

! コツのコツ・Tip on Tips

★ごまめがカリカリになるまで電子レンジにかけましょう。

★ Microwave the *gomame* until crisp.

第十五章
Chapter 15

Japanese Traditional Sweets

日本伝統のお菓子

日本の伝統あるお菓子は、食材の特徴をいかしたものが多い。ここでは、よくお菓子に使われる小豆あんの作り方はもちろん、古くから食べられる草もち、ぜんざい、大学いもなどを紹介。

Japanese traditional sweets make good use of the interesting characteristics of each ingredient used. In this chapter, we introduce recipes for frequently used sweet red bean paste, long-eaten mugwort-flavored rice cake, sweet red bean soup with rice cakes, candied sweet potatoes and more.

How to Make Chunky Sweet Red-bean Paste
小豆あんの作り方

about 150 min 約150分

2284 kcal 2284キロカロリー

ぜんざいや草もちに使う小豆あんをきっちり作りたい
Master sweet red bean paste which is the basic for preparing other red bean treats

■材料 (900g 分)

小豆	300g
砂糖	300 〜 360g
水	適宜

■ INGREDIENTS (makes about 32oz)

300g *azuki* beans
300 to 360g sugar
Water

■作り方

1 小豆はたっぷりの水に一晩くらい漬けておきます。漬け汁ごと鍋に入れ、強火にかけ、煮たったら差し水をし、再び煮たったらザルに上げ、ゆで汁を捨てます。

2 鍋に水をたっぷり注ぎ、1の小豆を入れ、弱火で約2時間、アクを取りながら指先でつぶれるくらい小豆を柔らかくなるまで煮ます。

3 鍋の大きさに合うふたで、鍋口をふたで押さえ、小豆が出ないようにして、煮汁をボウルにあけます。
※煮汁は使用しますので、捨てないでください。

4 3の鍋を再び火にかけ、砂糖を加え、混ぜながら汁けがなくなるまで煮詰めます。砂糖は好みの甘さに量を加減します。保存する場合は煮詰めてからバットに広げて冷まします。
※冷ましたものをタッパーなどに入れて冷蔵庫で保存するとよいでしょう。

❗ コツのコツ

★作り方3の煮汁はぜんざいの汁として、あんのかたさを調節する時などに使えるので残しておきます。

★砂糖の代わりにグラニュー糖や三温糖を使ってもよいでしょう。

★高級和菓子用の和三盆糖を使うと、風味と口当たりのよい上品なおいしさの小豆あんに仕上がります。

1

2

3

■ Directions

1 Leave the *azuki* beans in plenty of cold water over night. Place both the beans and the water in which they were soaked in a pot, and bring to the boil over a high heat. When it comes to the boil, add some cold water. When the water starts to boil again, drain the beans on a sieve.

2 Fill a pot with plenty of water, and add the *azuki* beans. Simmer over a low heat for about 2 hours while skimming off foam. When the beans are so soft that they can be crushed with your fingertips, remove from the heat.

3 Have a pot-size lid at hand. Cover the pot with the lid and pour only the simmering liquid into a bowl while holding back the beans with the lid.
※ Save the simmering liquid for later use.

4 Place the pot from step 3 over the heat again. Add the sugar, and simmer while stirring until all the liquid is gone. The quantity of the sugar to be added depends on how sweet you want the paste to be. If you intend to preserve the paste, spread it on a tray after boiling and let stand until cool.
※ You can put the paste in a plastic Tupperware for storage in the refrigerator.

❗ Tip on Tips

★ Retain the simmering liquid poured from the pot into the bowl in Direction 3. above. It can be used as a liquid ingredient for Sweet Red-bean Soup with Rice Cakes to adjust the thickness of the red-bean paste.

★ Granulated sugar or *sanonto* sugar can also be used.

★ Use *wa-sanbon-tou*, premium sugar made for Japanese traditional sweets, for more elegant and smoother red-bean paste.

第十五章・日本伝統のお菓子 ● Japanese Traditional Sweets

Mugwort-flavored Rice Cake
草もち

香り高いよもぎの風味と甘い小豆あんがおいしい
An excellent combination of aromatic mugwort and sweet red bean paste

■材料（12個分）

上新粉	180g
ぬるま湯	180cc
よもぎの葉（生）	100g
重曹	小さじ 1/5
砂糖	40g
小豆あん	180g

INGREDIENTS (makes 12cakes)

180g quality rice flour
180cc lukewarm water
100g fresh mugwort leaves
1/5 tsp baking soda
40g sugar
180g chunky sweet red-bean paste

■作り方

1 ボウルに上新粉を入れ、ぬるま湯を少しずつ3回くらいに分けて加えてよく混ぜます。

2 蒸気の上がった蒸し器に、清潔な濡れふきんを敷き、1を大きめにちぎって並べて強火で14〜15分蒸します。

3 よもぎの葉は葉先だけを摘み取って、重曹を溶かした熱湯で2分ほどゆでます。流水に15分くらいさらしてアクを抜き、水けをきつく絞ります。

4 3のよもぎを包丁で細かく刻み、ミキサーにかけます。

5 小豆あん（274・275ページを参照）は12等分にして丸めます。

6 2の生地をボウルにあけ、水で濡らしたすりこ木でつきながら、砂糖を2〜3回に分けて加えます。さらに、手に水をつけてよくもみ、混ぜ合わせます。

7 6の生地によもぎを加えて混ぜ合わせ、耳たぶくらいの柔らかさにします。

8 7の生地を棒状にし、12等分にしてから丸めます。円形にのばし、5の小豆あんをのせ、生地で包み込みます。

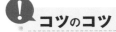
コツのコツ
★ゆでたよもぎは水けをよくきらないと、生地が水っぽくなってしまうので注意しましょう。

1-a

1-b

3

4

5

8

■ Directions

1 Place the rice flour in a bowl, and pour the lukewarm water gradually in three stages or so into the bowl while stirring well to make dough.

2 Spread a clean damp cloth over the bottom of the preheated steamer. Tear the dough into relatively large-sized pieces with your hands, and place in the steamer. Steam over a high heat for 14 to 15 min.

3 Pluck off the soft tips of the mugwort leaves, and boil the tips in water in which the baking soda has been dissolved for about 2 min. Rinse the boiled tips in running fresh water to eliminate bitterness. Squeeze hard to drain.

4 Chop the mugwort leaves from step 3 finely, and put them through a blender.

5 Divide the sweet red-bean paste (See P.274 and 275) into 12 equal portions, and roll into balls.

6 Transfer the dough steamed in 2. above to a bowl, and add the sugar over a few times while mashing the dough with a pestle moistened with water. Then, knead the dough with your hands while occasionally moistening with water.

7 Add the ground mugwort to the dough, and mix until the dough becomes as soft as an earlobe.

8 Knead the dough into stick form, cut into 12 equal portions and roll into balls. Flatten each ball into a circular shape, and place the 12 red-bean paste balls on top of each dough circle. Wrap the paste ball from step 5 with the dough to make a cake.

Tip on Tips
★ Drain mugwort leaves thoroughly after boiling, otherwise, the dough will become washy.

Sweet Red-bean Soup with Rice Cakes
ぜんざい

about **20**min 約20分

321kcal 321キロカロリー

甘い小豆あんと焼きもちで幸せになれる "ぜんざい"

Chunky sweet red bean paste and toasted rice cakes will make everyone happy

■材料（4人分）

小豆あん …………… 320g
小豆の煮汁 ……… 400cc
切りもち …………… 適宜

■ INGREDIENTS (serves 4)

320g chunky sweet red-bean paste
1 2/3 cups *azuki* beans simmering liquid （400㎖）
Cut rice cakes

■作り方

1 小豆あんの作り方は、274・275ページを参照してください。1人分80gに対して、小豆の煮汁 (274・275ページの小豆あんの作り方 **3** を参照) 100ccを加えて、鍋に入れてひと煮たちさせます。

2 切りもちは小さめに切って、焼き色がつくまで両面を焼きます。
※切りもちの大きさは、好みでよいでしょう。

3 **2** のもちを **1** の鍋に入れ、小豆あんと軽くからめます。それを器に盛っていただきます。

> ### コツのコツ
> ★煮汁の量を調整して好みの濃さのぜんざいにするとよいでしょう。
> ★小豆あんを焦がさないように弱火から中火で煮ましょう。
> ★小豆あんに塩をひとつまみ入れると、甘味が際立ちます。

白玉ぜんざい

Sweet Red-bean Soup with *Shiratama* Rice-flour Dumplings

■材料 (4 人分)

白玉粉	80 〜 90g
水	70 〜 80 ㎖
小豆あん	320g

■作り方

1 白玉団子を作ります。白玉粉に水を少しずつ加え、耳たぶほどのかたさになるよう練ります。

2 **1** を3cmほどの大きさに丸め、中央を親指で少しへこませます。

3 **2** の白玉団子を熱湯に入れ、浮いてきたらもう少しゆで、冷水 (分量外) に入れます。

4 小豆あんは 274・275 ページを参照してください。

5 の小豆あんに **3** の白玉を加えて温め、器に盛ります。

■ INGREDIENTS (serves 4)

80 〜 90g rice flour
70 〜 80 ㎖ water
320g chunky sweet red bean paste

■ Directions

1 Prepare *shiratama* dumplings. Add water to the rice flour little by little and knead until soft as an earlobe.

2 Divide the dough into about 1 1/4-inch size balls. Hollow the center a little with your thumb.

3 Put the dumplings from step 2 into boiling water. When they float, boil a little longer and transfer to chilled water.

4 Prepare chunky sweet red bean paste referring to P. 274 and 275.

5 Add the dumplings from step 3 to the chunky sweet red bean paste. Serve in a bowl when warm.

1-a

1-b

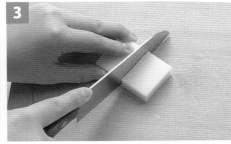

3

4

■ Directions

1 Place the chunky sweet red-bean paste (See P.274 and 275) and the *azuki* beans simmering liquid in a pot (one serving: 95g liquid per 80g paste). Boil briefly.

2 Cut the rice cakes into small pieces and toast until light brown on both sides.
※ Cut the size of the rice cakes as you like.

3 Place the rice cakes in the pot, and mix with the chunky sweet red-bean paste lightly. Arrange in individual bowls.

> ### Tip on Tips
> ★ You can vary the thickness of the soup by adjusting the quantity of the simmering liquid to be added.
> ★ Simmer the chunky sweet red bean paste over medium low heat so it doesn't burn.
> ★ Add a pinch of salt to the chunky sweet red bean paste to enhance the sweetness.

Tofu *Dango* Dumpling
豆腐だんご

豆腐だんごをみたらし風のタレでいただく

Enjoy tofu dumplings with sweet soy glazing sauce

■材料 (4人分)

絹ごし豆腐	100g
白玉粉	100g
じゃがいも	1/4 個
黒ごま	大さじ2

A
しょう油	大さじ2と1/2
水	大さじ5
みりん	大さじ1
砂糖	大さじ6

B
片栗粉	大さじ1
水	大さじ1

■ INGREDIENTS (serves 4)

100g "silken"tofu
100g *shiratama* rice flour for dumpling
1/4 potato
2 Tbsps black sesame seeds

A
2 1/2 Tbsps soy sauce
5 Tbsps water
1 Tbsp *mirin* sweet cooking sake
6 Tbsps sugar

B
1 Tbsp *katakuriko* starch
1 Tbsp water

■作り方

1 器に **B** を入れ、水を加えて溶き、水溶き片栗粉を作ります。

2 小鍋に **A** を入れて火にかけ、煮立ったら1の水溶き片栗粉を少しずつ加えてとろみをつけてタレを作り、火からおろします。

3 じゃがいもは水洗いして皮をむき（芽がある場合は包丁の角で芽を取り除く）ひと口大に切って、水にさらしてアクを抜き、水を入れた鍋で竹串がすっと刺さるぐらい柔らかくなるまでゆでます。

4 3をザルにあけて水けをきり、ボウルに入れて木べらなどで潰してマッシュポテトにしておきます。

5 別のボウルに白玉粉を入れ、4のマッシュポテト、軽く水けをきった絹ごし豆腐を手で崩しながら加え、耳たぶぐらいのかたさになるまで、へらなどでよく混ぜ合わせます。

6 5に黒ごまを加えてよく混ぜ、丸めてだんごを作ります。

7 鍋に湯を沸かし、6のだんごを入れてゆでます。

8 7のだんごが浮きあがってきたら、冷水に取って冷やし、水けをきります。

9 8のだんごを串に刺し、器に盛りつけ2のタレをかけていただきます。

コツのコツ

★5がかたい場合には、水（分量外）を加えてかたさを調整しましょう。

★タレを焦がさないように注意しましょう。

■ Directions

1 Put **B** into a bowl, add the water, and dissolve to prepare the dissolved *katakuriko* starch.

2 Put **A** into a small pot and place over a heat. When it comes to the boil, add the dissolved *katakuriko* starch little by little, and thicken to prepare the sauce. Remove from the heat.

3 Wash the potato in cold water and peel (remove any sprouts with the end corner of a knife). Cut into bite-sized pieces and expose to cold water to eliminate bitterness. Fill a pot with water and boil the potato until tender enough for a bamboo skewer to pierce without difficulty.

4 Drain the potato on a sieve. Transfer to a bowl and mash with a wooden spatula.

5 Put the *shiratama* rice flour in another bowl and add the mashed potato and the lightly-squeezed tofu by breaking into small pieces with hands. Mix well with a spatula until it becomes as hard as an earlobe.

6 Add the black sesame to the bowl prepared in 5. and mix well. Then make dumpling balls with hands.

7 Fill a pot with water and boil the dumplings.

8 When they come up to the surface, remove from the pot and soak into cold water to cool. Then drain.

9 Skewer the boiled dumplings, arrange on a plate, and pour the sauce prepared in 2.

Tip on Tips

★ When it becomes too hard, add some water (except quantity) to adjust the thickness.

★ Be careful not to burn the sauce.

Candied Sweet Potatoes

大学いも

about **30** min
約30分

178 kcal
178キロカロリー

古くから愛されている日本伝統のお菓子
A long-loved Japanese traditional sweet

■材料（4人分）

さつまいも	1本
炒りごま（黒）	小さじ1
揚げ油	適宜
水	大さじ2
砂糖	大さじ5
しょう油	小さじ1

■ INGREDIENTS (serves 4)

1 sweet potato
1 tsp black parched sesame
Oil for deep-frying
2 Tbsps water
5 Tbsps sugar
1 tsp soy sauce

■作り方

1. さつまいもはよく洗い、皮つきのまま縦4つ割りにしてから乱切りにし、たっぷりの水につけてアクを抜きます。水けをきり、耐熱皿に入れてラップをし、電子レンジで2〜3分加熱します。水けがあったらふき取っておきます。

2. 1のさつまいもを160℃の油でじっくりと揚げます。表面がかたくなってきたら、高温にして揚げます。

3. 鍋に水、砂糖、しょう油を入れてかき混ぜながら火にかけ、とろみがついたら火を止めます。

4. 揚げたてのさつまいもを3の中に入れて手早くからめ、炒りごまをふります。薄く油（分量外）を塗ったバットに広げて冷まします。

■ Directions

1. Wash the sweet potato well. Cut in quarters lengthwise with the skin still on, and chop into rolling wedges. Soak in plenty of water to eliminate bitterness. Drain, place on a heat-resistant plate, cover with plastic wrap and heat in a microwave oven for a few minutes. Wipe off any moisture.

2. Deep-fry the chopped sweet potato in oil at 320°F, slowly. When the surfaces harden, increase the oil temperature.

3. Place the water, sugar and soy sauce in a pot, and heat while stirring. When the liquid thickens, remove from the heat.

4. Place the just-fried potatoes in the pot with the sauce prepared in 3. above, mix quickly and sprinkle on the black parched sesame. Transfer to a tray thinly coated with oil (except quantity) to cool.

❗ コツのコツ・Tip on Tips

★さつまいもは、そのままで素揚げするより電子レンジで加熱することで、揚げ時間を短縮できます。

★ By heating the sweet potatoes in a microwave oven beforehand, the time it takes to deep-fry them can be reduced.

Japanese Table Manners

和食のマナー

おいしい料理を作っても、マナーが悪かったらせっかくの料理も台無し。ふだん何気なくおこなっている箸使いが、実はマナー違反だったり…。ここでは和食のマナーとして箸の使い方を紹介。

Though you prepared delicious dishes, everything would be spoiled if proper table manners were ignored. Sometimes, the unintentional use of chopsticks can be a breach of these manners. In this chapter, we'll introduce you to the correct use of chopsticks at the Japanese table.

箸の使い方
How to Use Chopsticks

正しい箸の持ち方 ● Proper Usage of Chopsticks

和食に箸は欠かすことの出来ない重要なものです。正しい使い方を身につけ、スマートに食事を楽しみましょう。

Using chopsticks is an essential part of dining in Japan. By following some simple basic rules, you can enjoy Japanese cuisine in a sophisticated manner.

箸の取り方と持ち方
How to Pick up Chopsticks and How to Hold Them

箸を取る時には、右手で箸の中ほどを上から取り（1）、下から左手を添え、右手で箸を持ち直してから使う（2、3）とよいでしょう。割り箸は、同じように持ち上げ、上下に割って使います。また、割った箸をすぐに使うのは失礼になりますので、一度箸置きに置いてから使いましょう。

To pick up chopsticks from the table, hold the middle of the chopsticks from above with your right hand, and pick them up while supporting them lightly from underneath with your left hand. Then hold the chopsticks with your right hand. To use disposable wooden chopsticks, pick them up in the same way as described above, and pull them apart. Using chopsticks immediately after pulling them apart is regarded as bad form, so place them on a chopstick rest in front of you first before using them.

器と箸の持ち方
How to Hold a Bowl and Chopsticks

ご飯や椀ものなどをいただく場合には、器を持ってから箸を取るようにします。両手で器を取り、左手のひらにのせ、右手で箸を取り上げます（1）。次に左手の人差し指と中指で箸をはさみ、右手で箸を持ち換えてからいただきます（2）。

When having a bowl of rice or soup, hold the bowl first before picking up chopsticks. Pick up the bowl with the both hands, and put it on the palm of left hand. Then take up chopsticks with the right hand, and put them between the index and middle fingers of the left hand before holding them properly with the right hand.

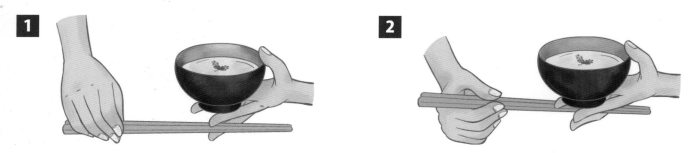

使い慣れると便利な箸ですが、食事の雰囲気をこわさないためにもタブーとされる箸使いを覚えておきましょう。

Once accustomed to using chopsticks, you should find them quite convenient. There are, however, some taboos related to the use of chopsticks, which you should observe in order not to spoil the merry atmosphere of the table.

してはいけない箸の作法
The improper use of chopsticks

■ 渡し箸（拾い箸）
Passing Foods

箸と箸で食べものを渡してはいけません。日本では納骨の時に行なうため決してしないように心がけましょう。

Never use your chopsticks to take something from someone else's chopsticks. This way of passing things relates to Japanese funerary custom.

■ 寄せ箸
Drawing Plates or Bowls Near You

箸で器を引き寄せてはいけません。

Don't draw a plate or bowl toward you with chopsticks.

■ 移り箸
Touching Foods Unnecessarily

一度箸をつけたのに、食べないで他の料理へ箸をつけるのは避けましょう。

Don't touch foods with chopsticks unnecessarily without eating them.

■ 横箸（もぎ箸）
Scooping

箸先についた料理を口で取るのは避けましょう。

Don't scoop up food by using chopsticks like a spoon and bring them to your mouth.

■ 込み箸
Shoveling Food into Mouth

器に口をつけて、箸でかき込むのは避けましょう。

Don't put your lips to a plate or bowl and shovel food into your mouth with chopsticks.

■ にぎり箸
Picking up Plates or Bowls While Holding Chopsticks

箸を持ったまま器を取ってはいけません。

Don't pick up a plate or bowl while holding chopsticks.

■ 指し箸
Pointing at Someone

箸で人を指すのは失礼になります。

Don't point at someone with chopsticks.

■ 渡し箸
Laying Chopsticks across Plate or Bowl

器に箸を渡してはいけません。

Don't lay chopsticks across a plate or bowl.

料理さくいん〈50音順〉

INDEX ⟨by alphabetical order⟩

● 編集協力／（株）ナヴィ インターナショナル
● 編集・プロデュース／菊池友彦
● 料理制作／藤田裕子
● 編集担当／田丸智子（ナツメ出版企画）
● レイアウト／北村香織、羽田眞由美〈（株）ナヴィ インターナショナル〉
● 写真／中島 劭一郎、木村 純
● イラスト／Mari
● 翻訳／鈴木さち
● ネイティブチェック／Megan Doyle Corcoran
● 写真協力／富岡八幡宮、京都市観光協会、祇園祭山鉾連合会、仙台商工会議所、国会国立図書館、東京国立博物館、DNP アートコミュニケーションズ、PIXTA（ピクスタ）

ナツメ社Webサイト
http://www.natsume.co.jp
書籍の最新情報（正誤情報を含む）は
ナツメ社Webサイトをご覧ください。

オールカラー 英語でつくる和食　完全版

2012 年 11 月 6 日発行

編著者	藤田裕子	© FUJITA YUKO, 2012
	ナヴィ インターナショナル	© NAVI INTERNATIONAL, 2012
発行者	田村正隆	

発行所　　株式会社ナツメ社
　　　　　東京都千代田区神田神保町 1 － 52 ナツメ社ビル 1F（〒 101 － 0051）
　　　　　電話　03（3291）1257（代表）　　　FAX　03（3291）5761
　　　　　振替　00130 － 1 － 58661
制　作　　ナツメ出版企画株式会社
　　　　　東京都千代田区神田神保町 1 － 52 ナツメ社ビル 3F（〒 101 － 0051）
　　　　　電話　03（3295）3921（代表）
印刷所　　株式会社リーブルテック

ISBN 978-4-8163-5318-5

Printed in Japan

〈定価はカバーに表示してあります〉
〈落丁・乱丁本はお取り替えします〉